VISION, VALUES,
AND
COURAGE

VISION, VALUES, AND COURAGE

LEADERSHIP FOR QUALITY MANAGEMENT

Neil H. Snyder

James J. Dowd, Jr.

Dianne Morse Houghton

THE FREE PRESS

A Division of Macmillan, Inc.

NEW YORK

Maxwell Macmillan Canada

TORONTO

Maxwell Macmillan International

NEW YORK   OXFORD   SINGAPORE   SYDNEY

The Free Press
A Division of Macmillan, Inc.
866 Third Avenue, New York, N.Y. 10022

Maxwell Macmillan Canada, Inc.
1200 Eglinton Avenue East
Suite 200
Don Mills, Ontario M3C 3N1

Macmillan, Inc. is part of the Maxwell Communication Group of Companies.

Printed in the United States of America

printing number
1   2   3   4   5   6   7   8   9   10

Library of Congress Cataloging-in-Publication Data

Snyder, Neil H. (Neil Harding)
    Vision, values, and courage: leadership for quality management /
  Neil H. Snyder, James J. Dowd, Jr., Dianne Morse Houghton.
        p.   cm.
    Includes bibliographical references.
    ISBN 0–02–929755–9
    1. Leadership.   2. Total quality management.   I. Dowd, James J.,
  Jr.   II. Houghton, Dianne Morse.   III. Title.
  HD57.7.S69   1994
  658.5'62—dc20   93–23935
                                                                        CIP

Excerpts in Chapter 7 reprinted from *Grinding It Out: The Making of McDonald's* by Ray Kroc with Robert Anderson, © 1977. Used with permission of Contemporary Books, Inc., Chicago.

CONTENTS

FOREWORD

Leadership has the power to make or break an organization. Not management but leadership. Leadership—shared vision, shared values, and the courage to act on them—is the difference between businesses that prosper over time and those that seem to just get by.

The distinction between leadership and management is important, and in their book, *Vision, Values, and Courage,* Snyder, Dowd, and Houghton do a terrific job of explaining the difference between them. But they do much more. In this book, they challenge the status quo, and they offer insightful perspectives on how and why leaders succeed. They explore dimensions of leadership that are often ignored and weave them into a model for understanding leadership behavior that will add real value to any organization.

Their discussion of vision is eye-opening and exciting. It will take hold of your imagination and help you uncover possibilities you did not know existed. Their focus on three critical values—an orientation to the customer as king, a commitment to continuous improvement, and the empowerment of people—provides a foundation on which strong, powerful, and successful organizations can be built. Finally, they stress the importance of courage to take action. Unless leaders are willing to take chances and to try new things, they will not know long-term success.

Long before TQM, continuous improvement, empowerment, quality circles and other late–20th century buzzwords were in vogue, great leaders practiced the substance of these techniques with startling results. This book takes these concepts and zeros in on their essence. It strips away confusion and explains what they mean in such a way that people can read the book, understand it, and use the information in it.

We all know, or have known, real leaders; those charismatic people we would follow anywhere. The people who could lead us into battle or who could draw from us things we did not know were there are real leaders. They are desperately needed in business today. Oddly, leaders are scarce. The traditionalist view of management seems to prevail— the view that large, complex organizations cannot be led. Thus, too many organizations have established large bureaucracies and layers of management to plan for the future and to deal with problems. The result is that they move into futures that are virtually identical to their pasts, and they go through a process of gradual decay. Many of them will not survive.

Vision, values, and courage can be observed in organizations that are led. They do not occur by chance. As organizations grow and leaders are moved further away from the action, the importance of these characteristics only increases. Size and prosperity do not necessarily go hand-in-hand. Leaders in growing businesses must learn to communicate in new ways if they intend for their organizations to continue moving down the road to prosperity. They must also learn to listen and to respond to what they hear.

Leaders are people who understand that without vision, there is no leadership; without honesty, there is no communication; without communication and shared values, there is no performance; and without the confidence to reach out and try new things, there is no risk taking or long-term success. As Ian Percy once said, "Managers count seeds in an apple, while leaders envision how many apples there are in one seed." This book is a great tool for teaching leadership. It deserves your attention.

Richard E. Fogg
Associate Vice Chairman—Taxes
Price Waterhouse
Washington, D.C.
August 1993

PREFACE

The world today changes more rapidly than ever before. Geographers must monitor geopolitical developments almost daily to track emerging nations and changing borders in eastern Europe; technological innovations that might have yielded years of competitive advantage in the past seem now to provide only a few months' head start before they become commonplace, and then obsolete.

More than a decade ago, the importance of quality became apparent as customers said in unmistakably clear language—with their wallets—that they would no longer accept inferior goods and services. Top quality products were entering markets in most industries, and firms producing them were winning competitive battles against well-established foes that had dominated these markets for almost half a century. General Motors, Sears, and IBM are examples of firms that found the pace of change too quick, and their inability to adapt did them, their shareholders, and their employees great harm. With new leadership, these companies have begun the process of change; if they fail, they will cease to exist.

But we may one day look back longingly on the time when simply producing quality products and services was enough to give a firm a competitive advantage in the market. That era is now passing, and firms that once possessed quality advantages are learning that such an advantage lasts about as long as a technological advantage—a few months at the most.

To compete effectively in today's global environment, businesses must produce quality goods and services at competitive prices, and they must continuously improve their products and services to have any hope of long-term success. From customers and competitors alike, the challenge has been made to every organization: what you do, you must do better. Inside the organization, the challenge to executives continues: you must do better with fewer people and with a smaller budget. Business as usual will suffice no longer. To be effective, executives must adjust their thinking and play different roles than they have in the past. They must learn to lead, not manage. If they fail to do this, their organizations will not survive.

Total quality management has been presented as the solution to many of our business problems, and there is no shortage of consultants and seminar leaders offering programs on the subject. In many organizations today, however, the very mention of the letters TQM will empty the room, and talk about empowerment will cause managers and employees alike to roll their eyes and shake their heads. What has gone wrong? In a word: leadership.

Without effective leadership, no quality program can succeed. Because he recognizes the essential role leaders play in successful quality programs, W. Edwards Deming, the quality guru, refuses to work in any organization unless he can begin with the CEO. This is why the first criterion examined for the Malcolm Baldrige National Quality Award is leadership. Leaders must show the way for their people by nurturing cultures that encourage and reward quality performance, and they must exhibit characteristics that inspire excellence. The payoffs include loyalty, commitment, innovation, quality, and profits. As Robert Galvin of Motorola said, "in my estimation, the real test of quality in the early part of the next century is going to be what I call the quality of leadership."[1]

Three leadership characteristics make the difference: vision, strong values and beliefs, and courage to take the actions that make the vision a reality. *Vision* helps each employee see what the future holds as a rational extension of the present. The vision gives meaning to the work of each individual and each group, uniting all for business success. *Values and beliefs* serve as the basis for direction and action. A quality business is marked by the making of value commitments, and the leader is an expert in the promotion and protection of values. But a person with vision who cannot articulate values and beliefs or inspire others is a dreamer—not a leader. *Action* is required for vision, values, and beliefs to become real. Leaders must possess the discipline and determination to actually do the job. Good intentions are laudable, but they are no substitute for getting the job done.

This book focuses on these three leadership characteristics and builds a foundation for leadership development that aims at producing quality results. By highlighting the leadership practices of such noted leaders as Walt Disney and Michael Eisner, Ray Kroc, and Sam Walton, this book demonstrates what leaders must do if they want their organizations to prosper and grow.

ACKNOWLEDGMENTS

Writing a book is a long and arduous task that requires the dedication and commitment of a host of people. We want to thank our colleagues at the University of Virginia's McIntire School of Commerce for their encouragement and support. We also want to thank Leonard Sandridge, senior vice president and chief financial officer at the University of Virginia, for insights shared as we explored leadership and quality issues in strategic management courses. In addition, we owe a special debt of gratitude to Cindy Orshek, assistant director for programs at the University of Virginia's Division of Continuing Education, for her support and encouragement as she arranged and coordinated seminars on leadership and quality for us.

Student interaction with faculty is a hallmark of the McIntire School of Commerce, and we strive to involve our students in our research and writing to help prepare them to compete in business. Involving them in our work also improves our productivity a great deal. A classic example of this involvement and its evolution over time is Dianne Morse Houghton, coauthor of this book. Dianne is a 1982 graduate of the McIntire School and was one of Neil Snyder's students at the time. After a successful career in business, she now joins Neil and Jim as a full-fledged member of the team working to improve leadership practices in business and nonbusiness organizations. She is our student no longer; she is our partner.

Other students deserve recognition for their contributions to this book as well. Joanna Blattberg, Angela Clontz, and Amir Iskander contributed chapters to this book on Walt

Disney, Sam Walton, and Ray Kroc, respectively. Several other students from the McIntire School provided research assistance and helped us develop our ideas over the past two years. They, too, made valuable contributions to this book, and we wish to recognize them here: Jennifer Gholson, Michelle Graves, Allison Schumacher, Vaishakhi (Tina) Shah, Kevin Phoenix, Andrew Priftis, David Wells, and Karen Maurer. We also thank those others, in many different roles, who have taught us so much about quality and leadership— demanding clients, knowledgeable coworkers and teammates, and nurturing professors.

Our families deserve more recognition for their patience and understanding than we could ever give them. For the times we were preoccupied, for the times we did not seem to care, and for the times we simply were not there, we want to thank Katie, Melanie, and Rebekah Snyder; Gabriele de Grace; and Paul Houghton. We love you all.

PART I

LEADERSHIP AND TOTAL QUALITY

CHAPTER 1

WHAT IS LEADERSHIP?

It is becoming increasingly clear that in many industries, American companies are lagging behind their foreign counterparts, struggling to catch up in the areas of product quality and operational efficiency. Although many U.S. firms are making great strides in performance improvements, foreign competitors continue to improve at an even faster pace. Thus the gap between the two is widening, not narrowing. If these current trends continue, the United States runs the risk of becoming a second-rate economic power.

In an effort to regain the market leadership position they have lost, many American firms have recently begun implementing various management methods and philosophies, hoping these new approaches will solve their business problems. Unfortunately, businesses often identify their so-called problems only in terms of the bottom-line results in their income statements and balance sheets. Because they attend only to financial problems, all too often the root cause of their difficulties—ineffective leadership—is overlooked.

Poor leadership is the primary cause of the declining effectiveness of operational methods and strategies of many U.S. industries over the past few decades. At the end of the operational process, poor leadership has resulted in product quality below most customers' tolerance for imperfection.

Although it has begun to improve dramatically, the U.S. automobile industry provides us with a good example of this trend. General Motors, formerly the model of industrial achievement, has come in the 1990s to represent what U.S. businesses should never be. GM was the world leader in automobiles following World War II, and judging by its income statements and balance sheets, it continued in this leadership position until the early 1980s. Since then, however, GM's financial statements show a different story—a story of poor performance that was years in the making. Although GM has been working on improving corporate operations and processes for over a decade, it is only now beginning to take steps that suggest a proper diagnosis has been made of the root cause of its poor performance: ineffective leadership.

The leadership problem at GM was never more evident than in the late 1980s when the board of directors offered to buy Ross Perot's stock in the company for almost $350 million more than it was worth if he would simply resign from the board and keep quiet about the problems at the company. But the stock price premium was just part of the problem, and not the most important part at that. Only a few weeks before the offer was made to silence Perot, the GM board had announced its intention to lay off personnel and close several plants, ostensibly to cut costs. These actions were supposed to save the company about $500 million. As it turned out, $350 million of that $500 million was earmarked for Perot. How do you think GM workers felt about this decision? What do you think it did to their morale, loyalty, commitment, and productivity? How could those workers have reconciled that decision with the company's push to improve the quality of its products? This action by the board, demonstrating a profound lack of understanding of human nature, speaks clearly about the poor quality of leadership at GM.

By contrast, consider Sam Walton and his company, Wal-Mart (the subject of Chapter 3). They stand as a shining example of what can happen when a leader understands and meets the requirements of an effective leadership role. Walton founded Wal-Mart in 1962 and turned the company into the most profitable retail firm in the country (surpassing even Sears and K-mart) in less than thirty years. He did that by believing in his people and by personally taking the initiative to make things happen. As Walton once said, "When it comes to Wal-Mart, there's no two ways about it, I'm cheap. A lot of what goes on these days with these overpaid CEOs who're really just looking from the top and aren't watching out for anybody but themselves really upsets me. It's one of the main things wrong with American business."[1]

Walton was right on target. Ineffective leadership is the most critical problem confronting American businesses today. Corporate executives have become "money men" interested more in finance and accounting than in manufacturing and delivering top quality products and services. If this trend continues, many U.S. firms will lose their ability to compete in global markets.

This book addresses the importance of effective leadership in reversing that trend. It explores the crucial role of leadership in producing long-term improvement in business operations and product and service quality, and it provides a timely message aimed at helping U.S. firms identify and deal with their leadership deficiency. To set the stage for our leadership discussion, we will first discuss the evolution of our current problem.

COMPLACENCY GETS A FOOTHOLD IN U.S. BUSINESSES

Between the end of World War II and the Arab oil embargo of 1973, the United States was virtually alone at the top of the world's economic ladder. Leaders in U.S. business could do just about anything they wanted and still succeed. Unfortunately, lulled by this stability and security, many chose to ignore important issues like modernization, quality improvement, and the development of the people who worked for them. These leaders forgot the important fact that businesses must move forward with as much vigor during periods of great security as they do during periods of strife.

With the luxury of an overwhelming competitive advantage, American executives failed to explore innovative management styles; instead they settled for the status quo, and management systems and organization structures grew excessively bureaucratic. But in the postwar period they continued to dominate the international business arena, largely because their weakened competitors remained so far behind. In their view from the top, it seemed they could do no wrong.

Sadly, it took twenty years to show us the true costs of that arrogance and complacency. In the 1980s, deficit spending by the federal government brought the illusion of economic prosperity to the United States, but the reality of the situation was the further erosion of our economic strength. The U.S. national debt ballooned from $894 billion to $2.837 trillion during this time, and it increased almost another trillion dollars in 1990 and 1991.[2] By 1990 it was also undeniably clear that businesses in many U.S. industries were far behind their foreign counterparts, and that many others were dangerously close to becoming followers in the global marketplace.

POST–WORLD WAR II DEVELOPMENTS IN JAPAN, EUROPE, RUSSIA, AND CHINA

For the reverse of this story we can look back to 1945 Japan. Decimated by the war, the Japanese were forced to rebuild their economy from the ground up. With active cooperation from the government, businesses in Japan launched an unprecedented rise from the ashes of wartime defeat to their current position of economic strength rivaling that of the United States. But the people of Japan deserve most of the credit for transforming their economy. While Japan is poor in natural resources, it is rich in tradition and culture. Its people were willing to sacrifice, save, invest, and work hard, and they laid the foundation for Japan's ascent to economic power. Business and government leaders in Japan harnessed the people's energy and determination and were thereby able to create one of the world's most powerful economies. Less than fifty years after World War II, with a population of 124 million people (about 50 percent of the U.S. population) and a land area the size of Montana, Japan is positioned for world leadership.

Japan has begun to exercise that economic power in its relations with the Association of Southeast Asian Nations (ASEAN). This economic union, comparable to the European Community in many ways, comprises some of the most successful economic powerhouses in the world. Although Japan is not a member of the group, its tremendous wealth and economic success give it great influence over member nations. History leads many in the region to be continually suspicious of Japan's motives, and the fear of Japanese domination of these smaller states will tend to limit Japan's sway in this developing region. Nonetheless, it appears that Japanese business leaders are quickly learning how to form and sustain mutually beneficial economic alliances. We should expect movement in this direction to continue, and as a result that Japan will be even more competitive in the future.

With some qualifications, we would predict the same for Europe. In the devastated aftermath of World War II, the nations of Europe were fragmented, suspicious of one another, and fiercely independent. They still are. Yet with the advent of the 1992 Single Europe Act, we are supposed to be witnessing the dawn of a new era of unity in the European Community (EC). With a combined population of 325 million people and a $4.6 trillion gross national product (GNP), the EC is, and will continue to be, a force to be reckoned with.

It will not be easy for the member nations of the EC to overcome their differences and learn to work together. For example, in June 1992 the people of Denmark rejected the Maastricht Treaty, which would have moved the EC closer to monetary union and common security. Later, the French approved the treaty by only the slimmest of margins. These actions cast doubts on the union itself. As in the Southwest Pacific region of the world, the nations of Europe are reluctant to give up their sovereignty and independence. The final outcome of the movement to unite Europe is uncertain as of early 1993, but political and economic realities suggest they will eventually see the advantages of working together.

Recent declarations of independence in Poland, Hungary, and other nations formerly in the Soviet bloc signal not only the end of the political threat from communist totalitarianism, but also the beginning of an expansion in the European market as these nations develop market economies. With a combined population of almost eight hundred million people, the economic potential of a union between the European Community and the nations of central and eastern Europe is breathtaking.

To take advantage of the opportunities before them, these countries must learn how to utilize their natural and their human resources. And in that effort, they face the daunting challenge of managing nationalistic tendencies. The peaceful division of Czechoslovakia in 1992 into two separate republics proves that these feelings run strong and deep, and the bloody battles in 1992 and 1993 to define the states of Bosnia, Serbia, and Croatia from the former Yugoslavia are painful reminders of what Europe risks as it moves toward unity. Here again, though, the political and economic advantages of cooperation should eventually persuade the people of Europe to settle their differences.

And what of the former Soviet Union? In August 1991, a stunned world watched as the USSR unraveled almost overnight and the Commonwealth of Independent States (CIS) emerged. One day we learned of a coup and the return of hard-line communist leadership; the next thing we knew, the Russian people stood up against the coup conspirators and said no. One by one, the Soviet republics declared independence, following the lead of the Baltic states a few months earlier.

And so after more than seventy years of communist rule, the Soviet threat ceased to exist. For decades the Soviet people struggled to survive without modern conveniences taken for granted in the West; indeed, many lacked adequate food and decent living conditions while their leaders poured money into the huge military apparatus required to suppress and sustain a far-flung empire. Following the collapse of the USSR, we learned that the nation was spending almost a third of its GNP on the military while the citizens of the country went without basic necessities. In that light, it was not surprising that the USSR fell apart; the surprise was that it took so long to happen (and that it happened so quickly once it started).

Fledgling democracies are now emerging throughout the republics of the CIS. It is not at all certain what form of government will exist in these nations as the twenty-first century begins, but the potential exists for the creation of a wealthy and powerful commonwealth founded on basic beliefs in freedom, human dignity, and democracy. Given the vast resources of Russia alone—its vast land area and its population—the introduction of a market economy could develop that republic into an economic power that could substantially alter the course of human events. The literacy rate in the old Soviet Union was about 98 percent, compared to about 80 percent in the United States.[3] Ironically, in future global competition with the United States, the CIS could find itself in the driver's seat by effectively utilizing its well-educated work force and its natural resource base.

And with a population of about one billion people and one of the most advanced military forces in the world, China should not be overlooked as a potential world economic power. The abundance of low-cost labor in China has already enabled that country to establish itself firmly as a leader in the textile industry. With the capacity to do the same thing in any labor-intensive industry, China can be expected to put significant pressure on firms that fail to modernize and keep pace with changes in technology and management practices. As the 1989 protests (and massacre) in Tiananmen Square showed the world, however, the change to a market economy has ignited the Chinese people's desire for political freedom and has posed a serious challenge to the leaders of this last major totalitarian communist state. With pressures from within and from the free nations of the world, China faces an uncertain future. If it can manage the coming political transition (transferring power from the old communists to the next generation), China may well develop its nascent economic power to rival the United States.

THE TASK FOR THE UNITED STATES

The United States must respond to these profound changes in the world around it.[4] Global competitive pressure and potential future economic threats are forcing U.S. business leaders and government officials to think seriously about the significant changes required to restore the nation's competitiveness in the global economy. The United States has formed a free-trade zone with Canada and will likely form a similar zone with Mexico to capitalize on the human, physical, and fiscal resources of each nation in global competition. Despite inevitable political resistance to such agreements in all three countries, economic realities again suggest that we will continue to move in the direction of increased cooperation with Canada and Mexico.

Our economic prosperity and the prosperity of our children and our grandchildren depend on the decisions our country will make in the 1990s. Never in our nation's history has leadership been more important than it is today. We lost sight of the leadership factor after World War II, and now we have no choice but to regain our perspective and to address the fundamental problems in both business and government.

Since the end of World War II, business executives have been told to monitor their environments closely and to be prepared to deal with unexpected changes if they want their firms to be successful. Those who followed this advice developed an appreciation for the importance of dealing not only with internal matters but also with the external environment. Additionally, business leaders have become more aware that successful managers in today's complex and rapidly changing world must confront current issues and must, at the same time, develop strategies for the future.[5]

But scanning the horizon for fluctuations that might affect the firm's survival is not the leader's job alone; everyone in the organization should do the same. Significant external changes may originate in industries or areas with which people are quite familiar, or they may come from people, places, or things altogether unexpected or unknown. Everyone in the organization must be on guard to detect changes that have the potential to threaten its well-being, and the leader's performance in motivating people to assume this responsibility can mean the difference between success and failure.

Consider the example of Baldwin Locomotive, the largest and most successful manufacturer of steam locomotives in the United States, put out of business after World War II by General Motors. During the war, GM developed the diesel locomotive. At first, it was a very crude and expensive technology that Baldwin's people chose to ignore, although they were aware of GM's work. Its preeminence in the industry and the belief that the diesel locomotive could not work brought Baldwin down. Had Baldwin's people been diligent, they would have studied the diesel locomotive, understood its advantages, and adopted *and improved* the new technology in a timely fashion. They did not; Baldwin is history, and Baldwin's leaders were responsible.

The leader's role in nurturing organizational cultures that encourage people to look beyond tradition and to excel is pivotal. In the 1990s it is not sufficient (in fact, it never was sufficient) for leaders to concentrate on controlling internal operations and such short-run performance measures as quarterly profits and production efficiency. They must also focus on finding innovative people and helping these people develop their abilities—an activity that only shows its true value over time. The payoffs for firms whose leaders assume these responsibilities include an increase in the loyalty and commitment of their employees and improved innovation, quality, and profits.

The importance of each individual's performance to the creation and maintenance of successful long-term corporate performance is being increasingly recognized.

> It is people within the organization who come up with new ideas, who develop creative responses, and who push for change before opportunities disappear or minor irritants turn into catastrophes. Innovations, whether in products, market strategies, technological processes, or work practices, are designed not by machines but by people. . . . And so, after years of telling corporate citizens to "trust the system," many companies must relearn instead to trust their people—and encourage their people to use neglected creative capacities in order to tap the most potent economic stimulus of all: idea power.[6]

People, not organizations, have ideas; people create, and people innovate. In the final analysis, individual efforts determine whether businesses succeed or fail. Thus, we turn our attention to the role leaders play in motivating individuals to exercise their creative abilities and to produce superior quality goods and services. Identifying and removing impediments to individual performance is one of the most important jobs leaders have. Failure in this role can be devastating.

CREATIVITY IN U.S. COMPANIES

For businesses to compete successfully in today's world economy, they must be creative, and their products and services must be regarded as being significantly better than those of their less creative counterparts. To be creative, firms must adopt an innovative, entrepreneurial, flexible, and responsive approach to solving problems and making decisions. They

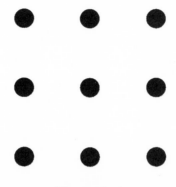

Figure 1–1

must also develop a capacity for renewing themselves and for continuously rethinking every phase of their operation. Experimentation is fundamental to this philosophy of corporate life, and disciplined management makes new ideas work once a decision is made to implement them.[7]

Unfortunately, for a variety of reasons, the people in most U.S. companies are not creative. Many companies foster large bureaucracies that generate unnecessary anxiety and effectively stifle innovation. Over the years, they have established deeply embedded traditions of deductive thinking and analytical problem solving, traditions that restrict the number and type of alternatives considered and perpetuate the status quo. To protect these sacred traditions and to minimize opposition to the way they do business, managers in these businesses recruit, hire, and promote people just like themselves. With no diversity in the work force and no creative role models, nothing new happens. And at the root of these problems you will find the people who run the company, the people who should be leaders, but are not.

In our leadership seminars, we use a simple exercise to show executives how pervasive this lack of creativity is. In Figure 1–1 you will see nine dots. We ask the executives to connect all nine dots using four straight lines without lifting their pens from the paper. Try it yourself; it is not as easy as you might think. Some of the executives in our seminars have seen this exercise before, but few of them remember how to connect all the dots. Rarely does a participant in the seminar figure out how to connect the dots in a reasonable amount of time.

Figure 1–2 shows the solution. Once we have shown it to the group, they understand immediately why they were unable to solve the problem and why their firms lack creativity. To solve the problem, they must extend their lines beyond the boundaries they see. What they see in our discussion after this exercise is that in fact *there are no boundaries.* They simply assume that they cannot go beyond the outer dots, and so they fail to solve the problem. This self-imposed constraint makes an otherwise simple task impossible to perform, yet it is a mistake repeated countless times each day by people in their organizations. This limited thinking within "rules" that do not exist keeps them from competing effectively, and it could, left unchecked, lead to their demise.

Creative companies are different. They attract and nurture intelligent, creative, and innovative people. They use a problem-solving philosophy that emphasizes *what* is right instead of *who* is right; they question assumptions, and they promote their best performers. Creative companies do not rely on close supervision and extravagant control procedures to get the job done. Instead, they rely on the character of their employees, expecting the latter to do what is right because it is right, not because they are told to do so. Leaders in these companies have a fundamental belief in and respect for their people, and they recognize that the company benefits when its people are allowed to "act out their aspirations."[8] This approach is especially appropriate in today's business environment. When the old rules and procedures no longer apply, we desperately need creative people with new ideas, new ways of doing new things we have never done before.

Executives must accept the fact that uncertainty and am-

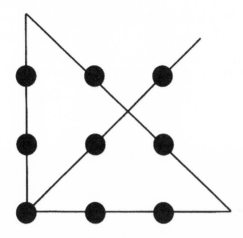

Figure 1–2

biguity will continue to be normal elements of their lives. Survival in this uncertain world of business will be determined more by the ability of leaders to marshal their forces to take appropriate action than by their ability to produce a few consecutive quarters of good financial reports. No longer will the mere application of policies and procedures suffice, even in industries that have relied on them almost exclusively in the past. Leaders must inspire their people with a shared vision and values, not just allow but encourage them to think and act accordingly, and reward them for doing so. It is this ability to make things happen that will separate the winners from the losers.

LEADERSHIP VERSUS MANAGEMENT

Most U.S. organizations are overmanaged and underled.[9] When leaders are more interested in looking good than in doing what is right and necessary, the results can be catastrophic. The U.S. experience in Vietnam illustrates what happens when management supplants leadership and form takes precedence over substance. Jeffery Record, a U.S. defense critic, made this point in his analysis of America's failure in Vietnam: "Too many military men forgot why they were in uniform. Promotion-hungry officers more interested in 'punching the ticket' too often forgot to lead their men and treated them like interchangeable parts in some vast machine. . . . Men cannot be managed to their deaths; they must be led there."[10]

Sadly, American graduate schools of business have exacerbated our leadership problem since the late 1950s. They have spent far too much time teaching students to use a rational, deductive, analytical problem-solving approach in managing people and things, and far too little time on leadership. Abraham Zaleznik, the former Konosuke Matsushita professor of leadership at Harvard Business School, distinguishes the two in this way: "Managers aim to shift balances of power toward solutions acceptable as compromises among conflicting values . . . [while] leaders develop fresh ideas to long-standing problems and open issues to new options. . . . [Leaders have] much more in common with artists, scientists, and other creative thinkers than they do with managers."[11]

In practice, leaders are team builders who draw forth the talent of individuals to produce results that satisfy both the team members and the team's customers. Managers, on the other hand, typically form committees to address issues and problems. And the difference is clear, according to Ralph Stayer, CEO of Johnsonville Foods: "A team has a vision. Committees have agendas—often, separate agendas."[12]

Until recently management textbooks discussed their subject almost exclusively in terms of what are known as the "management functions" (including planning, organizing, staffing, directing, and controlling). They, too, paid very little attention to questions about leadership. When they did address leadership issues they focused on psychological, sociological, and anthropological concerns, but they gave only scant attention to the roles leaders play in organizations. Although the management functions are important activities that are essential in keeping an organization running smoothly, merely performing them well is no guarantee of success. For that, leadership is required.

Fortunately, things are beginning to change. For example, it was reported in 1992 that General Electric had implemented a plan to reward and promote executives on the basis of demonstrated leadership ability and to remove those who do not lead. Under John F. Welch, Jr., chairman and chief executive officer, GE divides leaders into four groups. Type 1 leaders deliver on commitments and share the company's values. Their futures are bright. Type 2 leaders, on the other hand, do not deliver on commitments and do not share the company's values. They do not last long. Type 3 leaders are those who have difficulty delivering on commitments but who share the company's values; they are given a second chance and are relocated.

The final class, Type 4 leaders, deliver on commitments but do not share the company's values. They are autocrats who squeeze every ounce of productivity they can get out of their people. Their performance is good, but only in the short run. According to Welch, their inability to inspire their subordinates and to help them grow professionally is not acceptable "in an environment where we must have every good idea from every man and woman in the organization. . . . We cannot afford management styles that suppress and intimidate."[13] This type of leader may be able to manage, but he or she does not have a clue about what leading is.

As the matrix at General Electric implies, position in the management hierarchy is not always a good indicator of leadership ability. In late 1992 and early 1993 we have seen numerous examples of CEOs effectively forced out of office for failure to lead, including Robert Stempel of General Motors, James Robinson of American Express, and John Akers of IBM.

We take this as a positive sign: at the highest level, American business is taking a fresh, critical look at its leaders. The critical question for the future is, will their successors lead more effectively?

HOW LEADERS ARE DIFFERENT

In our view, three things distinguish leaders from managers: vision, strong values and beliefs, and the courage to act to make their visions real.

Vision

To a leader, vision is a reality that has not yet come to be; it is not a dream. This vision reflects a depth and breadth of understanding that enables one to detect patterns or trends as they unfold, and it guides a leader through the present and into the future.

> A true vision must provide a clear image of a desirable future—one that represents an achievable, challenging, and worthwhile long-range target toward which people can direct their energies. . . . For example . . . a corporate leader may have a "vision" of getting back to the basics or cutting the budget. As commendable as these goals may be, they hardly suggest a future distinctly different from and better than the past.[14]

A vision of the future is more than just a plan or a goal. It is a picture of what the future should and could look like; plans and goals operate as vehicles for making that picture a reality. "For leaders, the responsibility is to transform the vision into a reality. By doing so, they transform their dominion, whether an airline, a motion picture, the computer industry or America itself."[15] True leadership acts in direct opposition to mediocrity; it is concerned with greatness. As Henry Kissinger puts it: "Leaders must invoke an alchemy of great vision. Those who do not are ultimately judged failures, even though they may be popular at the moment."[16] True leaders possess vision, and having vision provides a leader with purpose. This will be crucial in moving businesses in our nation successfully into the twenty-first century.

Values and Beliefs

Values and beliefs are critical dimensions in leadership effectiveness because they serve as the basis for direction and action. According to management expert Philip Selznick, "The formation of an institution is marked by the making of value commitments . . . [and] the institutional leader is primarily an expert in the promotion and protection of values."[17] Put more simply, leaders in successful firms personify the values they profess, and they live the values the business represents.

Ray Kroc, founder of McDonald's, provides a good example of the leader's role in promoting and protecting values. The stated values of McDonald's are quality, service, value, and cleanliness. Cleanliness in particular is difficult to realize, and yet it differentiates McDonald's from the typical fast food restaurant. Like all other fast food franchisers, McDonald's relies on part-time, minimum-wage employees, many still in high school, to keep its stores clean. These are the same people whose mothers cannot get them to make their beds at home. How does McDonald's do it?

As the story goes, one day Ray Kroc walked into one of his franchise stores during the lunch rush, and the place was packed. In the corner of the store, someone had spilled a drink on a table, and it had rolled off the table onto a chair and the floor. The employees were so busy that no one noticed the mess, but Kroc saw it. He could have gone to the manager and brought it to his attention, but instead Kroc went into the back, got a mop and a rag, and cleaned up the mess himself.

No one in the store knew Kroc personally, so the employees must have wondered what was going on when the "old guy" took the mop and the rag. Some of them may have thought he was a thief. What did they think when they learned that the man who cleaned their floor was Ray Kroc, the multimillionaire chairman of the company? To say the least, if there were doubts in their minds about the importance of cleanliness, they were erased. Kroc's unspoken message was at McDonald's, cleanliness is so important that the chairman of the company will mop the floor if necessary. Knowing this makes it easier for the employees to work hard to keep the place clean. As a result, many customers will come to a McDonald's primarily to use a clean restroom, but then buy food while they are in the store. This is only a part of the vision that Ray Kroc's leadership made real; we will return to his example in more detail in Chapter 7.

A person with vision who cannot articulate beliefs and values and inspire others is a dreamer, not a leader. Values and beliefs are fundamental to what the United States stands for, and they continue to play an important role in maintaining the strength of our nation today. In 1776 one of our founding fathers, George Mason, said, "No free government, nor the blessings of liberty, can be preserved to any people, but by . . . a frequent recurrence to fundamental principles."[18]

Thomas Watson, Jr., the genius behind IBM, had a similar view. He believed that an organization must have a strong set of beliefs on which it bases all policies and actions. For each organization there is a core set of values and beliefs that determines the organization's survival and success. These are so fundamental that "if an organization is to meet the challenge of a changing world, it must be prepared to change everything about itself except those beliefs as it moves through corporate life."[19]

The founders and great leaders of a business inevitably

impart their own values and beliefs to the organizations they create. As a result, each company has its own unique set of core beliefs and values, much like an individual's character. In our research, however, we have found that organizations committed to quality share some essential beliefs and values. These may be expressed in different ways, but in essence they are the same. For example, in their book *In Search of Excellence,* Peters and Waterman describe the seven basic beliefs shared by the excellent companies they studied:

- Belief in being the best
- Belief in the importance of the details of execution (the nuts and bolts of doing the job well)
- Belief in the importance of people as individuals
- Belief in superior quality and service
- Belief that most members of the organization should be innovators (and its corollary, the willingness to support failure)
- Belief in the importance of informality to enhance communication
- Belief in and recognition of the importance of economic growth and profits[20]

Motorola, the first winner of the Malcolm Baldrige National Quality Award, is a company with a strong belief system. Its stated "seven attributes of a quality system" are strikingly similar to the beliefs found in excellent firms by Peters and Waterman.[21] The attributes are as follows:

- Extend leadership and quality commitment from top to bottom
- Communicate to every employee so that each knows that his or her individual contribution helps
- Train every employee and teach them the corporate language

- Establish challenging goals and very high standards
- Recognize successes in achieving quality through incentives and other rewards
- Create a participative and cooperative culture throughout the company and between divisions
- Develop a high quality, creative, receptive, and adaptive work force by developing employees to their fullest potential

According to George Fisher, chairman and chief executive of Motorola, the concept of *cycle time* ties these attributes together. Cycle time has been promoted by the Boston Consulting Group as an important competitive weapon for businesses competing at the global level. It is defined as either the time it takes to convert a customer need into a product that satisfies that need, or the time it takes to convert an idea into a product that is ready for the market. Cycle time can be used as a method to measure company effectiveness and improvement. The idea is that reductions in cycle time play a critical role in determining who wins and who loses in business. Reorienting U.S. businesses so that they consider a reduction in cycle time to be a competitive advantage in the global market will be an important job for leaders in the twenty-first century.

Our own research has led us to conclude that three primary values sum up all of these concepts. These three values are critical to success in today's businesses, and they will be dealt with individually in Chapters 8, 9, and 10 of this book. They are as follows:

- A focus on the customer
- Continuous improvement
- Employee empowerment

It should be noted that these values are found in excellent business and nonbusiness organizations. They may be adopted successfully no matter what products or services a firm sells and no matter how often those product or service lines change.

Courage to Take Action

Most important of all, leaders must possess the discipline, determination and courage necessary to get the job done. "A unique feature of the human brain is its ability to form mental images of the future and to translate these images into reality through leadership and action."[22] Good intentions are laudable, but they have no material value if they are not carried out.

The old adage that actions speak louder than words is especially true for leaders. They must possess more than vision and values. They must have discipline, energy, determination, zeal and courage to carry them through the difficult periods and, perhaps more important, to keep them moving forward during the good times as well. Teddy Roosevelt probably captured the essence of this leadership quality when he said:

> It's not the critic who counts, not the man who points out how the strong man stumbled, or where the doer of deeds could have done better. The credit belongs to the man who is actually in the arena; whose face is marred by dust and sweat and blood. Who strives valiantly; who errs and comes short again and again . . . who knows the great enthusiasms, the great devotions, and spends himself in a worthy cause. Who at the least knows in the end the triumph of high achievement; and who, at the worst, if he fails at least fails while doing greatly, so that his place shall never be with those cold and timid souls who know neither victory nor defeat.[23]

As we have said, true leaders share three basic characteristics: vision, strongly held values and beliefs, and the courage to take action. Possessing one or two of these qualities is not enough, because all three form a gestalt—an integrated whole. Most of the problems businesses face today result from a lack of leadership. We are witnessing a resurgence of creativity and innovation in this nation, however, and there is evidence of a similar resurgence in the recognition of the importance of leadership. Business people are realizing that the performance of the leadership role is essential not just for success, but for survival.

This book addresses the role of leadership in producing quality goods and services that are competitive in global markets. In the next chapter, we will review the views of the leading thinkers in the quality management movement before we move on to explore in more detail the role of leaders in producing quality results.

CHAPTER 2

LEADING TO QUALITY

W idely hailed as "the fundamental business strategy of the 1990s,"[1] quality is the hottest topic going in manufacturing, service, government, and not-for-profit organizations. In increasingly competitive and uncertain environments, all these organizations have learned that success depends on one thing above all else: meeting customers' demands for quality goods and services. And after years of hard work, practice, and patience, some of these organizations have learned to harness the creativity of their employees and to develop the flexibility required to deliver quality results consistently.

But if quality is the battleground on which global competition is taking place, studies conducted in the early 1990s by the American Quality Foundation in association with Ernst and Young suggest that U.S. firms are neither leading the battle nor winning the war.[2] To achieve true competitiveness in the global marketplace, many U.S. companies are developing so-called quality programs: planning and implementing a web of strategies, objectives, and tactics in an effort to help their companies develop "quality cultures" in order to catch up with their competition. Unfortunately, many of these programs are falling short of expectations. A 1992 study by McKinsey and Company of quality programs found that two-thirds had "stalled or fallen short of yielding real improvements."[3] Even winners of the prestigious Malcolm Baldrige National Quality Award, show kinks in their quality armor— one recipient has even gone out of business! Why is this happening? Has the quality movement turned out to be just another flavor-of-the-month management practice after all?

Must U.S. firms learn to accept and play the role of the provider of undifferentiated products for low margin mass markets?

We think not, and the facts suggest we are right. There are more than enough success stories that tell of the advantages of a quality strategy. When implemented correctly, a quality strategy can lead to excellence in operations. Failures are the results of poor implementation, often because the organization's leaders failed to understand and to fulfill their essential role in the effort.

It is the basic premise of this book that quality cannot be achieved without leadership. Leaders in U.S. businesses must lead the people in their organizations to a commitment to quality and to a quality culture. They must lead their organizations through a long and difficult process of change. With effective leadership, American business can improve productivity, eliminate waste, produce quality goods and services, and ultimately regain global competitiveness and guarantee the nation's long-term economic prosperity.

Transformation to a quality culture is both time-consuming and difficult, but it can be achieved if business leaders commit themselves to it. The success of an organization in developing a quality culture hinges on its leaders' possessing and then effectively communicating a quality vision, identifying and personifying the values and beliefs that define the vision, and taking the actions necessary to make their vision a reality. In Chapter 4, we will talk more about leadership and vision, but first we will lay the foundation for an understanding of what it means to be a quality-centered business.

A FRAMEWORK FOR LEADING TO QUALITY

"Total quality management" (TQM), "total customer satisfaction," "zero defects," "statistical process control," "Ishikawa diagrams," "quality improvement teams"—these buzzwords all represent different quality philosophies, programs, or techniques currently used by different organizations in their efforts to develop a quality culture. As we have said, however, quality philosophies and programs in and of themselves will not suffice; their value lies in helping leaders establish and communicate their vision and their values and beliefs, and in providing proven frameworks for action.

There is significant debate (and, some would argue, great confusion) about what quality is and how it becomes part of an organization's culture. Yet the fundamental principles underlying TQM are simple and easy to understand, and their importance to business leaders should be readily apparent.

The Quality Movement

Over the past few years, the success stories of companies that have implemented quality philosophies have appeared again and again in the business press, to the point where some companies are assuming legendary status. Xerox is an example of a company that made the transition to a quality operation. After years of complacency, the company awakened in the late 1970s only after seeing its market share drop from 18.5 percent to 10 percent over a five-year period. Its very survival threatened, Xerox responded by developing and implementing its Leadership Through Quality (LTQ) program. With this program, Xerox achieved astounding improvements in quality that in turn improved its market share and financial performance. By 1990 Xerox's LTQ program had produced the following results:

- Defects per hundred machines manufactured were reduced by a factor of ten.
- The number of production suppliers was reduced by a factor of ten.
- The defect rate on incoming parts was decreased from 80,000 to 325 parts per million.

- Fifteen million dollars was saved in receiving inspection costs.
- Unscheduled product maintenance was cut by 40 percent and customer complaints by 60 percent, and
- Unit manufacturing costs were reduced by 45 percent and defects per machine by 78 percent while product output quality was improved by 50 percent.

As Xerox and other companies committing to quality began to show such remarkable results, and their success stories were widely and repeatedly celebrated in the U.S. press, executives in other businesses rapidly developed an interest in total quality management. By the late 1980s, the quality movement in America was in full bloom. Interested managers soon learned, however, that developing and implementing a quality philosophy was no easy matter. From the start, they were faced with a number of quality philosophies from which to choose.

TQM Principles

There are many ways to define and measure quality, and just as many approaches for improving quality within an organization. All of these approaches, however, are very similar in substance. Stated simply, a quality product or service is one that satisfies and meets the requirements of its user. Thus, a customer focus is essential for developing a quality culture, and continually improving every aspect of its operations enables a firm to retain the customers it has earned. An easy way to understand the difference between a business that is working to achieve a quality orientation and one that is not is to compare some characteristics of their operations. Table 2–1 shows characteristics of typical U.S. companies alongside those of quality firms.

As Table 2–1 reveals, a quality orientation really does differ from the basic business culture and management philosophy of the traditional American company. A quality culture is the product of an integrated effort to improve products, services, and processes continually. It involves everyone in the organization and requires a new understanding of the relationships between a business and all its constituents, especially its customers and its suppliers. Business as usual simply will not suffice any longer. The day passed more than a decade ago when U.S. firms could ignore quality and survive.

A telling comparison of these two business cultures can be found in the experience of Motorola, which sold its Quasar television operations to the Japanese firm Matsushita. At the time, Quasar was recognized as a high-quality product within the American television industry. After buying the operation, Matsushita introduced changes in the operation's manufacturing process to improve product quality and reduce costs. Three years later, improvements were evident in the product's field failure data: the cost of annual service calls dropped

Table 2–1
COMPARISON OF BUSINESS CHARACTERISTICS

The Typical Business	Quality-Supporting Business
Short-term objective orientation	Long-term goals balanced with short-term objectives
Focus on financial performance	Focus on meeting customer requirements
Managing resources and performance personnel	Managing resources and leading personnel
Reactive/problem correction approach using intuition	Proactive/problem prevention approach using data
Acceptance of a margin of error	Striving for continuous improvement with a goal of error-free output
Inspecting product quality at the end of a process	Improving processes so as to build quality into the product
Nonparticipative problem solving/decision making	Empowered employees participating in problem solving/decision making

from $22 million to $4 million, and assembly line inspection and repair personnel decreased from 120 to 15.

There can be no more powerful lesson in the value of a real commitment to quality: the same operation, moving from American management working with the typical U.S. business culture to Japanese management working with a quality business culture, achieves remarkable improvements. Results like these make it easy to understand why many U.S. firms saw promise in the quality movement. Among those who learned this lesson was Motorola itself, first winner of the Malcolm Baldrige National Quality Award and one of the most successful businesses to implement a quality culture. Motorola's current goal is to achieve only 60 defects per *billion* product components! *That* is quality performance, and it is evidence of the profound impact of a quality philosophy on a business.

Numerous books have been written about what quality is and how it should be implemented. Quality has in fact become a big business, generating more than $750 million in revenue in 1991 for more than fifteen hundred quality and training consultants, earning an estimated 34 percent pretax profit.[4] Although each of these experts provides his or her own brand of quality to the consumer, they all are guided by the following principles:

- A quality product or service is one that meets customer requirements.
- Quality operations are achieved by continually improving all work processes. This is done by using tools, techniques, and training to plan new processes and to analyze and solve quality problems with existing processes, as well as by integrating efforts across all operations, involving all personnel in working toward a shared quality vision.
- Quality cultures are achieved by empowered employees who make quality a way of life, not just a buzzword, in their organizations.

Developing a quality culture in an organization most often requires a dramatic change in the way people in the organization see the world and their roles within it. It requires that they think and act differently. The extent of the needed change in culture can be traumatic for any organization and, like all change, it is often actively resisted by many. This is why the role of the leader in developing a quality culture is so critical. Only strong leadership communicating a shared vision can guide an organization through the change needed for a quality orientation. David Kearns was able to develop a quality vision within Xerox and lead the organization in changing to a quality culture. Without the vision and commitment of top management, achieving quality results will remain an illusive dream.

PROVEN QUALITY TECHNIQUES

Making the quality dream a reality for businesses worldwide has become a crusade for W. Edwards Deming, Joseph M. Juran, and Philip B. Crosby. These "quality gurus" have each developed quality philosophies and detailed approaches to implementing them. While the specifics of their approaches differ somewhat, the philosophies themselves are quite similar—so similar, in fact, that most organizations mix and adapt elements from all of them in an effort to determine their own approach to quality. (The International Quality Study found that 584 companies participating in their survey used 945 different quality management tactics in developing their in-house programs.[5])

The real difference between these men seems to be their teaching style. Deming, who is more than 90 years old, is known for his impatience and sarcasm with managers at all levels, often biting the hand that feeds him. No matter how much people have read about his crusty disposition, interaction with Dr. Deming often comes as a shock. Although his seminars were associated with George Washington University,

Deming carries his message as a virtual one-man show, keeping a pace considered hectic for men thirty years younger. Juran is approaching ninety as well; considered to be less abrasive than Deming (and known more for his bow ties and dry wit), Juran ended his one-man stint in 1979, when he founded the Total Quality Institute to carry on his work. Crosby is the youngster of the bunch—decades younger than his revered colleagues—but he makes up for his relative youth with his high energy and enthusiasm. Crosby founded the enormously successful Philip Crosby Associates (PCA) in 1979, which with annual revenue of more than eighty-four million dollars is by far the most profitable organization in the business. Both Juran and Crosby have recently left their organizations: Juran retired, and Crosby sold PCA and is now launching a new enterprise focused on leadership.

Through their efforts and enterprises, each of these men have made significant contributions to our understanding of what it takes to produce quality results, and we owe them a debt of gratitude. Although this book is not a primer on their differing quality programs and philosophies, the following pages are intended to provide a basic understanding of the fundamentals of each man's approach.

Deming's Management Method

W. Edwards Deming's goal is the transformation of American management. "American management on the whole has a negative scrap value. It's like an old refrigerator you can't sell. You have to pay someone $25 to cart it off."[6] This transformation "is not a job of reconstruction, nor is it revision. It requires a whole new structure, from foundation upward."[7] Dr. Deming, as he is called, preaches a philosophy that is embedded in the ideals of quality and continuous improvement, and he says he can direct a company through the needed transformation. Given the success of the many firms that have adopted his philosophy, including Ford and AT & T, it is easy to see why Deming is revered as the leader of America's quality revolution.

A Start in Statistics

Deming's approach to quality was conceived in the early 1930s.[8] While working for the U.S. Department of Agriculture, Deming was introduced to Walter A. Shewhart of Bell Telephone Laboratories. Shewhart had developed statistical theories of quality control that identified the role of random variation in work processes. These theories became the basis of Deming's now-famous statistical and quality management methods.

Many people have the impression that Deming's early statistical control applications were ignored in America, prompting him to seek another audience for his ideas. Surprisingly, however, much of American industry was educated in Deming's statistical control techniques during World War II. More than thirty-five thousand American workers learned Deming's Statistical Quality Control (SQC) methods as part of the government's drive for quality manufacturing for the war effort. In the rush of postwar industrial prosperity, however, Deming's SQC came to be considered cumbersome and costly. Much to his disappointment, these techniques were left behind following the war as U.S. firms rushed to produce goods and services for a market that was short on foreign competition and long on pent-up consumer demand.

Nothing could provide more of a contrast than the postwar industrial positions of the U.S. and Japan. U.S. industry was on the fast track from wartime expansion; Japan's industrial base had to be rebuilt from scratch. Enter Deming. First visiting Japan in the late 1940s to help plan for the Japanese census, Deming was invited back by the Union of Japanese Scientists and Engineers (JUSE), who had become familiar with his statistical control methods. By the time Deming accepted the invitation to instruct Japan's industrial leaders in

SQC, he had learned a lesson from his work in the United States. He was sure that his quality methods had not endured because America's corporate *leaders* did not understand their significance and were not committed to their use. In Japan, Deming targeted his message first to industry leaders—a strategy that he cites as critical to the successful adoption of his techniques throughout that country. For his work in Japan, Deming was awarded a medal by the emperor and had the country's highly coveted quality award, the Deming Prize, named after him.

It took more than thirty years for Deming's fame to spread to the United States. In 1980, a program about quality entitled "If Japan Can . . . Why Can't We?" aired on the NBC television network. Deming was featured at the end of the broadcast. He discussed his work and, with his now-famous candor, criticized corporate America for its lack of determination to achieve quality. Deming and his philosophy have been in great demand ever since.

The Deming Method

In the spirit of continuous improvement, Deming has been modifying and improving his management method for more than forty years. Starting with a set of statistical control and problem-solving techniques used to increase quality while lowering the cost of production, Deming has developed a complete management philosophy. His philosophy is simple: a company must continually improve the quality of its products or services with the singular goal of satisfying its customers. To be successful, says Deming, a company must embrace and implement his philosophy in its entirety throughout the organization—in effect, transforming the company's current culture to a quality culture. According to Deming, this transformation must begin with, and be led by, top management.

Deming's quality transformation is accomplished by following his now-famous "fourteen points" for management, avoiding his "deadly diseases," and overcoming frequently seen "obstacles."⁹ These guidelines, presented in the Appendix at the end of the book, involve every aspect of an organization, including its purpose, philosophy, culture, and operations, as well as the roles of and interactions between management and employees. Briefly, Deming asserts that organizations must do the following:

- Adopt the philosophy of quality improvement in full. This includes defining a single overriding corporate commitment to continually improving products and services and the work processes that produce them.
- Build quality into work processes; do not "inspect" them into the products or services at the end of the process.
- Work with suppliers to develop long-term quality relationships rather than awarding business merely on the basis of price.
- Take fear out of the workplace and provide workers with the training required to ensure that they have the information and resources they need to do the job right.
- Educate workers about quality improvement, eliminate numerical quotas, and remove barriers to pride of workmanship.
- Break down barriers between different groups within the organization.
- Develop and carry out a plan of action to accomplish all of the above.

Management Must Lead the Transformation

Implementing Deming's philosophy requires time, resources, and most importantly, the complete commitment of top management. Demonstrating his belief in leadership involvement, Deming will only work with a company at the invitation of its CEO. (He also requires a contract agreeing to complete conformance to his directions, and if he does not get things done to his satisfaction, he will fire a client!) Deming stresses management's role because he believes that management is responsible for as much as *94 percent* of a company's quality problems. This view is a constant source of irritation for many managers, who blame employees for the majority of quality problems. Not so, says Deming, pointing out that although they are held accountable for the quality of their work, employees are usually not allowed to make changes in the way they do it. Furthermore, employees often do not have the knowledge, skills, or proper equipment needed to do the job correctly. All these things are under management's control, and so, Deming concludes, are the problems. It is management's responsibility to make the changes that will solve quality problems.

Using Statistical Process Control (SPC)

SPC is a technique used to monitor changes, or variation, in whatever a process produces. If you are making ball bearings, for example, SPC can track the changes in the weights or diameters of the ball bearings rolling off the assembly line. The measurement of variation is important, according to Deming, because the quality of what you produce improves as process variability decreases. SPC is a tool to help develop quality processes; however, it is just a tool, and only one of many parts of a quality culture. Unfortunately many firms learn about SPC, put these measures in place, and then think that they have completed their transformation to a quality culture. Their lack of results soon teaches them otherwise!

SPC has two basic benefits: it can identify sources of quality problems that must be fixed to bring a work process under control, and it can spot areas where quality can be improved. When used to bring work processes under control, SPC techniques help distinguish the normal, random variation that is in any work process (very few ball bearings will have *exactly* the same weight) from any abnormal or unusual variations that might also be present. SPC determines the normal limits of a process (say 1.2 to 1.4 ounces for our ball-bearing weight limits) and measures products coming out of the process to ensure that they are within those limits. If they are, the process is considered to be in control. Measurements beyond those limits signal that there is a problem somewhere in the process, which is then considered out of control.

Problems that throw a process out of control are sometimes attributable to "special causes" (such as bad raw material) that can be traced to an individual worker or an activity, but according to Deming, only 6 percent of a company's quality problems come from such causes. The other 94 percent of quality problems are due to "common causes," or faults in the system. Because management alone can change the system, it bears responsibility for these problems. Deming recommends that management use SPC to identify these common causes and then eliminate them. This is the second purpose of SPC: to improve processes, even those in control.

According to Deming, the result of implementing his philosophy is "continual reduction in mistakes, continual improvement of quality, mean lower and lower costs. Less rework in manufacturing. Less waste—less waste of materials, machine time, tools, human effort. Your costs go down. So many ways they go down. As costs go down, through less rework, fewer mistakes, less waste, your productivity goes up."[10]

Juran's Approach to Quality Improvement

Dr. Joseph M. Juran is a pioneer of the quality movement and a rival of Deming for decades. In a career that has spanned almost seventy years, Juran has worked as an industrial executive, government administrator, university professor, labor arbitrator, author, and management consultant. Today, Juran's name is synonymous with the concept of managing for quality. He has written extensively on the subjects of quality control and quality management; *Juran's Quality Control Handbook* (fourth edition, 1988) is the international standard reference work on this subject.

As an electrical engineer with Western Electric Company in the 1920s, Juran, like Deming, was influenced by Walter Shewhart and his statistical control theories. Also like Deming, Juran and his theories first gained respect and prominence in Japan. Invited to that country by JUSE in 1954, however, Juran was quick to distinguish his quality methods from Deming's. While Deming was advocating the application of statistical controls to identify variation, Juran was addressing methods of managing for quality. And although Japan's quality award is named for Deming, Juran's work is often cited as having the greatest long-term impact on Japanese industry. In fact, his approach is said to be responsible for the evolution of Deming's own theories of quality from a narrow focus on statistical process control techniques to a comprehensive management philosophy. Regardless, the two men are quick to point out differences in their approaches and, while always polite to each other, are said to be keen rivals.

Juran's Quality System

To Juran, quality is a customer-oriented concept that he defines simply as "fitness for use." After all, only the user can really judge how well a product fits its planned use. A product is fit for use when it satisfies the customer's needs with its design, operation, and service. By meeting its customer's needs, a product will generate income for a company. And yes, income is important; as Juran points out, "if you don't have the income, all the rest is academic"! Juran lists the following cost-oriented elements of a product's fitness: freedom from waste, freedom from trouble, and freedom from failure.

Juran focuses on organizing and implementing a "quality system" with the objective of nurturing a commitment to providing quality to the customer in every phase of business operation. A quality system includes Juran's three quality processes, which are often combined in the term *total quality control:*

- *Quality planning,* to develop products and processes that meet customers' needs as well as to establish quality objectives and to develop plans to meet those objectives
- *Quality improvement,* to break through to new levels of quality peformance by eliminating the causes of chronic waste in work processes
- *Quality control,* to maintain quality processes at optimal effectiveness by measuring performance against standards and taking the necessary corrective action to bring processes back under control

The Role of Management

Juran is a strong advocate of employee involvement in implementing quality improvement, stressing that the entire organization must become involved in implementing a successful quality system. Like Deming, Juran places the responsibility for the success or failure of a system squarely on management. Quality improvement requires an "ongoing shift in corporate consciousness," which can only be accomplished by an organization's leaders. To infuse quality successfully into its operations, an organization must develop the habit of making annual improvements in quality and annual reductions in quality-related costs. On a practical level, this means that quality must become part of a company's formal planning system along with strategic business plans and operating budgets, and it must be given constant attention by the company's leaders.

Management must not delegate these responsibilities and simply play the role of the "quality cheerleader." Leadership is necessary if quality is to be a priority in the organization. To lead the organization to quality, says Juran, management must do the following:

- Undergo training in how to think about quality, how to plan for quality, and how to measure improvement. Management must create "the quality improvement program—including setting quality policies, goals, plans, controls, and incentives."
- Make the organizational changes necessary to meet the new quality goals and implement the new quality policies, focusing on coordination, teamwork, and the elimination of departmental boundaries.
- Personally review and reward performance through a revised compensation system that includes measures of performance on quality improvement and control. This requires the development of accurate measures of quality.
- Stay personally involved as the quality goals are communicated to lower levels of the organization.
- Approve and fund expenditures necessary to achieve the established quality goals.[11]

The Cost of Quality

To help managers understand the impact of poor quality, Juran invokes his "cost of quality" accounting system. This system identifies the true cost of quality as that of making, finding, repairing, or avoiding defects. Juran uses these terms largely to get management's attention and their commitment for improvement efforts.

Juran also uses this cost-of-quality system to identify the

point at which additional improvements are no longer cost-effective for a process. Here Juran's approach differs from Deming's and Crosby's. He does not identify zero defects as a goal; instead, he emphasizes improvement and suggests that it should be the goal until the cost of improvement analysis becomes greater than improvement savings.

Organizing for Quality

To implement a quality system, a company has to organize for quality. Juran recommends developing a hierarchy of quality boards or councils and quality teams. Such a structure helps to identify and carry out improvement projects, and using this approach gives top management an opportunity to lead by example.

Quality Improvement, Planning, and Control

Quality planning and quality improvement teams are trained together in Juran's planning and improvement approach. Process improvement projects are not developed for sporadic problems; rather, they focus on an organization's chronic problems of waste—the waste that has been built into daily operations. Juran estimates chronic waste to consume as much as 20 percent of an organization's revenues.

Problems found in a process are identified as either management-controllable or operator-controllable. Juran defines operator-controllable problems as those in which operators know what they are expected to do, know how their actual performance measures up to requirements, and have the means to regulate and change what they do.[12] All other problems are management-controllable, and Juran estimates that these represent 80 percent of problems found during process improvement projects (a figure a bit lower than Deming's 94 percent common-cause statistic, but still high enough to get managers' attention).

The goal of quality improvement project teams is to apply Juran's analysis and problem-solving processes to achieve "breakthrough" improvements (those that eliminate the causes of chronic waste). These can only be achieved on a project-by-project basis. Opportunities for breakthrough improvements dwindle as an organization becomes more entrenched in a quality culture; companies reach a point where poor-quality processes have been improved and subsequent processes have been developed using Juran's quality-planning techniques. When this happens, the tendency is to become complacent. Thus, leaders must be vigilant in their pursuit of quality even after they have achieved their quality goals. An emphasis on continuous improvement requires real dedication and commitment.

Juran also uses quality control techniques to hold onto the gains that have been made by implementing the improvements. This control phase measures the actual performance of a process and compares it to its defined performance; corrective action is taken if the performance level is not up to the established standard. Quality control is used only to maintain the level of quality attained from an improvement. Improvement projects are needed to boost the quality of the process further.

Using SPC

Statistical controls and techniques have a critical role in Juran's quality system approach as well. Statistical analysis helps improvement teams identify areas where improvements are needed. Like Deming, Juran cautions against implementing statistical techniques unless they are part of a broader and more comprehensive quality approach. Too many companies, he feels, emphasize the quality control process without paying enough attention to the quality planning and quality improvement processes.[13] Quality control alone will not produce a quality organization or quality goods and services. Juran identifies the necessary components of companywide quality management as follows:

1. Focusing on customers
2. Extending the quality effort to all products and processes
3. Increasing awareness of the costs of poor quality
4. Accelerating quality improvement
5. Making quality planning pervasive
6. Using complete quality control[14]

Crosby's Quality Approach

Among the leading quality gurus, Philip B. Crosby is often identified as the most inspirational. He has been described as a "formidable motivational speaker, known for whipping his audience into an emotional frenzy that leaves them waving his quality banner in evangelical fervor."[15] It is no wonder that the quality award given out by the company Crosby founded is called the "Quality Fanatic Award."

Crosby's quality roots can be traced to a U.S. Army Pershing missile. In the early 1960s, the Martin Company promised and delivered the Pershing missile to the U.S. Army at Cape Canaveral, Florida. It was an outstanding example of a quality product. By developing this missile, Martin showed that it could deliver on a zero-defects pledge. Crosby worked for Martin in the 1960s and was exposed to this zero-defect philosophy, which he would later popularize in his best-selling book *Quality Is Free*.

While working for ITT later in his career, Crosby convinced management of the advantages of improving quality. To get his ideas across, he cornered the CEO in an elevator to discuss quality issues, telling him that improved quality could increase company sales by as much as 20 percent. Crosby's arguments were persuasive, and his subsequent work lifted him to the position of vice president for quality. Crosby left ITT in 1979 to start Philip Crosby Associates (PCA) with the goal of educating executives about quality and assisting them in establishing their own corporate quality improvement processes.

Crosby's approach to infusing quality in an organization is based on his four "absolutes of quality management," which are detailed below.[16]

Absolute #1: The Definition of Quality is Conformance to Requirements

Under this definition, a quality product is one that follows its design specifications. Any product or service that conforms to its predetermined requirements is a quality product. The power of this definition, Crosby feels, is that it leaves no room for subjectivity, and it permits everyone in the organization to know when they have achieved a quality result.

Crosby defines requirements as "the specific needs a product or service must meet if they are to be of value to a customer."[17] It is, he argues, management's role to create the proper requirements for the organization: "One of the problems of quality is that managers don't know how to explain what the requirements are. If you want your people to do it right the first time, you've got to tell them simply and clearly what 'it' is."[18] Requirements are determined, says Crosby, by finding out what the customer wants. After that, it is management's job to describe and communicate precisely what those requirements are and the company's intention to meet those requirements.

Because of his belief in the crucial role of management in defining the requirements to be met, Crosby (like Deming and Juran) preaches that commitment to quality must start with senior management. Crosby feels it is the "leader's job to make employees and suppliers successful." Quality is the outcome of an organization's policy and its management's actions. Thus, Crosby directs his message to the top of the corporate hierarchy.

Absolute #2: The System of Quality is Prevention

Too often, says Crosby, systems to improve quality are aimed at the end of an operation: the final 10 percent of the output receives 90 percent of the quality improvement effort. Work processes that include quality inspection at the end of the operation are, therefore, "dedicated to the inevitability of error."[19] To produce quality products or services, organizations must enact a process of prevention and quality in the design of work processes, rather than relying on appraisal or inspection at the end of the work process.

To make this happen, everyone in the organization must be aware of and committed to the quality improvement effort. This can be done only when an organization creates and embraces an "attitude of change" and a philosophy that emphasizes continuous improvement. Crosby's philosophy emphasizes management commitment, the application of his quality measures, raised quality awareness, employee involvement and motivation, and the recognition that quality improvement is an ongoing process.

Absolute #3: The Performance Standard Is Zero Defects

The performance standard Crosby tells executives to set for their work processes is the now-famous "zero defects" standard. This means that products or services conform to requirements *completely*. For quality to be achieved, top management's expectations must be converted from "X percent of error is adequate" to "the requirement is zero defects." A management that expects imperfection, Crosby says, will always get imperfection. When perfection is the communicated goal and the entire organization becomes committed to this goal, everyone will strive for improvement continuously. To make zero defects a reality, top management must establish the policy of delivering defect-free products or services on time. Nonconforming products, says Crosby, must not be delivered under any circumstances.

Absolute #4: The Measurement of Quality Is the Price of Nonconformance

Crosby measures quality for an organization in terms of the price of nonconformance, that is, the price paid for failing to meet the requirements set for a product. The price of nonconformance includes scrap expenses and rework expenses, including all the costs associated with wasted time, effort, and material. Crosby's approach calculates a price for this waste and then uses the cost to direct improvement efforts and, later, measure the improvement in work processes.

Crosby calculates the total cost of quality as the price of conformance plus the price of nonconformance. The price of conformance will always exist; it is the cost of producing a product or providing a service. The price of nonconformance, says Crosby, can be reduced in an organization through the application of quality improvement principles. Crosby pegs the average organization's price of nonconformance to be about 20 percent of sales. Having improved quality by improving a product's conformance to requirements, a company can reduce the cost of nonconformance. Quality is free, insists Crosby, because improved product quality decreases the total cost of production, thereby improving a firm's profitability.

In summary, Crosby identifies zero defects as the appropriate goal for a company working to improve quality and says simply that companies must stop doing the things that work against that goal.

WHICH APPROACH IS BEST?

Although Deming, Juran, and Crosby differ on a few points, their messages are fundamentally the same. It does not matter which approach is used in the quest for quality, and as we said before, it is not unusual for companies to combine elements of the different approaches to meet their specific needs. More important than the approach chosen is the willingness and ability to commit to and persevere in implementing that approach until quality is achieved. As Deming points out, the change to a quality organization requires that "management must awaken to the challenge, must learn their responsibilities, and take on leadership for a change."[20]

As we said earlier in this chapter, this book focuses on the role of leaders in quality management. It is not a handbook on TQM methods and approaches, although we believe understanding the views of the quality gurus is an essential step in understanding the unique contributions required of business leaders. As we noted in Chapter 1, leaders bring to the table vision, strongly held values and beliefs, and the courage to take action. Each of these is crucial in the successful implementation of a quality management program. When implemented correctly and led by committed leaders, a quality initiative can help to establish the long-term improvement in business operations and product and service quality needed for competition in today's global economy.

In the next chapter, we focus attention on a man regarded by many (including the authors of this book) as one of the truly great business leaders of all time, Sam Walton. There can be no doubt that Mr. Sam, as he liked to be called, revolutionized discount retailing, and he left a legacy that reached beyond the Wal-Mart corporate boundaries. Wherever there is a Wal-Mart, there are competitors who have been forced to improve their operations and pay attention to customers simply in order to survive. Ironically, Wal-Mart achieved its success without a formal TQM program. The company owes its prosperity instead to the leadership of Sam Walton, whose vision, values, and courage created a truly great company.

CHAPTER 3

SAM WALTON

Leadership at Wal-Mart

So I thought that larger stores could be put in smaller towns than anyone had tried before. There was a lot more business in those towns than people ever thought.

—Sam Walton[1]

As kids, we all worked for the company. I got to work behind the candy counter when I was five years old. The business was always included in the dinner conversation. We heard a lot about the debt it took to open new stores, and I worried about it. I remember confiding to my girlfriend one time, saying, "I don't know what we're going to do. My daddy owes so much money, and he won't quit opening stores."

—Alice Walton, Sam Walton's youngest child[2]

This is hard to believe, but between my paper route money and the money I saved in the Army—both of which I invested in those stores—it's worth about $40 million today.

—John Walton, Sam Walton's second son[3]

One time Sam and I got invited to a fancy quail hunt on one of those South Georgia plantations. They told

This chapter was written by Angela P. Clontz, who is an associate consultant with A. T. Kearney, Inc., in Dallas, Texas.

us they'd pick us up at the landing strip. So we flew in there, and there were all these corporate jets lined up. Well, this guy in a Mercedes pulls up to get us. You should've seen the look on his face when Sam opened up the back of that plane, and his five dogs came flyin' out of there. They weren't expecting anybody to bring their own dogs. They had to haul them in that Mercedes.

—Bud Walton, Sam Walton's brother[4]

It was a deceptively simple vision, but Sam Walton believed in it—a discount store with nearly wholesale margins on every product, but also offering easy shopping and friendly service. This vision, in combination with his deep-seated values and dedication to action, enabled Walton (with the help of thousands of employees) to make Wal-Mart the premier American retailer and even redefine the way consumers shop.

But what made Sam Walton different from the 90 percent of entrepreneurs who fail? What made Wal-Mart such a financial gold mine that it catapulted Walton's family into the public eye as the richest in America? In part, it was Walton's ingenious concept and his knowledge of retailing. And in part, it was also the absence of competition in rural markets, joined with the explosive financial power of the 1980s. But the critical and irreplaceable ingredient to Wal-Mart's success was Sam Walton himself—his overriding vision, unflinching values, courage to take action, and uncanny ability to motivate and inspire his "associates" to carry on, even after his death in April 1992. In simple terms, it was Sam Walton's leadership that made Wal-Mart a success.

Sam Walton made things happen despite many setbacks. In fact, the major obstacles Walton had to overcome became the opportunities that gave birth to Wal-Mart's distinctive advantages, opportunities that led him to take even more progressive steps both in retailing and in management practices.

THE LEARNING PROCESS BEGINS

Walton began shaping his vision back in the 1950s. At that time, he was already fully entrenched in the retailing world as the Chicago-based Ben Franklin Stores' largest franchisee. He knew there were greater opportunities beyond the typical Ben Franklin variety store, and he set out to investigate a new concept of discounting. He traveled to several stores, taking detailed notes, building the arguments he would need for his proposal to Ben Franklin that he act as a guinea pig for this new idea. But Ben Franklin's management passed on Walton's offer. According to Walton, Ben Franklin used 20 to 25 percent margins, "didn't want to give on their end to the degree that it took for the prices to be as low as I felt they should be. . . . If they had been able to sell to me on a 12% range, I probably would not have put together the organization that we did. . . . I was forced to build my own team."[5]

Following Ben Franklin's refusal, Walton continued the learning process that would shape his vision. Don Soderquist, former president of Ben Franklin and later a top Wal-Mart executive, recalls running into Walton at a local K-Mart the day after Ben Franklin had rejected his proposal. When Soderquist asked why Walton was busily interviewing stock clerks and taking notes about these new, large urban stores, the latter responded, "It's all part of the educational process. I'm just learning."[6]

To become an independent discount retailer, Walton would have to assume responsibility for buying, warehousing, and distributing merchandise—all activities previously handled by Ben Franklin. But in 1962 he set out with his brother, Bud Walton, to realize his vision: rural stores of thirty-five thousand to sixty thousand square feet that offered discount prices on everyday consumer items. With his "We Sell for Less" motto, Walton moved forward as an old-fashioned entrepreneur, one step at a time: store by store, employee by employee. Walton knew he had a lot to learn. His open-minded understanding that neither he nor anyone else had all the answers was an integral part of Wal-Mart's development, success, and corporate culture.

With Wal-Mart's rapid success came a multitude of revised goals and objectives from Walton. Never losing sight of his "everyday low prices" vision of retailing, he continually pushed himself and his associates toward daily improvement. Even when Wal-Mart was a mere ant among such retail giants as Sears and K-Mart, Walton had already set his mind on making Wal-Mart America's largest mass merchandiser—an almost unthinkable goal for a store with only regional presence.

Yet in 1991 Wal-Mart, still without the benefit of national coverage, took the number one spot from Sears, posting sales of $42 billion from nearly two thousand stores. In typical fashion, Walton quickly announced new corporate targets of $100 billion and three thousand stores by the twenty-first century. The 125 percent leap in sales supported by only 33 percent more stores seemed outrageous, but Walton provided a simple framework by breaking it into manageable pieces: sales per square foot would increase from $150 to $400, thereby achieving $32 million in sales per store. As Walton noted, one hundred stores were already doing that kind of business. Walton provided the vision and left the details of implementation to the creative ingenuity of his "associates."[7]

SHAPING AN ORGANIZATION

It is commonly stated that Sam Walton overcame formidable barriers and competition and achieved success through the sheer force of his personality, his belief in his vision, and the integrity of his leadership. This is only partly true, because Walton knew he could not and did not achieve this success all alone. Instead, he shaped an organization and provided the infrastructure that could achieve his objectives. David Glass, CEO of Wal-Mart since 1988, agrees: "You can't replace a Sam Walton, but he has prepared the company to run well whether he's there or not."[8]

Walton painstakingly searched for every individual who made up his management team. He sought individuals like himself, individuals who believed in the discount concept and were dedicated to working long hours to see the vision become reality. He cleverly and unceasingly wooed people from his competitors, many of whom (like David Glass and Don Soderquist) joined him more than ten years after his initial offers. He also developed people from within; for example, Ron Loveless rose from his 1964 position as a stock boy to head Sam's Warehouse Clubs, then proceeded to an early retirement as a wealthy man at 42.[9]

In 1982 Sam Walton was diagnosed with hairy-cell leukemia, an incurable form of cancer. During its remission, Walton turned his attention to developing the company's leadership and improving its dynamics. He took some unorthodox steps to shake up his management team and better prepare them to carry out the Wal-Mart vision in his absence. While struggling over the question of who would be his successor, he masterminded a switch between his two top lieutenants, CFO David Glass and president Jack Shewmaker—a switch that left Shewmaker reporting to Glass until Shewmaker retired and Glass moved into the CEO spot. Glass, a native Missourian, keeps a low profile but is said to understand better than Walton's family what Sam envisioned for the company. A part of Wal-Mart for more than twenty years, he knows he cannot reproduce Sam Walton's charisma, but by 1993 he had given the company four years of dramatic growth, as sales tripled and compound earnings increased by 26 percent annually. Guided by Sam Walton's enduring vision, David Glass sees no limits to Wal-Mart's growth and vows to fend off "big-company disease" at all costs.[10]

But to Walton, leadership went further than spreading his vision among those at the top, because in his eyes there was no top or bottom at Wal-Mart. He actively worked to inspire every Wal-Mart associate with his vision—from part-time cashiers to full-time department managers, from the new clerk to the nearly retired truck driver. During his lifetime, every one of Wal-Mart's nearly three hundred thousand associates had met, heard, or seen Sam Walton via store visits or companywide satellite addresses. Walton provided the framework of friendly service and value merchandising; he left it to the associates to use their hard work, creativity, decision-making skills, and customer contacts to carry out the details needed to make the Wal-Mart vision a shared reality. Walton transferred his vision and Wal-Mart's fate to associates—many of whom were unskilled individuals working for $5 per hour—by giving them pride in themselves and the possibility of ownership (in the form of stock options) beyond their imagination. And they loved him for it.

PERSONAL VALUES

Embedded in Walton's vision for Wal-Mart was his rock-solid set of personal values, including humility, honesty, frugality, and trust. Sam inherited many of his beliefs from his father and developed others during the Great Depression. His small-town roots and down-home style are visible in Wal-Mart's simple, no-frills headquarters in out-of-the-way Bentonville, Arkansas. And despite his $9 billion family fortune, Sam held on to his Ford truck, casual clothes, and modest ranch-style house. He saw no more need for flash in his personal life than in his stores; he applied the same standards to both.

Walton's personal values were translated into three key business principles: provide the customer with value and service in a clean and friendly shopping environment, create a partnership with the associates, and maintain a commitment to the community. He also never forgot what he learned during his trainee days at JC Penney; that company, too, had a set of values, many of which Sam Walton brought to Wal-Mart. He focused on the "we," "us," and "our" in the organization long before "employee empowerment" came into vogue. Furthermore, he continuously pressured his people to focus on the many small transactions and details of daily life at Wal-Mart—every customer, every display, every promotional decision. Nothing was left to chance; nothing (and no one) was too small to matter.

WAL-MART PEOPLE

Sam Walton believed in his people. He tore apart the traditional organizational structure, placing great emphasis on the salesclerks: "I've always appreciated what it meant to be a sales clerk and how much a salesperson can influence a customer in a business relationship. . . . If we don't have the customers satisfied at the cash registers, none of us has a job."[11] He gave his associates motivation, spirit, guidance, and support. It was these tools that allowed them to exercise their creativity without fear of failure or repercussions. Sam Walton was guided by the philosophy that "if people believe in themselves, it's truly amazing what they can accomplish."[12]

Sam Walton had specific notions about the responsibilities and roles of his associates and management team. He demanded that the salesclerks make the seat-of-the-pants judgments that really counted—those that involved satisfying the customer. He urged his people to try new ideas and classified failures as learning experiences. Walton criticized "management by intimidation" as "chicken management," and called on his managers to "make our positive discipline philosophy in dealing with our associates work. . . . You must be a master at communicating with them all aspects of the business and their place in it. The only way you can let them know how much you value their contribution is to show them and tell them." He expected all of his managers to be leaders, urging them to "put their people before themselves. If you are able to do that your business will take care of itself."[13]

Leadership at Wal-Mart, however, is not all cheerleading,

coaching, and optimism. Wal-Mart leaders "know how to raise the roof off the place" when they want to, says an eleven-year employee. For example, on one of his many surprise visits, Walton launched into a tirade about operational efficiency after discovering surplus Christmas merchandise in a stockroom in midsummer. And in 1972, Sam caught an associate sleeping in the storeroom atop a box of merchandise. Only after the store manager's assurance of the employee's dismissal and a glass of water did he regain his composure and continue his tour.[14] Unceasing attention to details, to daily activities, was not simply an ideal for Walton, it was his way of life.

Like so many other qualities that distinguish Wal-Mart, the emphasis on people evolved from a challenge that Walton turned into an opportunity. During the 1960s, two of Wal-Mart's twenty stores began unionization drives. Labor lawyer John Tate, now an executive vice president at Wal-Mart, advised Walton, "You can approach this one of two ways—hold people down, and pay me or some other lawyer to make it work. Or devote time and attention to proving to people that you care."[15] Walton took the latter approach and within a month developed the company's first management seminar, entitled "We Care."

Such was Sam's ability to perceive hidden opportunities and adapt to changing environments. As he explained:

> We are willing to change. . . . We have been very flexible and have been looking every day for changes that need to be made. . . . These people out here are smarter and more capable than many of us recognize, and they understand our business and certainly know what the company wants. . . . But change, and the willingness to change, to try anything, try anyone's ideas, might not work. But it won't break the company when it doesn't.[16]

Although they sound familiar today, Walton's ideas were nothing short of revolutionary in the 1960s and 1970s, and

Sam Walton's leadership was essential in carrying them out. The paradoxical combination of Wal-Mart's nearly Bible Belt values and its aggressive innovations in management gave Wal-Mart people a solid foundation from which they could work together to change the rules of retailing.

Walton was a champion of what Tom Peters has called the philosophy of "management by walking around." Walton knew of no better way to scrutinize the stores than to talk to associates, shaking hands and meeting people, all the while keeping a sharp eye out for ideas, successes, and failures. Even after his cancer was diagnosed, Walton kept up his grueling schedule of self-piloted visits to out-of-the-way stores. He instilled a fervor in his people; he was out on the floor with them, and that gave them pride. His hard work and encouragement led them to satisfy the company's ambitious performance and customer service objectives. His challenge to the associates at a new Sam's Wholesale Club was typical of his signature blend of goading and praising: "Have you only just begun? Will you do as well the second year as the first? Are you taking care of your customers everywhere? Congratulations on being one of the finest wholesale clubs in our company."[17]

IDEAS JOINED WITH ACTION

Sam Walton demanded the same dedicated action from every associate in the company. Senior and regional managers are expected to spend at least two days a week visiting stores, with Friday and Saturday reserved for meetings to evaluate performance, operational observations, and strategic initiatives. Store employees are given objectives and policies and then expected to handle the details themselves. As Walton said:

> Our folks don't expect something for nothing, and they don't expect things to come easy. Our method of success is

ACTION with a capital A, and a lot of hard work mixed in. . . . Nothing in the world is cheaper than a good idea without any action behind it. . . . Do it. Try it. Fix it. Not a bad approach—and it works.[18]

The overriding theme of all Wal-Mart activities is cooperation—between stores and warehouses, suppliers and distribution centers, associates and management, and salesclerks and customers. Partnerships and sharing occur at all stages of the business processes and are an integral part of the organization's culture.

In eliminating the traditional corporate hierarchy, Sam Walton redistributed responsibility, laying it at the feet of his store personnel. Much of Wal-Mart's openness stems from this one simple change. Wal-Mart teaches its associates to be "merchants" by giving them full access to data on costs, markups, overhead, profits, and store performance; they can then make well-informed decisions that affect operating performance in thousands of little ways. Each month, Wal-Mart distributes performance summaries ranking every department in every store: overachievers are recognized and rewarded, while subpar performers are sometimes demoted.[19] Every associate knows the objectives at the corporate, store, and even departmental levels. If a store surpasses its objectives, all store associates share in a portion of the excess profits.[20] And the reward goes beyond year-end bonuses. Wal-Mart employees are owners, shareholders in the corporation who attend annual meetings and reap the benefits of overall strong performance.

A LOW THRESHOLD FOR CHANGE

As part of Wal-Mart's universal belief that change must be sought out and embraced, every store manager speaks individually with each associate to hear the latter's ideas on improvement opportunities. Wal-Mart managers and associates live by Walton's "low threshold for change" (LTC) theory, jointly nurturing a culture that is comfortable with challenging and changing policies; at Wal-Mart there is no standard operating procedure. The company's "letter to the president" program offers associates a direct pipeline to senior management for complaints and ideas. Each letter receives a response, and many have helped alleviate problems of shoplifting and pilfering and have raised employee morale.

Sam Walton himself was a champion of soliciting and implementing employee requests. For example, one sleepless night Walton climbed in his truck, picked up some doughnuts, and headed to one of Wal-Mart's nearby loading docks. In conversation, he asked associates there what was going well and what needed to be changed. They responded not with a barrage of complaints, but with a simple request for two more showers in the locker room. The next day they had their showers.[21] Word of Walton's action spread rapidly across the company, boosting both morale and corporate loyalty. This was not a calculated ploy, but an example of a leadership that recognized the importance of people and their needs.

Until his death, Sam Walton was a beacon, the embodiment of the company's commitment to continuous improvement. CEO David Glass recalls that "the one thing I underestimated about Sam is that he has an overriding something in him that causes him to improve every day. . . . As long as I've known him, he's never gotten to the point where he's comfortable with who he is or how we're doing."[22]

As an embodiment of Walton's philosophy and actions, Wal-Mart is a company that values humility. According to Sam, "ego is one of the worst things that can happen to a company," and he fought it by keeping everyone focused on the "thousands of little things" that contribute to Wal-Mart's success.[23] CEO Glass described Wal-Mart as having "no superstars. . . . We're a company of ordinary people overachieving."[24] So management continues to pore over details. Each week the top one hundred managers discuss thick printouts representing product performance and evaluate merchandising techniques, pricing, and competitor practices. Many of these managers were handpicked by Walton; they log fourteen- to sixteen-hour days, and those aspiring to senior management must give top priority to the team.

On every team, however, the captain finally calls the shots. And when tough decisions came around, Sam Walton rose to the occasion, more than once declaring, "I still own most of the stock in this company, and this is the way we're going to do it."[25] He evaluated available information and then never looked back. Even when he made a mistake, he transformed it into a learning opportunity. Walton "made a lifetime of learning and observing from other companies . . . just trying to get ideas, any kind of ideas that will help our company."[26] That was Sam Walton, and that is also the Wal-Mart culture that was created by Sam's total quality leadership.

THE PRODUCTIVITY LOOP

Wal-Mart's success rests on what has been called its "productivity loop": low prices and better service attract a greater number of shoppers, thereby enhancing sales and making the company more efficient, which in turn makes it possible for Wal-Mart to lower prices even more.[27] The productivity loop is the result of four fundamental Wal-Mart initiatives uniting the efforts of all associates and linking together the key business processes: its distribution system, supplier partnerships, cost control, and customer service.

Distribution System

Wal-Mart's distribution system—to many, its major competitive weapon—grew out of a lack of available resources. When Wal-Mart started, because of the stores' rural locations, few distributors could supply the stores in a cost-effective manner. Sam Walton went to his people for suggestions. Ferold Arend, company president until 1983, pushed Sam to invest in company-owned warehouses and distribution centers. Despite his cost consciousness, Sam was willing to invest in any initiative with long-term advantages. As a result, the hub system now in place at Wal-Mart consists of nineteen distribution centers, each capable of serving 150 stores within two days. More than 85 percent of all products sold at Wal-Marts are shipped from the distribution centers on the company's two thousand trucks.[28]

Not only have internal distribution capabilities removed the 15 percent cut for external distributors, but the centers alone are singly responsible for scanning and tracking every product with bar coding, mechanized conveyors, and computerized inventory. Even though company executives knew Walton never liked computers, they jointly convinced him of the technology's incredible potential. Between 1975 and 1979, Sam Walton approved $500 million in expenditures on a modern computerized communications system, and by 1979 every store had twenty-four-hour access to distribution centers and headquarters.[29]

Throughout the 1980s, the company continued its commitment to information systems. Walton often used the system to broadcast live messages over a six-channel video satellite, personally contacting every store and distribution center. As a former president and CFO explained, "Systems are not intended to replace people, or to take the place of their judgments; systems are intended to help them do their jobs better."[30] And doing the job better at Wal-Mart means satisfying the customer with informative and friendly service.

None of Wal-Mart's achievements would have been possible without senior-level leadership in terms of financial commitment, stated goals, continuous review, and tolerance of failure. Wal-Mart's managers, led by Walton's example, provide not only the infrastructure but the personal level of support needed to succeed in these operational total quality initiatives.

Supplier Partnerships

Sam Walton and his management team have also taken bold steps to develop management processes with their external partners. Because of Wal-Mart's nearly 100 percent on- line quick-response capabilities, Wal-Mart has product, inventory, sales, and customer data that can be extremely valuable to suppliers. Bobby Martin, senior vice president of information services, describes the relationship: "Customers tell us what they like or don't like every day with every purchase they make. But our merchants had to guess before at what our demand would be. Now they can know tomorrow what we sold today."[31]By sharing this knowledge and ordering in bulk, Wal-Mart helps its suppliers achieve more accurate forecasting and production planning. Furthermore, Wal-Mart is quickly moving toward paperless invoices to decrease its turnaround time to less than ten days.[32] All of these initiatives provide suppliers with improved efficiency and cash flow and thus serve as valuable bargaining chips for Wal-Mart.

As part of such lucrative partnerships, Sam Walton demanded high standards of workmanship, low prices, on-time delivery and trust. Wal-Mart buyers "are very focused people, and they use their buying power more forcefully than anybody in America," says a major supplier.[33] To keep that focus, Walton initiated a no-perks policy: buyers cannot accept meals, trips, or gifts from suppliers. When one buyer violated this policy, he received a quick demotion and two weeks off without pay.[34]

Wal-Mart has notified its suppliers that it will only deal with them directly, thus eliminating the sales-representative interface and another layer of costs. This closer relationship enables buyers to provide direct input into product designs and colors with detailed pricing negotiations, down to garment-specific characteristics.

In the early 1980s, Sam Walton took the concept of supplier partnerships one step further. Following the lead of Roger Milliken of Milliken & Co., Sam investigated instituting the "buy American" philosophy at Wal-Mart. He sent a letter to manufacturers offering to work with them to develop and produce goods that were competitive with imports, both in price and quality. He urged them to respond, but made clear his guidelines:

> Our American suppliers must commit to improving their facilities and machinery, remain financially conservative, work to fill our requirements and most importantly, strive to improve employee productivity. Wal-Mart believes the American workers can make the difference, if management provides the leadership.[35]

When he began receiving calls and letters of interest, Sam Walton followed through. One apparel manufacturer, Farris Fashions, had struggled since Sears and JC Penney had taken their Van Heusen shirt orders to China. But Walton gave Farris a shot, keeping it in business with his order of fifty thousand flannel shirts in 1984. By 1990, Farris had tripled its employment and was producing more than two million shirts annually for Wal-Mart. In appreciation, Farris employees received a $25 gift certificate redeemable at the Wal-Mart of their choice.[36] Owner Farris Burroughs recalled, "Sam Walton is the only guy that I've ever worked for who looked me right in the eye and said, 'Son, if you can't make money off this project, don't do it.' Most people could care less whether you made money."[37] That was the key: Sam Walton would not support unprofitable business or buy at higher costs, but he would work with the supplier to reach a win-win level in supplier partnerships.

Walton worked diligently with his suppliers to lead others by example. Wal-Mart managers estimate that the company has created or retained more than one hundred and fifty thousand jobs and converted or saved more than $3.8 billion in purchases at cost that would otherwise have gone offshore.[38] While imports still generate nearly 40 percent of Wal-Mart's sales, the company has enhanced its image by effectively publicizing its "buy American" initiatives and merchandise. Sam's motivation in this and in all his initiatives was tied to his primary company values: "The best part of the program, as important as any other, is to try to get our manufacturers to create a partnership with their workers the way we've tried to do with our people, and share the profits with them."[39]

Cost Control

The basic retailing concept at Wal-Mart is discount pricing, and cost control is essential to that idea. With the efficiencies and economies of scale achieved through its interlocking distribution network, information systems, and supplier partnerships, Wal-Mart is able to sell products at prices 5 to 50 percent lower than the competition. In the face of these advantages and Wal-Mart's success, Sam Walton has fought frills and perks at every opportunity. From charging ten cents for coffee at headquarters to flying his own plane on trips to driving his old pickup truck, Walton has set the example of frugality and ingrained cost cutting in Wal-Mart's corporate culture. As a result, Wal-Mart spends only 15 percent of sales on selling, general, and administrative expenses, a vast improvement on the 20 percent spent at K-mart.[40]

Cost reductions at Wal-Mart are achieved not through complicated programs or in-depth studies, but through commonsense ideas. For example, Walton wanted to reduce shrinkage (shoplifting, pilferage, damage, etc.) at Wal-Mart from the industry's average level of 2 percent of sales. He went directly to his associates and offered them a shrinkage bonus of up to $200 if their entire store held shrinkage below corporate objectives. The associates went to work. Some discovered that customers were switching the tops on paint cans to get a better brand at a lower price, so they put the price tag on the can rather than the cap. They made special price tags for sales to avoid tag switching, and they began monitoring dressing rooms more closely. Store managers began to have mandatory meetings where they highlighted results and further trouble areas. The combined efforts of the associates yielded a 50 percent reduction in shrinkage from 1980 to 1990, and millions of dollars in increased profits.[41] This might seem to have taken a long time by most planning standards, but Walton kept the heat on, redefining the objectives and reinforcing the rewards of reduced costs, and the end result was worth it.

No area of the Wal-Mart business escapes scrutiny. When a new store is built, the company trains the store manager to run the security cables through the store in order to avoid the additional cost of an electrician. Even periodic lock changes are performed by in-store personnel.[42] Moreover, each store's lighting and air conditioning are centrally controlled in Bentonville to maintain an optimum cost-efficient environment; Wal-Mart also keeps advertising costs below all of its competitors, at 0.5% of sales.[43] Wal-Mart primarily advertises through in-store flyers, using associates and their children as models to perform the dual service of keeping costs low and building the store's "real family" image. Rather than simply serving as advertising vehicles, these flyers provide a wealth of information: profiles of "buy American" efforts, letters from manufacturers, and accolades from customers. Wal-Mart's everyday low prices eradicate the need for constant product promotions, thereby making sales more predictable for suppliers and holding stockouts and excess inventory to a minimum.

The way Wal-Mart is run feeds into the Wal-Mart vision at many levels. Even the board of directors cuts corners, as is related by Jack Stephens of Stephens, Inc., the country's largest regional investment bank:

> At Wal-Mart, we never knew where we were going to meet. We'd take any room that was available. The chairs were kind of rickety. Our sandwiches were cold, but we had

potato chips. And if we brought our own quarter, we could buy a Coca-Cola. That's the philosophy of the company. That's what makes it lean and strong. . . . Now the other boards I've sat on—linen, china, cocktails, jets. Not Sam Walton—he lives and breathes efficiency.[44]

Regardless of corporate performance, Walton never made more than $350,000 in annual salary. CEO David Glass earns two-thirds the salary of K-mart's Joseph Antinoni and less than half as much as Dayton Hudson's Kenneth Macke.[45] But Walton, Glass, and every Wal-Mart associate all benefit handsomely from the lucrative stock options that reflect the success of Wal-Mart's initiatives. Regardless of these rewards, David Glass fights the complacency of success: "We can become far more efficient. We can lower our cost of business for lots of reasons."[46] This is the consistent response to Wal-Mart's successes, and this response necessarily generates even greater success.

Customer Service

The fourth initiative in Wal-Mart's productivity loop is its aggressive dedication to customer service. Sam Walton would do anything to satisfy a customer, and he ceaselessly reminded his associates to follow his lead. Once the live satellite addresses were functional in the late 1980s, Walton used these addresses to motivate his employees to display "aggressive hospitality to the customers. . . . It's simple. It won't cost us anything. And I believe it would just work magic, absolute magic on our customers, and our sales would escalate, and I think we'd shoot past our K-mart friends in a year or two and probably Sears as well." He then called for action—approach every customer who comes within ten feet of you, look them in the eye and ask if you can help. He continued with a more personal message:

> It would, I'm sure, help you become a leader, it would help your personality, you would become more outgoing, and in time you might become a store manager, you might become a department or district manager, or whatever you choose to be in the company. . . . It will do wonders for you.[47]

Sam Walton set the example by constantly talking to customers, both in and out of the stores, soliciting their comments and suggestions. More than four thousand letters reach Wal-Mart headquarters each month; every one receives a response, and many result in companywide change. One disgruntled customer complained, "That [Wal-Mart] truck almost killed me and my wife. You ought to do something about it." So Walton did. He set up a driving awards program that even contract drivers must follow, and the program turned Wal-Mart's truck fleet into the most accident-free in the retail marketplace.[48] Again, by his own actions, Walton had set the standard for all Wal-Mart associates: listen to the customer, and learn to do it better.

Wal-Mart managers and associates have taken it from there. One of them suggested employing a "greeter" in each store. Walton liked the idea, and soon every store had a greeter by the front doors, usually an older person passing out information on store specials, offering to help, smiling, and simply contributing to the hometown atmosphere that makes customers feel good at Wal-Mart. Another customer wrote to Wal-Mart regarding his experience while shopping: he saw Margaret Chambers, a salesclerk, reading Valentine's Day cards to an obviously illiterate person so he could make his selection. When the shopper left with his card in hand, the observing customer commented on the salesclerk's kindness. "Oh, I don't mind," she responded, "he's been here before—he's a customer."[49] These small, simple decisions and actions by Wal-Mart people at all levels cannot be taught. They require a genuine commitment to customers, a commitment that comes from the example of Sam Walton.

Even the stores themselves are designed and operated to cater to the customer. In contrast to K-mart's plan of five merchandise sections, Wal-Mart stores are broken into thirty-six specific departments.[50] This layout helps customers quickly and easily find exactly what they need. Wal-Mart provides detail-oriented training to associates and to managers, ensuring that customers can obtain the information they need on product features and benefits. In-store flyers describe specials and compare prices to those of nearby competitors, drawing shoppers to the bargains and lengthening their time in the store. Cleanliness and neatness are priorities as well; Walton has been known to close an entire store until it met the company's high standards. And once the shopping is over, Wal-Mart strives to make the checkouts hassle free. Rows of registers and cashiers work industriously to live up to the store's stated goal that "at Wal-Mart, you're always next in line."[51]

Its extraordinary customer service is the culmination of Wal-Mart's productivity loop. The commonsense distribution system, linked to a state-of-the-art information system, keeps the store shelves full while reducing the already-discounted product costs. Internal cost cutting provides additional value to the customer while rewarding the associates and owners with stock appreciation. And in the end, Wal-Mart associates, trained to know the products and to serve the customer, provide the kind of service that will keep customers coming back to shop at Wal-Mart.

THE LEGACY OF VISION

The results speak for themselves. Wal-Mart has succeeded in satisfying not only its customers but its employees, suppliers, investors, and host communities. Wal-Mart outshines the rest of the industry in growth, sales, earnings, margins, and employee and floor productivity. Since its incorporation in 1970, Wal-Mart's compounded annual growth rate has remained well over 30 percent each year. There have been occasions when Sam Walton himself sometimes underestimated the power of his associates. In 1984, he vowed that if Wal-Mart topped 8 percent pretax earnings, he would hula down the center of Wall Street; Wal-Mart's historical high had been 7 percent, well above the industry average of 3 percent. At year's end Wal-Mart closed with 8.04 percent earnings, and as promised, Sam Walton shimmied in lei and grass skirt, to the delight of investors, reporters, and associates.[52] Even during the October 1987 stock crash (in which he lost $2.6 billion in net worth), Walton maintained his calm demeanor and faith in Wal-Mart's resilience, noting that "it's only paper."[53] Led by Sam Walton, Wal-Mart has been the darling of Wall Street for more than twenty years.

But financial success is only the beginning of the story. Wal-Mart continually ranks among *Fortune* magazine's "most admired" companies. A variety of surveys have revealed that Wal-Mart is consumers' preferred place to shop for reasons of location, service, and price. Furthermore, Sam Walton directed that Wal-Mart would benefit the communities in which it operates. Schools, fire departments, disaster victims, scholarship recipients, and disadvantaged citizens receive money and merchandise every year through in-store fundraisers and focused contributions. Although Wal-Mart giving as a percentage of earnings is one of the lowest in the industry, Wal-Mart receives a great deal of local publicity by keeping the money at the community level.

A similar philosophy underlies Wal-Mart's profit-sharing plan. Early on, Sam Walton decided to make his associates partners with him in owning stock. Employees can receive stock through a managed profit-sharing plan that totaled more than $800 million in 1990, up from $18 million in 1980. By giving employees a stake, Walton effectively decreased turnover, increased loyalty, and provided an incentive for employees to work harder and keep their money in the company. Those that do remain reap a handsome reward upon retirement. One hourly associate with twenty-five years under his belt received more than $1 million as a retirement nest egg.[54] According to a veteran assistant store manager, "The stock is a prevailing theme for everyone at Wal-Mart. . . . There's sort of a promise that if you hang around long enough, you can make a fortune on the stock."[55] But "hanging around" is an inadequate term to describe the hard work and productivity that Walton and the Wal-Mart leaders request and receive from every associate.

With Sam Walton's death, both insiders and outsiders have wondered if his handpicked team can provide the leadership and dedication to excellence he epitomized. Walton himself stated that he could "walk away and the company wouldn't lose a step." As George Billingsley, a family friend, stated prior to Walton's death, "you will not find people in Wal-Mart today—least of all Sam—who feel they are solely responsible for its success."[56] As Wal-Mart moves forward, CEO David Glass recalls the spirit of Sam Walton in his own humility and optimism:

> There's more opportunity ahead of us than behind us. We're good students of retailing and we've studied the mistakes of others. We'll make our own mistakes, but we won't repeat theirs. . . . The only thing constant at Wal-Mart is change. We'll be fine as long as we don't lose our responsiveness to the customer.[57]

But this aside, no one would deny that Sam Walton was integral to the creation of Wal-Mart as it stands. He was Wal-Mart's leader, providing the vision, values, and courage that have made the company admired across America. He did not accomplish his goal by merely implementing popular management techniques, creating committees, policies, and rules to achieve success. He had a vision, defined his objectives, and then allowed his associates and partners to shape the way Wal-Mart does business. He provided honest feedback to people on an individual basis and sought partnerships with all parties to produce win-win results.

Among business leaders, Sam Walton stood apart. He had the rare gift of inspiring others to greatness and then stepping back to let them succeed. Having created Wal-Mart, he could have made himself irreplaceable there, making every decision and never developing leaders who could take his place. But Walton had a rare foresight that led him to invest in people and leave an organizational culture that would spur Wal-Mart to even greater heights without him.

In its values and beliefs, and in his continuing vision for the company, Sam Walton is still present at Wal-Mart. He left a great legacy to the Wal-Mart associates and the leadership team he nurtured. The challenge remains, however, for Wal-Mart to continue thriving without him. It remains for the people Sam Walton left behind to live out his values, to improve on what he did, and to continue striving to achieve his vision for Wal-Mart.

PART II

VISION: CONCEIVING REALITY

CHAPTER 4

LEADERSHIP AND VISION

In his speech accepting his nomination as the Democratic party's 1992 presidential candidate, Bill Clinton reminded the nation what the Book of Proverbs tells us: "Where there is no vision, the people perish." What is true for nations is true for corporations, too—companies whose leaders have no vision are doomed to function under the burden of mere tradition. They cannot prosper and grow, because they are reduced to keeping things the way they have always been; they seem to be guided by the premise "If it ain't broke, don't fix it." True leaders see things differently. They are guided by another premise: "If you think it ain't broke, you're not looking hard enough." They know there is always room for improvement, and they are not threatened by the fact that no one has ever done anything so well that it cannot be done better.

We said in Chapter 1 that to a leader, a vision is not a dream but a reality that has yet to come into existence. The ability to see that reality gives the leader the inner strength required to devote long hours over many years in order to make the vision real for others. In this way, a vision acts as an inner force compelling a leader to action. As it becomes the leader's purpose, the vision's power and the leader's dedication to it work to inspire others.[1] When people sense a deep purpose and a personal commitment in the leader, they are more than willing to be led; they choose to follow.

After years of working with leaders, Warren Bennis concluded that "while leaders come in every size, shape, and disposition—short, tall, neat, sloppy, young, old, male, and female—every leader I talked with shared at least one characteristic: a concern with a guiding purpose, an overarching vision. They were more than goal-directed."[2] Peter Kreeft, a professor of philosophy at Boston College, says that in order "to be a leader you have to lead people to a goal worth having—something that's really good and really there."[3] That essential "something" is the vision.

A DEFINITION

What is vision? Because it operates on many levels, it is difficult to define simply. A vision is more than an idea. At once it is a picture both of the future and of the present, appealing simultaneously to logic and to feeling; first it makes sense, and then it inspires strong, simultaneous feelings of hope and pride in its accomplishment. When we say a leader has vision, we refer to the ability to see the present as it is and, on that foundation, to define a better future. A leader with vision is able to see far into the future without being farsighted and remain rooted in the present without being nearsighted.

In the history of nations, political parties, social movements and religions and other groups, we have repeatedly seen the power of leadership with vision. In the world of commerce it is no less essential. A vision for a company is a target at which the leader directs the organization's energy and resources. With an eye on that vision, the leader keeps the organization moving forward in spite of personal, organizational, and environmental challenges and resistance, including a fear of failure; suspicion, derision, or sabotage from superiors, peers, or subordinates; competitor attacks; government obstructions; economic disruptions; and any and all other external events. By imparting that vision to their people, leaders enable and inspire themselves and others. A work force can become much more than just a collection of employees defined by their job descriptions, brought together by the coincidences of having been hired by the same organization. When they are striving to achieve a shared vision, the people work together as a team.

VISION ADDS MEANING TO CORPORATE LIFE

When employees understand the leader's vision, they understand what the organization is trying to accomplish and what it stands for; each person can see what the future holds as a natural, rational, and exciting extension of the present. In addition, the vision conveys meaning to each job, each work group, and each department, affirming the value of every contribution to the organization's success. This is possible only when the vision is plausible and at the same time challenging and creative, able to capture the imaginations of the individual contributors.[4]

Ironically, as Frank Kessler, a real estate developer, pointed out to us, the bigger and more challenging the vision is, the fewer competitors there will be with which to contend. Most leaders think too small, and as a result, they do not capture the imaginations and the deep-rooted commitment of their people. At the same time, by choosing a modest path, they encounter a horde of other marginal leaders who do not possess the inner strength to pursue great visions. Instead of blazing new, exciting, and rewarding trails, they join the pack of mediocre leaders and accept modest results. That is unfortunate indeed, because they deny us all a better life in the process.

The leader's role is not simply to describe the vision. Leaders "create meaning for people" by amassing large amounts of information, making sense of it, integrating it into a meaningful vision of the future, and communicating the vision so that people want to participate in its realization.[5] Such visions have the power to lift employees out of the monotony of the workaday world and to put them into a new world full of opportunity and challenge. Jerry Wind, a professor at the University of Pennsylvania's Wharton

School, refers to a vision as "something to rally around, a glue pulling the organization together."[6]

Although vision guides a company in a particular direction, leaders do not typically produce specific plans for making the vision a reality. They usually leave the more detailed planning to managers. Nevertheless, "unless the leader has a sense of where the whole enterprise is going and must go, it is not possible to delegate . . . the other functions."[7] It is just as dangerous to leave others to drift by being too general as it is to cage them in by being too precise. "Typically, a vision is specific enough to provide real guidance to people, yet vague enough to encourage initiative and to remain relevant under a variety of conditions."[8]

Because the vision may seem almost impossible to some employees, it is also the leader's responsibility to bolster their courage with understanding. Experienced leaders can do this so naturally that people do not even realize how courageous they are, instead simply doing whatever is needed in pursuit of the vision.[9] Leaders themselves "lean on" the vision, drawing from it the strength to overcome adversity and to cope with doubt. Leaders must impart that same strength to their people, enabling them to carry on through all the confusion in the workplace and to focus on the things that really matter.

EMPLOYEE BUY-IN AND COMMITMENT

To be effective, a leader cannot simply force his or her vision upon the rest of the organization. Any attempt to do so will invite rejection and cost time and money. Additionally, such an approach will lead to frustration and anger among the people and in the leader as well. Autocratic leadership in business today generally brings only compliance with the rules, not commitment, and commitment is required for the long-term success of a vision. Ideally, a leader will express the vision in words and actions, continually communicating its essence; as people come to comprehend the vision, they commit to it. We will discuss this process in greater depth in Chapters 5 and 6.

Having committed to the leader's vision for the company, people begin to participate in shaping it, and it comes to reflect their personal visions—the images they have in their hearts and minds about what their futures will be like and how they will contribute to the organization. At this point, the leader's vision becomes a shared vision, and people in the organization become even more committed to it. Shared vision creates a commonality of interest that enables people to see meaning and coherence in the diverse activities of the typical workday. Furthermore, a shared vision causes people to focus on the future and what it holds, not simply because they must but because they want to.[10] The realization of a shared vision results in the "alignment of the individual energies" of all who take part in it. The realization of what an organization can actually achieve will generate a "unique rush of power," a level of energy high above what is considered normal and that can be sustained for a relatively long period of time.[11]

Possibly the most important variables contributing to a leader's success in implementing a vision are the leader's level of commitment to that vision and the level of commitment they can inspire in their employees. If a leader is wholly committed to a vision, he or she will find it much easier to motivate people and to direct their energy toward making that vision a reality.

OVERCOMING THE FEAR OF FAILURE

The fear of failure prevents many otherwise capable people from pursuing their visions, and leaders must overcome this reluctance to risk failure if they hope to succeed. Fear of failure is a natural phenomenon, but true leaders do not allow it to paralyze them and prevent them from pursuing their vision.

In 1982, at the lowest point of the most severe recession in the United States since the Great Depression, Kemmons Wilson, the founder of Holiday Inns, spoke with a group of students at the McIntire School of Commerce at the University of Virginia to discuss the opportunities he saw for entrepreneurs in the future. His view of the future was bright. Wilson kept telling the students how fortunate they were to be living at a time when there was such an abundance of opportunity to be pursued. Wilson was challenged by one student who told him that it was easy for him, an extremely successful businessman, to say such things since he had never experienced failure. Wilson responded, "I have failed more times than you've tried."

Wilson's point was that it is not how many times you try and fail that matters, because everybody fails. What matters is your ability to get up and try again following each failure. A leader simply must expect and deal with failure, because it is a fundamental part of the learning process. Everybody fails in the process of learning to do anything they intend to master; it is unavoidable. The point is that these failures are part of a process that leads to success.

Consider for a minute how much effort goes into learning the game of golf. The truth is you never really master the game; you are always learning to play golf, no matter how good you are at it. Even professional golfers seek instruction from people who can help them improve their game. We bring this up because it is easy for most golfers to remember how atrocious they were when they started playing, with those duck hooks and vicious slices. A good golfer is one who has kept playing, who has learned from the problems that kept him or her from succeeding. If your vision is to become a good golfer, you must deal with your failures along the way or it will never become a reality. This applies to leadership as well: your vision will never become a reality if you are not able to deal with your failures.

Another example is that of professional baseball. In the

major leagues, if a player hits above .300, he is considered to be a very good hitter. If he hits around .320 or .330, he is among the best in the league. But even a .350 batting average means that 65 percent of the time, the player either did not get on base or got on base only as a result of someone else's error. In major league baseball, a player who fails to hit the ball safely 65 percent of the time is heading toward the Hall of Fame. Interestingly, Babe Ruth is known as a great home run hitter, but he was also a leader in strikeouts. Leaders must learn to deal with failure; they must master this experience. If they cannot cope with failure, they cannot lead.

Albert Einstein had great vision, and he was a leader in the scientific community. His theories literally changed the way we see the universe. But when Einstein was once asked how many ideas he had had in his lifetime, his answer was two. (Einstein considered ideas to be only those thoughts nobody had ever thought of before.) The point is that a person can have an abundance of ideas, but success depends on what is done with them. Chances are that an idea a person believes to be original has already been thought of by somebody else, somewhere, only that person failed to do anything about it. As the story of Einstein shows, it only takes one good idea to be a stunning success, but you must act on and build on that idea. The fear of failure prevents many talented people from mentioning their ideas to others or from following through completely on them. As a result, we deprive ourselves and others of many benefits.

Nevertheless, many people believe the key to success is to avoid failure. Thus they stay with things they know, seldom trying anything new. These people fail because the surest way to fail in the long term actually is to continue doing what you did yesterday, to follow proven tradition mindlessly. Things are changing, and times are changing. If we do not change along with them, we will eventually fail.

The willingness to confront and deal with failure is an important attribute of a leader. But how many times should a leader try and fail before deciding it is time to quit? One? Two? Three? When Thomas Edison was working on the electric light bulb, he had to deal with a great deal of failure. He is said to have tried thousands of filaments before he found the one that worked. He did not quit after the first, five hundredth, or thousandth try. He believed in his vision, and he wanted to succeed more than anything else; so he dealt with his own daily failures and kept his eye on the long-term success. Today we all benefit because Thomas Edison did not choose to give up.

CHALLENGING THE STATUS QUO

Leaders must make certain that their people do not give up either, and that they continue to strive for success. It is natural for some people to quit before they begin, but organizational pressures can hobble those who would take the risk to try a new idea. As John D. Rockefeller III wrote: "An organization is a system, with a logic of its own, and all the weight of tradition and inertia. The deck is stacked in favor of the tried and proven way of doing things and against the taking of risks and striking out in new directions."[12]

Walter Ulmer, Jr., president of the Center for Creative Leadership, says that "the natural state of an organization is conservative, to maintain the status quo."[13] Many people in organizations that have been around for a long time believe their primary responsibility is to protect the status quo. They are obstacles in the path of success, and leaders must learn to deal with them and to protect those who question the way things are done. Ram Charan, a management consultant, believes "divine discontent with the status quo" is an essential quality of a leader, and we agree.[14] Abraham Zaleznik says that people who have leadership talent have "a real fire in their belly . . . a fire that has to do with having an effect on the world."[15] You can tell when a leader has been in an organization because he or she leaves a mark and, as a result, affects the destinies of many others.

Ridicule: A Technique Used to Make Leaders Quit

When employees in most organizations encounter a person with a vision that is significantly different from the status quo, it is common for them to resist the suggested changes and to put obstacles in the way of success. Their rationale is easily understood: change means work and exertion for them. By preventing change, they save time and energy in the short term, although in the long term, their resistance may be their ruin.

If the leader refuses to quit, employees turn to ridicule in the hope that shame and humiliation will keep the leader from moving forward. Leaders must learn to deal with this ridicule, understanding that great leaders before them faced and prevailed over it. Marconi was ridiculed as he sought support for the wireless radio. Imagine him trying to convince a group of would-be investors that his invention was capable of capturing "little waves" out of the air that could not be seen, then converting them to sound that would come from a little box. A fair number of the investors must have thought he was crazy. It is natural for some people to exhibit disbelief when unusual ideas are presented to them. It is also natural for them to ridicule the people who present those ideas.

When Success Is Dismissed as Luck

Suppose a leader develops a vision to which he or she is committed, shares it with people, accepts failure, deals with ridicule, and after working tirelessly for many years, actually turns that vision into a reality. It is now time for him or her to reap the rewards and hear praise for an amazing accomplishment, right? Wrong. In all likelihood, what he or she will hear is, "Oh, you were just lucky"—meaning, of course, "if it wasn't just plain dumb luck, I would have done it myself." In this situation, a leader should find comfort in the words of Emerson: "Shallow men believe in luck, wise and strong men in cause and effect."

Luck cannot explain accomplishment. Winning the state lottery may seem like a matter of luck, but you have to buy a lottery ticket to win. Ara Parseghian, football coach at Notre Dame several years ago, led his team to beat the University of Alabama for the national championship two years in a row; Alabama was favored to win both times. Both years, Alabama took an early lead and held that lead until the end of the game. Both years, Notre Dame came back in the closing seconds of the game and won. When a reporter asked Parseghian after the second victory about "the luck of the Irish," he is reported to have said, "If you mean by luck the place where preparation meets opportunity, then we were lucky."

In this world, there is an abundance of opportunity for everyone. Parseghian knew that the Alabama football players were not infallible and that they would give his team opportunities to win. If his team prepared well and was ready for the game, it could take advantage of those opportunities. It took hard work and practice to be able to see and take advantage of the openings provided—for preparation to meet opportunity.

There is a story that is often told about professional golfer Gary Player's struggle to win the U.S. Open. To stay in contention, he needed to par a certain hole. He hit a terrible tee shot into the rough. His second shot sliced unmercifully, yet it rolled onto the green a few feet away from the pin. As he walked toward the easy putt for par, someone in the crowd yelled "Gary, you're lucky." He is reported to have turned to the man and said, "The more I practice, the luckier I get." Commitment, not luck, produced his success.

COMMUNICATING VISION

Communicating vision is the subject of Chapter 6, but a few words about that topic are in order here. A leader must communicate his or her vision to others in order for it to become a shared vision. To accomplish this, the leader should act in a manner consistent with the vision in everything she or he does.[16] A leader must set a personal example; she or he cannot afford to send mixed signals by saying one thing and doing another.

The first step in communicating a vision to a group is to stress its importance so people will take an interest in it. If they believe the vision is important and worthwhile, many of them will want to be involved with it, even if they do not understand all the details. As John W. Alexander, vice president and general manager of 3D Distribution Systems, puts it, "Most people will cooperate and follow the leader with only a vague idea of what their participation, contribution, and reward might be" if the leader's vision excites them.[17]

In his book *A Force for Change,* John Kotter offers several suggestions for sharing a vision. Delivering a single clear and credible message is important in helping people understand the goals at hand. In order to communicate clearly and reinforce the vision, it is necessary to send frequent messages orally and in writing, and these must be more than the typical day-to-day orders coming from "the boss."

Communication that motivates people to action should focus on the core values and beliefs supporting the vision. Effective communication of these values and beliefs speeds implementation by conveying simple images or words that make the vision easier to remember. In addition, repeating simple words and symbols communicates the message without clogging already overused communication channels. Written communication can be used in a similar manner to reinforce the vision by reporting progress for everyone to see, and progress toward achieving goals keeps people's spirits up and helps convince them that they can do it.[18]

GOING FROM COMMUNICATION TO COMMITMENT

After the vision has been explained simply and directly, people must decide if they want to be a part of it.[19] If they do not want to follow, they cannot be forced to do so. They can be forced to do some things, of course, but they will abandon these quickly as they figure out how to get out from under the strong arm of a leader who has not earned their commitment. Autocratic leaders do not typically last long because the cost of using this approach is too high: halfhearted efforts produce goods of inferior quality, continual turnover drains the organization of employees with skills and ideas, and time, money, and effort are lost. Moreover, forcing people to do things they do not want to do requires a great deal of energy—more than most people can expend on a sustained basis.

Over the long term, most people are not motivated by being pushed. They are motivated by the desire to satisfy their own very basic human needs for achievement, belonging, recognition, self-esteem, control over their lives, and the sense of having lived up to their ideals. To be successful, leaders must connect with these human needs and let their people become excited about a vision. Furthermore, the leader must involve people in deciding how to achieve the vision, or at least to achieve the part of it that is most relevant to them. Their involvement must be real, and the rewards and recognition they receive must be sincere.[20]

To win continued support from a group, a leader must be willing to share his personal views with them, and he must also listen carefully to theirs. Ultimately, the leader must be willing to assume a vulnerable position and ask a difficult question:

"Will you follow me?" In reality, the leader is asking, "Is this vision worthy of your commitment?"[21] Being vulnerable in this manner is difficult for many people who have grown up during a time when employees were expected to comply with the leader's orders and not to ask too many questions.[22]

Although a leader is responsible for introducing the vision to the group, the people want and need to become personally involved with the vision. As we have said before, they cannot do this unless the vision reflects, to some extent, their own personal visions. Thus it is critical for a leader to keep an open mind to employee suggestions and ideas that can improve the vision. Too often leaders present their visions to employees as cast in concrete, and they send the subtle (or not so subtle) message that there is no room for compromise. As a result, the employees either reject the vision or simply go through the motions of supporting it. In either case, it is doubtful the vision will ever become reality.

The introduction of the word *compromise* may surprise many people because they have been led to believe that once the leader is committed to the vision, he or she cannot afford to be flexible. While it is true that the leader's commitment to the vision must be strong and unwavering, it is also true that the leader is incapable of predicting in advance precisely what the future holds. Thus, as the leader and the group move together toward making the vision a reality, they both learn more about their vision and have opportunities to improve upon it. Compromise as the vision unfolds should not be interpreted negatively; in fact, the leader's willingness to accept suggestions that result in some change in the vision will benefit the leader and will improve the quality of the vision and the intensity of the employees' commitment to it.

Stated another way, the development of a vision is an evolutionary process. As noted by Peter Senge, "At any point there will be a particular image of the future that is predominant, but that image will evolve."[23] A vision should be constantly examined and modified to reflect important changes in the environment and to assure continued support and enthusiasm from everyone involved.

As their commitment to the vision grows, it becomes more real to employees, and they will find it easier to dedicate the time and energy necessary to make the vision a reality. Those who have expertise in a particular field should be encouraged to use their knowledge to improve parts of the vision that are related to their specialty. According to John W. Alexander, employees supply "the details, missing steps, and concerns that confront the leader's visionary goals. When leaders solicit input, they discover the knowledge, interest, and evident parameters of support they can expect from others."[24] A leader should expect parts of the vision to undergo alteration, but the essence of it will remain intact.

If a leader cannot see the value in compromises and is too inflexible to accept them, the vision will never achieve its full potential. "When more people come to share a vision, the vision becomes more real in the sense of a mental reality that people can truly imagine achieving. They [the leaders] now have partners, co-creators; the vision no longer rests on their shoulders alone."[25]

EMPOWERING PEOPLE TO DO THEIR JOBS

Communicating the vision accurately and fully has the added advantage of creating the conditions under which employees can be empowered to do their jobs. The term *empowerment* is used frequently today; unfortunately, many people using the term do not really understand what it means. Some people who are familiar with management literature interpret empowerment to mean delegation of authority. Strict literalists will be quick to point out that a manager can delegate authority, but not responsibility. To them, empowerment is a formal (almost legalistic) passing on of a task from one level in the organization to another. But while delegation is not empowerment, empowerment does require good delegation.

Empowerment means giving employees jobs to do and the freedom they need to be creative while doing them. It means allowing employees to try new ideas, even if these ideas have never been considered or have been previously rejected. It means allowing employees to experiment and fail on occasion without fear of punishment.

Having said this, we must point out that leaders take big risks only after carefully considering the consequences. They must exercise judgment, and as a general rule, they should establish an understanding with employees about the risks they are willing to take in any experiment. But as we said earlier, experimentation is essential, so leaders must not be so restrictive that their employees fail to try new ideas. Empowerment means giving employees more than the mere authority to do the job.

AN EXAMPLE OF VISION

Look at Figure 4–1 for a few moments. What do you see? We have used this example in leadership seminars for many years, and it is interesting what people think they see in this picture. Some people think it is a satellite photograph; we have frequently been told with supreme confidence that is is a picture of the Black Sea. Others tell us that it is a cloud, or a dog, or a cat, or a woman. It is actually, however, a picture of a cow—not a very good one, but a picture of a cow nonetheless. A small percentage of the people in our seminars see the cow quickly without assistance (about 5 percent); and some people never see it at all (about 5 percent). In Figure 4–2 we have outlined the cow so that most of you will be able to see it.

The picture of the cow is like a leader's vision in many respects. When we tell the groups what it is, most of them just laugh at us as if we are joking. The laughter is similar to the ridicule a leader receives when presenting an idea that is not readily understandable. Of course, we do not back off when they laugh at us because we know what it is, and we know from experience that we can help most people see what it is eventually.

But what would happen if, after trying for several minutes to show the cow to the group, we could not get anyone to see it? Although this has never happened, our guess is that the exercise would be a complete failure, and we would lose our credibility instantly. So we risk failure and accept ridicule simply by showing a group of people a picture that is unclear. Leaders take the same chances when they present their visions to groups from whom they need support. Faced with this prospect, many people who could be leaders are afraid to present their visions.

But, as we said before, only about 5 percent of the people see the cow without assistance; the rest of the group, troubled that others can see what they cannot, accuse us of "setting them up" by enlisting confederates for this exercise. After we outline the cow, most of the people can see it, and those who cannot still have doubts. When 95 percent of the group sees the cow and spontaneously attempts to help point it out to the 5 percent who cannot see it, however, the remainder accepts that it is a picture of a cow even if they still cannot see it. Even those who cannot understand a vision can contribute to it, and will, if they observe confidence in and commitment to the vision on the part of their colleagues.

THE DIFFERENCE BETWEEN PERCEPTION AND REALITY

Showing the difference between perception and reality is very simple in this exercise. We ask a participant in the group who thought the picture was a satellite photograph in the beginning, "What was the picture before you saw the cow?" Without exception, the participant says the picture was a satellite photo. Notice that we do not ask them what they *saw* in the beginning; we ask them what the picture *was*. Of course, the correct answer is that regardless of what they thought they saw in the picture, it was always a picture of a cow. Their seeing the cow, or not seeing it, had absolutely no bearing on what the picture actually was: it was, is, and always will be a picture of a cow.

It is common for a member of the group to say, "To you it's a picture of a cow, but to me it's something else [like a satellite photo]. That's what I see." That would be fine, except for one thing—it is a picture of a cow. Still, there are people who say, "To hell with the facts, I have my opinion." They may not be able to support their beliefs, but they hold fast to them nonetheless.

This attitude is not surprising in our society, and leaders

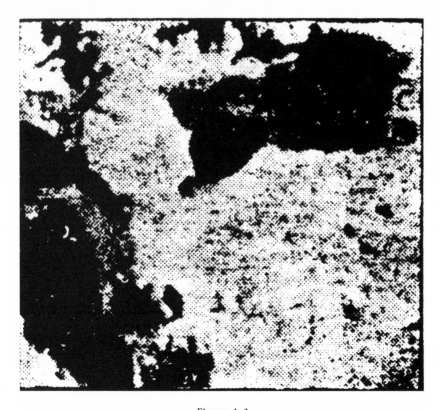

Figure 4–1

need to be prepared to deal with it. In marketing classes, for example, students are taught that perceptions are reality, and they learn to manipulate those perceptions. Politicians learn to play the perception game as well, and they hire "spin doctors" to cast a positive light on things that are far from positive. For example, politicians who have no real understanding of education may visit public schools to show they are serious about education. What they are doing is creating the perception that they are concerned about education, but the facts may tell a completely different story.

Remember the old question, "If a tree falls in the woods, and no one is around to hear it, does it still make a sound?" The answer is yes, of course. Sound is vibrations, and the vibrations occur regardless of our perception of them. It is difficult to understand how anyone could be so arrogant as to believe there would be no sound unless he or she were present to hear it, but some people do. Reality is not affected by our presence or absence; it is what it is.

Leaders need to take heed of perceptions, but they need to focus greater attention on reality. If a leader's vision is accurate, people will make it a reality with hard work and persistence. But if the vision is fundamentally flawed, no amount of salesmanship and effort can make it a reality, and it should be changed. As the old adage says, you can't make a silk purse out of a sow's ear.

THE MAJORITY CAN BE WRONG

In our seminar exercise, we ask the group what the picture would be if 60 percent of them had voted that it was a satellite photo. The group responds by saying that the picture is a cow even if the majority believes it is something else. This is an interesting occurrence in a democratic republic where the majority rules; we make the point that the majority can be wrong and that leaders often blaze trails that are not well traveled by the majority. When they do, they assume the risk associated with taking a different path (the possibility of failure and ridicule), but they also position themselves to win big when their visions become real.

INFLUENCING REALITY

Leaders are not magicians. They do not just predict future events; they are strategic thinkers who are willing to take risks. Leaders determine what they want the future to be like, and then they figure out how to make things happen. Rather than create something out of nothing, they look at what they know to exist and search for relationships, for the way things

Figure 4–2

are meant to fit together. Once they find the connections, they share them with other people. In their minds, leaders maintain a balance between a clear understanding of the present and a clear focus on the future. Peter Senge calls this balance "creative tension," and maintains that "an accurate picture of current reality is just as important as a compelling picture of a desired future."[26]

We all have the potential to influence reality by taking steps today to bring about some desired condition in the future. Leaders in particular have a tremendous opportunity to change things for good and for bad because they control vast resources (financial and human) that can be used to bring their visions to life. But they do not determine what reality is; they only influence it.

As leaders move toward converting their visions into realities, they exert an influence that may shape the course of destiny, but the resulting reality has a life of its own that is much greater than the leader who conceived it. Steve Jobs learned this lesson the hard way at Apple Computers when he was removed as chairman of the company. He conceived the notion that computers could be manufactured for sale to individuals and that the market would be huge. He got the ball rolling, but in no time at all it developed beyond his wildest dreams. Quickly, he became a small player in a very big game, and he became irrelevant to the industry.

CHAPTER 5

LEADERSHIP AND COMMITMENT

Many business leaders today profess to be guided by a vision. Seeking to shape a productive and efficient company, they emphasize satisfying customer requirements through the principles of customer focus, continuous improvement, and employee empowerment. They know that achieving their vision is possible only if they can secure the commitment of their people, and they know that the creativity unleashed with that commitment will propel the organization to ever-increasing levels of quality and productivity. Many leaders know that commitment is necessary—but they do not know how to get it.

To cultivate commitment in others, leaders must communicate both their vision and their commitment to it to the people in the organization. Therefore, before communicating with others, leaders must first understand the scope of that commitment that they themselves must make (and communicate) if they are to bring their vision to reality. They must commit themselves not only to the vision, but also to the *process* of realizing it.

This chapter discusses the elements of leadership commitment, the first and most critical step in developing the organizational commitment to a collective vision of quality and performance excellence. In the next chapter we build from this discussion, exploring the opportunities and methods a leader can use to communicate the vision and his or her commitment to it clearly to the organization, the second step to developing the organizational commitment to a shared vision of performance excellence.

THE POWER OF COMMITMENT

Like *quality* and *excellence, commitment* is a word that enters our conversations every day. We may use the word as a synonym for duty and obligation when discussing our work lives, or for dedication and devotion when discussing our personal lives. For the most part, though, we speak of commitment without thought to the potential force the word holds locked within.

True commitment is a wondrous power. When people are committed to a vision, their lives and the lives of those around them can change dramatically. Time and again we find ourselves shaking our heads in wonder when commitment to the vision of being the best propels an injured athlete beyond seemingly hopeless setbacks to the status of a world champion, or when a fierce commitment to survival enables the victim of an earthquake to endure days of entrapment under a destroyed building and emerge from the rubble to continue on with life.

When commitment to a vision is shared by many, its power can develop into an immense force. Throughout history the fervor of commitment so characteristic of religious and political ideals has radically and forcibly transformed societies, continually restructuring the nations and peoples of the world and the complex relationships they share. People have lived wretchedly and died tragically because of the completeness of their shared commitment to a leader's vision. Such a commitment was evident in Guyana in 1978, when 912 men, women, and children were led to their deaths by drinking cyanide-laced Kool-Aid. These followers were committed to a leader's vision: the Reverend Jim Jones's vision of himself as "the living God" and his promise of ultimate personal transformation for each committed follower.

Lest we think this occurrence will not be repeated, a similar incident occurred in 1993 when David Koresh, a self-proclaimed messiah from Waco, Texas, established a group of committed followers that he called the Branch Davidians. They had been taught and they believed that the end of time was near and that Koresh was going to lead them through a final battle into the promised land. Instead, more than 70 men, women and children, lost their lives in a fiery inferno after negotiations with federal authorities reached an impasse.

The world was amazed at the commitment gained by such manipulative leaders and their destructive ideals.

Yet commitment to a collective vision, even when realized through struggle and conflict, can also bring its followers a sense of elation and fulfillment. We can only imagine the feelings of triumph soaring through colonial Americans as their commitment to a vision of liberty secured their independence and brought about the birth of this nation at the end of the Revolutionary War. Or those of nineteenth-century abolitionists who listened with joy as President Lincoln proclaimed as a law of the land the emancipation of all slaves living, until that point, in bondage within the United States.

Between the extremes of tragedy and euphoria, but no less important in our own lives, is the strength that can come from the quiet belief in and commitment to what we do every day. When we commit ourselves to a vision and understand our own role in accomplishing that vision, we achieve an increased sense of purpose and fulfillment. Like the commitment that has moved groups to act in extremes, the power of everyday commitment is a force that can, albeit more slowly, change both the world in which we live and our role within it.

COMMITMENT IN ACTION

A leader's role is unique within an organization. So also is the essence of the commitment required by the leader to realize his or her vision for the organization. We have described leaders as those individuals with vision who possess strong values and beliefs and who, through the courage of their convictions, are willing to take action to make their vision a reality. And we have described leaders' great visions as those that, when clearly articulated, bond together the vigor and the objectives of individuals into a common, energized purpose.

Often we think of visions associated with movements and purposes of a grand scale, but this need not be the case. Upon reflection, each of us can most likely remember a moment where the veil of the present was lifted, revealing with stunning clarity a picture of a future state that made us think, "Yes, that's how it *should* be." Perhaps these experiences have not occurred about a matter we consider to be of remarkable magnitude; they are nonetheless true experiences of vision. From these experiences we realize that many men and women have formulated visions. Not all of these individuals, however, have acted on those visions, and fewer still have seen their visions become realities.

Why is this so? What distinguishes a vision that becomes reality from one that lingers only in the mind of its creator? If a leader is indeed committed to the vision he or she holds, why does it not naturally follow that the vision will be realized?

Visions are sometimes not realized because commitment to what the vision *is,* on the part of both the leader and his or her followers, is not enough. A leader who has developed a vision and wants to ensure that it becomes reality must also be committed to the process that is necessary to make the vision reality—in other words, committed to the *action* of leading to the vision, which is a separate commitment from belief in what the vision represents.

Commit comes from the Latin word *committere*, which includes in its definition this element of action: "to bring together, join, entrust, and *do*."[1] This idea of commitment as an inherent element of leadership is echoed by J. F. T. Bugental. In describing the essence of the commitment of a leader to a vision, he wrote, "Commitment is, in a paraphrase, the statement, 'This I am; this I believe, this I do. . . .' "[2]

In developing the vision and then committing to what it represents, the leader can become the champion of the vision simply by believing in its rightness. But it is the embodiment of the vision, the *doing* of leadership, that personifies commitment, giving it life and making it possible for that vision to become a reality. Creating a vision will never suffice; a leader must commit herself or himself to making the journey needed to achieve the vision. It is unwavering commitment to the actions necessary to implement the vision that brings power to it—the power spawned from joining together the focus of mind and the energy of action.

Martin Luther King, Jr., had a truly great vision, expressed powerfully in his "I Have a Dream" address at the Lincoln Memorial in 1963. This was a vision of absolute power, expressed with ringing clarity and truth, shared by millions of people across the world. But the formation and declaration of the vision was not enough: King had to prompt and direct action on the vision. The power of the vision came with those who first embraced it as their own, and then acted on it, venturing down the difficult, even life-sacrificing path toward making this dream a reality. King was able to articulate this vision eloquently, but just as importantly, he actively led its followers on the difficult journey of its realization. It was his commitment to both the vision itself *and* the struggle needed to bring it about that has kept King's vision (still yet to be fully achieved) alive in the hearts and souls of many.

The world of business is filled with leaders who have bonded together the individuals within their organizations, inspiring them to new plateaus of excellence. From his first day as the leader of Corning Glass Works, Jamie Houghton has articulated a vision of quality and excellent performance for his organization. But more importantly, he has also championed the process of change that is taking Corning from its performance level of the past to what has become its collective vision for the future. In the 1980s David Kearns brought Xerox back from the brink of disaster by first formulating, and then actively leading, the process to fulfill his vision of Xerox as an organization capable of rivaling its competition in the areas of customer satisfaction and product excellence.

These accomplishments were possible not just because Houghton and Kearns were committed to the vision of quality they had developed for their organizations, but because they became committed to the long process necessary first to direct the focus of the organization to the vision, and then to lead employees on the journey to achieve the vision.

THE LEADER'S COMMITMENT TO THE JOURNEY

Many organizations insist on carrying the baggage of their past. "We've always done things that way," "We're comfortable with how things are now," "We know the routine"— these are the common signs of minds set against change. The resistance to change inherent in any organization is the most powerful constraint an organization faces as it begins the journey of improvement. The gap between what an organization is today and what its leaders envision it to be in the future can be immense, often requiring the organization to undergo substantial changes during the long and rocky journey to reach that future destination. The leader must be committed to *personally* guiding the organization through this journey, helping the organization shed the mind-set of the past and plunge ahead into the changes that must be made to bring it into the envisioned future state.

Why must it be the organization's leader who leads this

journey? The answer to this question lies in the inherent role of the leader in the organization. Although inclusive of the role and influence of the leader as a figurehead, it goes beyond this role to include the more *functional* elements of the leader's position in influencing and directing the organization's management issues and actions. Leadership commitment to the process of transforming the organization is necessary because it is this leadership that provides an organization with the "integrative thinking and necessary resources"[3] required to operate the organization. If the organization is to change, so too must the entrenched operations of the organization change, not only to support the vision's end state, but also to be able simply to survive the process of change. It is the leader's role to "understand the interaction between strategy, structure, and making it happen, and to chart a course that carefully blends the hard and soft aspects of the desired change in corporate positions and capability."[4]

When a leader commits to the process of realizing the vision of performance excellence, his or her vision and commitment evolve from an intangible idea to a series of very tangible actions and plans. These actions and plans become "focused on a single overwhelming objective: the creation of the right environment for each and every person in the organization to truly perform"[5] and so contribute to moving the organization closer toward the vision. As the vision becomes more real and defined through this process, more applicable to what the organization is and does, so also does the commitment of the leader to the vision become more real and applicable to each member of the organization.

COMMITMENT SHOWS IN A LEADER'S BEHAVIOR

A leader supports and nurtures an environment that fosters transformation to a vision—from its more intangible atmosphere or work culture to its more concrete organizational structure—through his or her direct and indirect behavior and actions.

> I discovered that people watched my every action to see if it supported or undermined our vision. They wanted to see if I practiced what I preached. . . . Eventually I came to understand that everything I did and said had a symbolic as well as a literal meaning. I had to anticipate the potential impact of every word and act, ask myself again and again if what I was about to do or say would reinforce the vision or undermine it.[6]

This example drives home the most important commitment a leader makes in realizing his or her vision: *the commitment to model the vision through one's own behavior in a visible and consistent manner.* If the leader is not committed to the rigors of modeling the vision through his or her actions and attitudes, the process of transforming the organization will end before the first step is taken. "The only way leaders can make values tangible and real to followers is through their behaviors and actions. Employees look to their leaders as role models of how they should behave. And when in doubt, they believe actions over words, without fail."[7]

Leaders are continuously under scrutiny by members of the organization, who critically observe the leader's personal and operational actions, taking cues from and tailoring their own actions to their *interpretation* of the verbal and nonverbal signals observed. We have all worked for and with people who have said one thing and done the opposite: closed doors or obvious glances at watches greeting those who came seeking a frequently pronounced open-door policy, or invitations to submit ideas for improvements that, when submitted, are left to collect dust in a file with little or no feedback given to those making the effort to participate. In a very short time the real message shines through these paper policies and spreads throughout the organization: "This is another gimmick that sounds good, but it obviously isn't going to happen. It's just another example of management saying one thing and doing another."

For an organization to move toward a vision of quality and continual improvement, its leader must develop a visible link between the articulated vision and the personal attitudes and behavior he or she displays on the job every day. The vision must be used by the leader, and eventually each member of the organization, as the filter for understanding information and the basis on which all decisions are made and actions taken. Simply put, the leader's attitude, behavior, and actions must support the ideals that the organization is striving to achieve: focusing on the needs of the customer, treating employees with respect and empowering them to do their jobs well, and striving for quality output and continuous improvement. Every question, every action, every decision from the leader will either reinforce or undermine the vision.

Although this scrutiny at first may be somewhat overwhelming, it offers continuous opportunities for the leader to set the tone and expectations for the organization. Leadership commitment must be translated through and evident in a leader's actions in two areas: personal behavior, and operational behavior.

Personal Behavior

A leader's personal behavior and actions are the most powerful indicators of his or her commitment to the vision and the process of reaching it. Until his death in 1984, Ray Kroc was known to appear at McDonald's restaurants around the country, mopping floors and washing windows along with other members of the crew. What more effective way was there of showing his commitment to the value of cleanliness than by actually wringing out a mop? Sam Walton, one of the richest men in the world, would show up at any one of a number of remotely located Wal-Marts and proceed to model the importance of customer satisfaction by directing customers down aisles and personally answering their questions and concerns.

These stories of Kroc and Walton have entered business folklore, partly because their success in developing quality organizations staffed with committed individuals is proof of the importance of a leader's everyday behavior. We must take their actions to heart, and when we do so a clear lesson emerges: organizational leaders are most effective when they commit to modeling the values and beliefs that have been set for the organization in their personal attitudes and behavior.

When a leader must change the direction and culture of an organization to become focused on quality and continuous improvement, the leader's personal behavior becomes even more important. As depicted above, members of the organization will be watching the leader's personal behavior critically to see if the behavior is consistent with the new vision and values espoused for the organization:

- How open and willing is the leader in undergoing personal change? Have the leader's personal actions changed in keeping with the new direction for the organization?
- How does the leader interact with and use inputs from others in the organization? Is the interaction honest? Are inputs of others listened to, respected, and *acted on*?
- How does the leader react to criticisms, mistakes, or bad news?
- How does the leader make decisions? Are they informed, information based, and consistent with a customer focus?
- How does the leader spend his or her time?

Each of these areas represents an opportunity for the leader's personal actions either to reinforce or to invalidate the organizational vision of quality and continuous improvement.

Operational Behavior

In addition to personal behavior, a leader must commit her or his operational actions to be in sync with and support the desired end vision of performance excellence. Leaders can actively leverage the power of their management position to ensure that the transformation of the organization to the vision is operationally possible.

In their organizational role, leaders can ensure the development and allocation of structural and operational resources needed to set the context of continuous improvement within the organization.

> I had come to realize that . . . I did manage the context. I provided and allocated the resources, I designed and implemented the systems. I drew up and executed the organizational structure. The power of any contextual factor lies in its ability to shape the way people think and what they expect.[8]

Continuation of or transformation to a desired level of performance cannot take place if an organization's structure, processes, and systems impede the organization's ability to change and improve. Because of this, a leader must be proactive in using the power of his or her position to make and carry out specific operational policies that support the changes to come. The leader's specific managerial decisions can provide the incentive and the resources to remove the barriers and encourage the analysis and improvement of the organizational structure and work and planning processes. Modeling the vision through appropriate operational behavior includes ensuring the procurement and development of the appropriate technical and human capabilities, knowledge, and skill required for the organization to make the improvements in what it does and how it does it.

It is no coincidence that exemplary business leaders (including Sam Walton, Ray Kroc, Walt Disney, Robert Galvin, and David Kearns) who have successfully fostered the development of quality organizations were all visibly committed to focusing their personal and operational behaviors to reflect the vision for their organization. From them, we learn that modeling the vision of quality and improvement in personal and operational behavior requires a leader to commit to actions that do the following:

- Embrace personal and organizational change as a positive force rather than a threat
- Foster personal and organizational learning and growth
- Encourage risk taking and innovation
- Inspire enthusiasm and excitement for the transformation itself

EMBRACING CHANGE AND CONTINUAL IMPROVEMENT

As we have said, the transformation of an organization's culture to enact the values of quality performance and continuous improvement often requires an organization to undergo an extensive amount of change. The leader's willingness and ability to change his or her own behaviors and actions, as well as encourage and support change in others in keeping with the created vision, will determine the success of this transformation. If the leader does not embrace change in his or her actions and attitudes, employees will certainly not feel the need to change their own actions. It follows, then, that when committed to modeling a vision of continuous improvement, a leader becomes a champion of change.

As well as championing personal change, a leader's actions must reflect the acceptance and importance of change in an organizational and operational context. Through his or her management position, the leader can ensure that changes made in the organization do in fact facilitate moving the company toward the end vision. This does not mean that the leader must foresee and personally implement every change that an organization undergoes. Rather, the leader should use his or her position to ensure that the resources are available to allow employees first to identify what to change and then to make the changes happen.

In leading the transformation of Xerox to a customer-driven quality organization in the 1980s, David Kearns not only endeavored to model change in his personal behavior but, as CEO, supported and approved a multitude of structural and operational changes in the organization. The operational changes Kearns supported included changing Xerox's organizational structure, management processes, allocation of resources, and cost base. Additionally, new systems (such as a customer satisfaction management system and numerous benchmarking systems) were developed to provide the organization with the information needed to understand how to focus and maintain the transformation process. Over time, these changes enabled the organization to make the intangible vision of quality tangible as the changes improved operations, which in turn led to increased quality, productivity, and customer satisfaction—all driven by the commitment and supporting action of Kearns in his leadership role.

And Kearns is not alone. Robert Galvin effectively used his position as CEO of Motorola to ensure employees were given the resources needed to identify and implement better ways of doing business, and George Fisher has followed his lead. After embracing the need for change in his personal behavior, Galvin committed to educating Motorola's employees to understand the inevitable need for and opportunities that come with change. He then capitalized on the authority of his position to create "tool management culture" (TMC), providing employees with the tools and skills necessary to deal with changes in their work environment.

Even organizations that are committed to a vision of quality and customer satisfaction and to excellence, such as Disney or Wal-Mart, need leadership that continues to champion a positive attitude toward change. To Sam Walton, being flexible enough to "look every day for changes that need to be made"[9] was a belief he modeled for—and in turn expected of—each employee. Over time, Walton's personal attitude that change must be not just accepted but sought out and embraced became known as his "low threshold for change" (LTC) theory. Wal-Mart managers continue Walton's commitment to lead the change process, actively working with each store employee to solicit ideas for improvements in the organization's operations.

FOSTERING INDIVIDUAL AND ORGANIZATIONAL LEARNING AND GROWTH

Critical to the success of an organization's ability to implement quality concepts and continually improve is its capacity to learn. An organization must be able to learn and grow if it is to generate and take advantage of innovative technologies and work processes, and so keep ahead of its competition. The willingness to learn is also a key element of developing the flexibility required to respond to and capitalize on the changes in an organization's environment.

In his book *The Fifth Discipline: The Art and Practice of The Learning Organization,* Peter Senge makes clear that over the long run, superior organizational performance depends on superior learning. Senge reminds us of the learning potential inherent in every person within an organization and links that individual learning capacity to the learning capacity of the organization as a whole: "An organization's commitment to and capacity for learning can be no greater than that of its members."[10] This in turn clarifies the role of the leader: "Leaders in learning organizations are responsible for *building organizations* where people are continually expanding their capabilities to shape their future—that is, leaders are responsible for learning."[11] By personally modeling the incentive to learn, a leader can do much to influence individual employees' (and thereby the organization's) incentive to learn.

There is no finer example of the impact a leader can have in transferring the value of continued learning and growth through personal actions than Walt Disney. Through his life, Disney continued to learn, to grow, and to reach for the stars. Every day in his role as the leader of the company that "manufactured happiness," Disney embodied an intense commitment to learning, exhibiting an insatiable level of interest and curiosity not only in things that were, but also in things that might be. His desire was so great that he came to resent the limitations of his own imagination. Disney's propensity to experiment, explore, and discover was the catalyst for the same behavior in his employees, which in turn spawned the marvelous creative insight and technical techniques pioneered in Disney films, television, and theme parks. Disney instilled his value for learning by personally encouraging and supporting his employees in the development of both their artistic and technical work techniques. He once described his role as that of a bee collecting and distributing pollen, going from area to area within the organization, stimulating people to learn and create new things.

Operationally, leaders must support the more tangible aspects of learning within their organization. Training opportunities and resources are required if employees are to be able first to perform their job, and then to stretch beyond it and develop ways to improve the work process. The commitment of a leader to develop a learning organization is evident when that leader ensures that the systems and resources that support this message are provided throughout the organization.

Again, we see this behavior as an important factor in the

success of Disney. Beyond the inspiration to grow ideas and stories, Disney recognized the need for and benefit of training his employees. He supported the learning and growth expectations he held for himself and communicated to his employees by providing them unique technical and personal development training opportunities—even sending personnel to art school. Imagination was critical, but if employees were to translate their ideas into a quality product, Disney knew they had to be supported with the right equipment, instruction, time, and encouragement.

One of the first, and still critical, actions by the leaders of Xerox and Motorola in moving their organizations to performance excellence was the allocation of resources for training and educating their personnel. Motorola's success today is due largely to the learning environment fostered by Robert Galvin. In implementing the new vision of quality for the corporation, Galvin committed to the virtual reeducation of every employee within the organization. Motorola has invested millions of hours in knowledge and skills training, which has enabled its employees to develop and maintain expertise in an environment of rapidly changing technologies and techniques. Additionally, the company's leadership has committed resources to special learning programs to facilitate a means of stimulating new ideas about what the company does and how it does it.

ENCOURAGE RISK TAKING TO ACHIEVE INNOVATION

In extending the commitment to foster learning and growth actively, a leader must also commit to encouraging risk taking within the organization. The ultimate outcome of learning and risk taking is improvement and innovation; conversely, innovation will not come to a firm whose leaders or employees are afraid to take risks.

Firms can profit enormously when their employees feel

free to take risks and experiment. This freedom, however, will only surface in the actions of employees if it is evident in the actions of their leaders. Leaders must model risk taking that works toward the desired vision in their personal and operational actions, exhibiting and rewarding fearlessness in their organization. (Let us be sure, of course, to distinguish between fearlessness and foolishness.)

Along with the innovation and successes that can result from taking risks come inevitable mistakes and failures, but mistakes can quickly become learning tools when honestly and nonpunitively communicated within the organization. A telling example is that of the top-level manager who came in to a staff meeting one day and laid a $50 bill on the table. He proceeded to tell the participants about a risky decision he had made the week before that turned out to be a mistake. After finishing, he offered the bill to anyone in the meeting who could best the story. Reluctantly at first, managers took turns relating their own "worst mistake." Not surprisingly, everyone attending was able to relate such an experience— many of which had been covered up as much as possible to avoid punishment or embarrassment. The learning experience of that meeting was unmatched, as was the resulting openness to share lessons learned when it became apparent that the organization's leader was truly committed to taking risks and learning from mistakes.

Leaders' actions must encourage and reward the honesty that is shown in admitted mistakes. There is no better way to show a commitment to the value of continuous improvement than for a leader to applaud well-developed risk-taking efforts that do not succeed. It is the leader's role both to encourage others to take risks and to support their honest failures as well as their successes.

The true value of taking risks is the opportunity it brings for innovation. Disney clearly understood the relationship between risk taking and innovation. The innovations developed by his organization, both aesthetically and technologically, would never have come without the personal risks he took, such as borrowing against his life insurance policy in order to finance the development of Disneyland. Disney both exhibited his own attitude of fearlessness and supported the actions made in the same mind-set by his employees. Beyond modeling this characteristic in his personal behavior, Disney ensured that even in tight times, his employees had the sophisticated tools, techniques, and time for experimentation. Disney's determination to have his employees take creative and technical risks paid off as the continual innovation in the company's products ultimately transformed not only the organization, but animation art and the entire film industry as well. Today, more than twenty-five years after Disney's death, Michael Eisner portrays the same personal and operational commitment to risk taking that has spawned Disney's more recent successes, such as Touchstone Pictures and Euro Disneyland.

INSPIRING ENTHUSIASM

Perhaps the most important (and often most challenging) element of a leader's role in guiding an organization to a vision of performance excellence is inspiring a shared enthusiasm for both the vision and the process of transformation required to reach the vision. A leader's conscious commitment to act in a way that inspires his or her employees is a powerful tool in overcoming apathy, mistrust, and frustration about the change process.

It is important to note that the leader's role cannot simply be that of a cheerleader for the vision. Success in reaching the vision requires that the leader commit to the tangible personal and operational actions that we have addressed in this chapter. But the enthusiasm a leader exhibits for the organization's plotted direction can greatly ease the rough spots along the way, inspiring the organization to continue on in its journey. A leader's enthusiasm for a vision is contagious and often is responsible for arousing interest in and convincing others of the rightness of the vision, thereby obtaining commitment. "You cannot command commitment, you can only inspire it. . . . Leaders cannot ignite the flames of passion in their followers if they themselves do not express enthusiasm for the compelling vision."[12]

No matter what their personal style, leaders possess a natural excitement when truly committed to their created vision. It is this excitement that must be harnessed to the leader's everyday attitudes and actions, inspiring others throughout the organization by giving encouragement and support to employees as they meet roadblocks and suffer the inevitable setbacks and disappointments that go along with the change process. Enthusiasm is ignited when a leader provides positive feedback for a job well done, or simply says "thank you" for support—in short, making time for the small actions that ensure no employee effort is taken for granted. These are the actions that foster the spirit of enthusiasm and perseverance necessary to achieve a vision.

We need only turn once again to Walt Disney to see the power of a leader's ability to inspire enthusiasm within an organization. Disney's obvious excitement about possibilities yet untapped was evident to each of his employees through his commitment to provide the time, resources, and constant personal encouragement to experiment and explore. As his staff caught his excitement, Disney was able to inspire his employees to achieve the impossible, spurring them to "come up with things you didn't know were in you and that you'd have sworn you couldn't possibly do,"[13] thereby reaching the breathtaking levels of creative and technical innovation that were the hallmark of the organization.

A leader can also infuse enthusiasm for the vision by using her or his operational position to ensure that organizational incentives are tied to behavior that supports the end vision. Formal systems that reward traditional behaviors do little to inspire employees to change their actions or attitudes in keeping with the new vision. Many organizations undergoing the transformation to quality use assessment plans that tie promotion specifically to quality performance. It is impossible, for example, to be promoted at Xerox without specifically being identified as a quality performer.

Informal and spontaneous recognition of vision-supporting behavior also goes a long way in inspiring employees to support others who act the same way. Study after study has shown that small, inexpensive symbols of appreciation for a job well done or an effort well attempted can be just as motivating as larger financial incentives.

THE FIRST STEP: LEADERSHIP COMMITMENT

In summary, the first step in leading an organization to a vision is to establish a leader's unwavering commitment not only to the vision but also to the *process* of realizing that vision. Committing to this process requires that a leader model the espoused vision, values, and beliefs in his or her personal and operational mind-set, attitudes, and actions.

Unless convinced beyond a shadow of a doubt of their leader's commitment, employees will never buy into the organizational vision. Building organizational commitment to the vision, however, requires that the leader communicate continuously, to everyone, both the vision and his or her personal commitment to it. This topic—communicating for commitment—is the focus of our next chapter.

CHAPTER 6

COMMUNICATING FOR COMMITMENT

When a vision of performance excellence permeates an organization's mind-set and work processes, the momentum of its force can propel the enterprise along the path of improvement, giving it the power to break through obstacles and to reach the final destination. As we said in the previous chapter, no matter how essential or right it is for an organization, no vision of excellence can be realized without the full commitment of the organization's employees to that vision. Organization-wide commitment, however, is possible only after a leader has first clearly articulated his or her vision for the organization and then inspired those within the organization to embrace the vision as their own. It is the skillful, effective communication of a leader's vision and its underlying values and beliefs that instills a sense of direction and positive motivation in an organization's work force, enabling commitment to the vision to take root in the hearts and minds of employees.

Challenging visions require change, and change is always difficult. The leader's role during change periods is, more than anything else, a task of *persuasion*—persuading each individual of the vision's importance and vision's rightness for both the organization and himself or herself. This task of persuasion represents at once both the greatest opportunity and the greatest threat a leader faces when seeking to transform an organization. If the vision is communicated thoroughly, clearly, and with personal relevance to the employees of an organization, the vision has the chance of becoming reality. Conversely, if the vision is communicated poorly or haphazardly, so that employees feel no personal relevance in its message, it is doomed.

To communicate the vision effectively, the leader must convey a clear understanding of the future that it represents, instill a sense of connection to it in others, and foster a sense of shared ownership of it. The vision must be described in a way that becomes meaningful and inspirational to *each* person within the organization. And the leader must strive to communicate not only her or his vision of what the organization can be, but also the importance of this future state as it relates to each employee and the role each has in making the vision reality. Employees must be convinced of the vision's rightness before they can become inspired by its possibilities.

Specifically, developing commitment to a vision requires that a leader clearly communicate the following:

- The message of the vision
- The need for the vision within the organization
- The rightness of the vision for each employee
- The commitment of the leader to the vision
- The role of each employee in realizing the vision

By translating these concepts in a way that enables employees to understand and *relate personally* to the developed vision, a leader is able to convince employees of its rightness and so secure their personal commitment to it. This personal commitment on the part of employees forms the foundation for the organization-wide commitment that is critical to an organization hoping to achieve its vision of performance excellence.

We begin our discussion on communication by addressing each of the elements that a leader must include when communicating a vision to the organization. We then look at the processes of communication from a leader's point of view. Finally, we identify specific tactics a leader can use when communicating the vision he or she has developed and identified as the future for the organization.

CONTENT

As described by David C. Limerick, a leader's task in developing commitment to the envisioned future is to "communicate the very identity (vision, mission) of the organization and manage the field of shared meanings, values, and beliefs that surround the identity to make the vision credible and persuasive."[1] This begins with the clear articulation of the vision of excellence that the leader has for the organization.

1. The Message of the Vision

A leader must translate his or her vision into a message that can be clearly expressed, and so understood by those who hear it. In doing this, the leader is defining both the future identity of the organization and the philosophy of underlying values and beliefs that will guide it in adopting this identity. This is a tremendous task: trying to sum up in a concise manner the very reasons for the organization's existence and its aspirations for the future.

Simply translating the vision into words, much less a concise, focused statement, can be challenging. A study of fifty CEOs revealed the difficulty and frustration encountered when they tried to establish a concise description of their vision:

> During the interviews, no one statement or phrase communicated the CEO's vision. Rather it was revealed through a whole series of allegories, metaphors, slogans, and myths. . . . As one CEO complained: "Every time I try to communicate the image, I cheapen it."[2]

Yet visions can indeed be set in the simplest of terms. Walt Disney said, "If you can dream it, you can do it"—a vision expressed so simply, so truly it makes the heart sing. More often, however, describing a vision in such clear terms can be distressingly difficult. More often, a simplistic vision has evolved from a more complex message. For example, Xerox's vision, as contained in its "quality policy," is stated as follows:

• Xerox is a quality company.
• Quality is the basic business principle for Xerox.
• Quality means providing our external and internal customers with innovative products and services that fully satisfy their requirements.
• Quality improvement is the job of every Xerox employee.[3]

This description of Xerox's vision of commitment to quality is quite clear, but hardly inspirational. It was not until almost a decade into Xerox's journey of improvement that David Kearns was able to describe this vision in much simpler terms: "The goal of Xerox is to achieve and maintain 100 percent customer satisfaction."

It is important to note that when Xerox started its journey to become a quality organization, not only was the vision of 100 percent customer satisfaction not formed in Kearns's mind, but even if it had been formed and translated into those words, it would have meant little to the employees within the organization. The organization itself had to grow into this wonderfully concise vision, to understand the importance of customer satisfaction, and to believe that 100 percent was not just a fantasy goal but could indeed become reality. If this vision had been communicated in the early 1980s, it would have had little relevance to the organization or its individual members. In the 1990s, it is a clearly understood beacon guiding the organization into a future of continued improvement in quality and customer satisfaction.

2. The Need for the Vision

A vision of change holds little interest for an employee who does not understand why the vision was developed or that there even exists a need for this new direction. A vision of continuous improvement means change, and resistance to change is best overcome by showing a convincing, relevant need for a new direction. A leader can overcome such resistance to the change that the vision represents by ensuring that the need for the new vision is established and understood by everyone in the organization.

Doing this, however, can require something that is often taboo in our business culture: sharing strategic and operational information with employees. How can an employee be motivated to put forth the effort necessary to help change the organization if he or she has not been shown the need for this change? And how can this need be understood if organizational performance and planning data is withheld? "Managers must be open and willing to share information on such potentially sensitive topics as profits, strategies, and new product plans. . . . Employees operating in ignorance resist change, harbor mistrust, and will never develop commitment to the changes required."[4] Competitive and operational performance information has long been deemed the exclusive property of upper management, but this must change. When a leader asks the organization to change based on information available to her or him, people in the organization will be more easily convinced of the need to change when the same information is made available to them. A concern for proprietary information is often cited by managers who are reluctant to share this data, but employees need and want information because of its value in helping them better understand the issues they face. The cost of not providing it is greater than the risk that it may fall into competitors' hands.

Once the operational and strategic implications of the organization's environment are known, the need for change can be understood. This need can then be simplified for easy communication and reinforcement, as shown by this statement developed by Xerox:

The Need

In recent years we have not been able to effectively meet the competitive challenges due to our high cost of doing business and the lack of quality in many of our products and services. To remain an industry leader we need

- A renewed and heightened commitment to meet the requirements of our customers.
- To make better use of the energies, talents, and ideas of Xerox people.
- To bring more discipline to the way we manage and work, to be achieved through a progressive step-by-step process.[5]

Xerox ensures that employees are kept informed of the company's objectives and priorities in an effort to have them understand their own role in fulfilling the organization's strategy.

Understanding the need for the organization to change can also be reinforced in employees by sharing information about the environment in which the organization operates and the customers that it serves. For example, do employees really know the impact that one disgruntled customer can have on future sales? How can they understand the need for "100 percent customer satisfaction" if this knowledge has not been communicated to them?

3. The Rightness of the Vision

Beyond understanding the need for and message of the vision, each employee must understand and become persuaded of the *rightness* of the vision as it applies to his or her own life. Communicating the rightness of the message requires that a leader go beyond simply developing acceptance of the vision as the new direction for the organization. The leader must communicate the changed organizational direction in a way that connects the individual and his or her personal needs with the organization's stated purpose and future.

It is when an individual feels the rightness of the vision to himself or herself that the leader's vision truly becomes a shared vision, inciting employees to commit both to what the vision represents and to making the vision their own. It is this sense of ownership on the part of each employee that brings power to the vision within an organization. To instill this connection with the vision in the organization's members, a leader must "discover what aspirations, goals, interests, needs, or dreams they have in common . . . detecting the tie that binds."[6] The implication for the leader, of course, is that this awareness must have had a part of the formation of the vision in the first place.

The leader of a historic nonprofit foundation who has experience in bringing new visions to changing organizations told us, "Part of shaping the vision for an organization is getting to know the members of the organization, talking with and listening to these people in a continued dialogue." This CEO then processes what he has learned during these personal interactions, synthesizing the information received on a higher plane to find the common threads that surface in his discussions. These repeated themes, he stresses, signal problems or opportunities that can then be woven together with the leader's insight into a vision for the organization. When such a vision is communicated to the members of the organization, they are able to recognize the shadings of their own interests, and so understand the rightness of the vision to themselves and their work.

4. Commitment of the Leader to the Vision

As we stressed in Chapter 5, paired with the actual message of the vision is the need for a leader to communicate his or her commitment to the vision. Consistent, visible commitment goes a long way in persuading employees of the seriousness of the new direction for the organization, and so in convincing them that their own efforts in this direction will be worthwhile. A leader's commitment is best communicated by modeling the vision, and its supporting values and beliefs, in personal and operational actions every day.

5. The Employee's Role in the Vision

Even when a vision, its need, its rightness, and the leader's commitment to it have all been effectively communicated, organizations have been thwarted in their efforts to achieve quality results. This is often due to the unintentional but substantial gap between the time these concepts are communicated to the organization and the time that the organizational structure and processes are ready to support the employees' actions.

Members of an organization must hear the vision in a way that encourages them to take an active role in making it a reality. To do this, the communicated message must include goals and objectives that the employees are able to relate to their everyday work—goals that help foster the sense of personal, tangible relevance of the vision. Additionally, any communication that the leaders make about this new vision must be accompanied by immediate opportunities for employees to act on it. As with the operational actions required to make tangible a leader's commitment, operational factors must be in place for motivated employees to be able to act. Nothing will smother commitment to a vision faster than inspiring people to action on the vision and then not having the operational considerations in place to direct their energy and efforts.

In fact, providing avenues for action in itself will help increase the overall commitment of employees to the vision. This idea is supported by the theories underlying behavioral change: psychological research indicates that changing people's attitudes does not necessarily change their behaviors, which of course must be the end result if an organization is to change. Rather, a change in behavior often initiates a change in attitude. A leader, then, must successfully communicate a call to action that specifically informs employees what behaviors must be changed and provides them with the direction and mechanisms for the change.

In 1990 a satellite facility within what used to be Honeywell's Marine System Division (now part of Alliant TechSystems) was developing a pilot workshop in an effort to instill in employees a more personal understanding of the changes the organization's vision would ask of them. It was soon realized, however, that although the workshop would seek to modify employees' attitudes and beliefs, the operational structure to support the hoped-for changes in their actions had not yet been put in place. The training was postponed until the operational systems needed to support the desired actions were ready to support the newly trained employees. Once given, the workshop itself ended with the presentation and discussion of the new systems that awaited the employees when they returned to their jobs. (An added advantage of having the operational support ready was the strong sense of leadership commitment that it gave to the concepts that were communicated to the employees—when resources were allocated, employees knew the organization's leaders meant business.)

PROCESS

We have identified the elements of what a leader needs to communicate in order to develop commitment to a vision. But how should this information be communicated? Some may view this as no problem; after all, we all know how to communicate. In fact, we spend an estimated 70 percent of our waking hours communicating—writing, reading, speaking, and listening[7]—and almost 80 percent of our working hours doing the same.[8] Communicating is such an important part of our everyday existence that we rarely stop to think about it. By adulthood we assume that communication skills are something inherent, requiring little thought and even less practice.

A simple example will show the dangers of these assumptions. John, like many managers, finds communicating with his subordinate Chris to be quite simple: John talks, Chris listens. Of course, John assumes the message Chris receives is the message John intended for him to receive. Therefore, if Chris does not act on the message in the way John expects, John knows Chris has either willfully disobeyed his direction or simply misunderstood it because he was not listening. The flaw in John's viewpoint is obvious. He has forgotten a crucial element of communicating, that "Communication must include both the *transference* and *understanding* of meaning."[9] Perhaps the idea John strove to communicate was clear in John's mind, but perhaps it was not. Perhaps John translated this idea clearly into his verbal and nonverbal messages to Chris, but perhaps he did not. Perhaps Chris did clearly hear the message and then translated it to understand exactly what John intended, but perhaps he did not. With so many parts of this simple communication in question, is it really fair for John to assume Chris was either insubordinate or unintelligent?

Of course, we are overstating our point with our example of John and Chris. But it reminds us that we do need to pay heed to some of the basic principles of communication that we neglect so often in our race to manage our daily work loads. How much more important, then, that we take a moment to consider the intricacies of communication before trying to convey a life-changing message to a complete organization!

Successfully communicating even a simple message requires a linked chain of events: the communicator must identify the message she or he wishes to communicate, decide how to express the message (translating the idea into words or symbols), and decide what channel to use to send the message (written, oral, face-to-face, telephone); and the receiver must hear the message and then translate it for understanding, attaching personal meaning to the message. Each step within this process, however, provides an opportunity for the intended message to become distorted:

- The message of the sender is affected by such things as the sender's skill in speaking or writing, knowledge of the topic, and attitudes.
- The physical product of the message itself is affected by the "code" of symbols used to transfer meaning, including the message content and the decision the sender makes in selecting and arranging the content.
- The channel used by the sender to communicate flavors the content of the message.
- The receiver must decode the message received, and is restricted in this effort by his or her skill in listening or reading, knowledge of the topic, and attitudes.[10]

When we realize the possible distortions surrounding our ability to communicate, it becomes surprising that we are ever able to communicate effectively, and we are almost thankful that we are able to understand each other at all. Yet maintaining an awareness of these intricacies and reflecting this in our approach to communication will go a long way toward improving our skill in this area, and so will improve the likelihood of communicating with success. For a leader faced with the task of communicating a vision that is to become the future of the organization, communicating effectively is not a luxury, it is a necessity.

The steps of simple communication that we just described are, the reader will realize, a *process*. Within an organization, communication can be viewed as a work process. Indeed, if as managers we spend more than three-quarters of our time communicating in the organization, the communication process can fairly be called the most important management process in the organization. As such, communication must be managed and thought of just as if it were a more traditionally defined work process, such as a manufacturing process or a payroll process.

As we noted in Chapter 2, organizations working to achieve quality and performance excellence must focus their time and efforts to improve their work processes continually. Unfortunately, many organizations fail to recognize communication as a key work process, and so do not give any attention to this process in their improvement efforts. Although it is by nature less controllable than other processes, the content, organization, style, and approach used in the communication process should be analyzed and continually improved just like any other work process in a quality-driven organization. This is true for communication both at an organizational level and at an individual level.

It should, then, come as no surprise that a leader must *plan* her or his communication approach, developing a strategy for communicating effectively. This can be done if leaders take the perspective of a supplier planning a work process: they must consciously identify how they (the supplier) will use existing and new communication avenues (the process) to develop the product (the message) in a way that meets the requirements of the customers (the members of the organization). As with other work processes, they must ensure that mechanisms are in place to receive feedback from their customers about how well they are meeting these requirements, and then improve and adjust the process as necessary.

In treating communication as a process, the leader should develop an easy-to-understand, written description of the vision's end state and how the organization will get to that state. Although it sounds simple, this exercise can be quite strenuous and time-consuming. Each thought and word must be weighed and examined for meaning and clarity. Performing this exercise, however, is beneficial to the leader in two ways: the process of developing such a description tests the soundness of the message and ensures that it can be communicated as effectively as possible, and the resulting document will be a useful tool for communicating within the organization.

Beyond the initial conveyance (and then continuing iteration) of the vision message for the organization, the leader must be sensitive to the communication process embedded at the organizational level. As the organization starts buying into and working toward the vision, interaction and information sharing among employees becomes even more critical, soon involving everyone in the organization. Communication becomes an important part of maintaining the improvement course; informing the organization's members about objectives, policies, and plans; assisting in process problem-solving and improvement efforts; and sharing information and feedback. For this reason, the skills knowledge that would become part of any process training must become part of the organization training: leaders must champion the idea that employees be provided the opportunity to learn how to excel in this very critical work process.

METHOD

Great leaders are often thought of jointly as great communicators—Churchill, FDR, Martin Luther King, Jr., Gandhi—individuals whose natural communication style fits powerfully with their vision, message, and circumstances. But few of us are masters of the level of inspiring rhetoric found in these individuals. We know that a leader's communication task goes beyond creating understanding of the vision: it is to convey the vision in a way that compels the individuals within the organization to claim it enthusiastically as their own. But all leaders do not have the natural inclination for effective communication. Like other skills required to operate an organization, the ability to communicate effectively is most often a learned skill that must be given the attention of conscious development, practice, and improvement.

Simply by virtue of his or her position, a leader's communications have a great impact on the organization. The leader commands the attention of and is more closely and critically watched than anyone else within the organization. As unsettling as this might be, it also provides a unique opportunity for the leader to draw in, inform, and persuade employees about the direction of the future. The effectiveness of this communication, however, will depend on the integration of a leader's position, style, language, actions, channel, delivery, and of course, message content.

Style and Language

The style and delivery of a leader's message must be persuasive; after all, the leader is attempting to convince the employee of the rightness of the vision and the need to embark on what might be a difficult journey to implement it. A person's communication style will always be a function of his or her personality and communication skills, but care must be given to develop the ability to tailor the message and delivery style to the audience. The language a leader selects is important to this. A leader can go far in communicating her or his vision when she or he uses "clear, vivid, and emphatic language that is appropriate in the mind of the receiver"[11] and grounded in meaning for the audience. Not only is language important in the initial communication of the vision, it can also provide a common thread as an organization continues down its journey (for example, Disney calling its employees "performers," its customers "guests," and its personnel department "central casting"; or McDonald's calling its employees "crew members".)

The impact of language can also be enhanced by the

framework in which it is used. Using metaphors, stories, and analogies goes a long way in clarifying a leader's message. Such methods

> can capture and experience by appealing simultaneously to the various senses of the listener . . . there is an appeal to the emotions, to the intellect, to imagination, and to values. This variety of stimulation ensures a more vivid experience for the listener. . . . Listeners are engaged, not passively listening, they decipher and experience insight.[12]

The right story or analogy can transcend the many barriers that exist between the leader's idea and an individual's understanding. Surely, very few people could mistake Ross Perot's meaning in the third 1992 presidential debate when, asked whether Bill Clinton's tenure as governor of Arkansas qualified him for national leadership, he compared that proposition to calling the owner-operators of a mom-and-pop grocery store qualified to run Wal-Mart.

Physical Communication

Nonverbal or physical communication elements can also be harnessed by a leader in developing an effective communication style. This includes a leader's actions, as well as his or her use of symbols and space. As we discussed in detail in the last chapter, a leader does much to communicate convincingly his or her commitment to a vision and its underlying values by modeling the vision in his or her personal and operational actions. Employees will not commit to the vision if they are not convinced of the leader's commitment; they must see this commitment in the actions and attitudes of the leader every day. What a leader says, how she or he says it, the body language she or he uses, the expressions she or he crafts: all are worthless if her or his actions do not support the message she or he is communicating.

Leaders can communicate their direction and vision

through other physical mediums. Symbols associated with the leader or the organization itself, as well as the actual space within an organization, can be used to capture a spirit or feeling. When Michael Eisner built Disney's headquarters in Florida, for example, he selected a building design and style unique in shape, colors, and lighting, all to convey the Disney values of imagination and innovation. Although less resplendent, Sam Walton's vehicle of choice—a pickup truck—was a powerful symbol evoking his baseline values. The nondescript truck has been cited in almost every article ever written about the man because of the powerful meaning it conveys.

Listening and Feedback

To communicate successfully, a leader must develop and use the skill of listening. Deborah Hopen has drawn this distinction between mere hearing and real listening: "Hearing is the ability to process transmitted sound waves; it is a neurological process. On the other hand, listening involves making sense out of what is heard. Good listening takes time, effort, and energy. Indeed, active listening can be more stressful than active speaking."[13] Leaders must listen to their employees, management, and customers to sift through input in developing a vision that can be shared by the organization, and then receive and understand feedback as the organization moves toward the vision.

In addition to seeking feedback from others, a leader can bolster the effectiveness of his or her communication by personally providing feedback to others in the organization. Thomas Connellan discusses the importance of a leader providing interpersonal feedback to members of the organization—letting them know when they are doing a good job and when their actions are supporting the improvement effort. Interpersonal feedback can be positive, negative, or all too often, nonexistent. "Not giving feedback communicates a powerful message. Curiously enough, the message it communicates can have a more negative effect than punishment. It communicates not caring, not noticing, unimportance."[14]

As the journey to the vision is progressing, people within the organization are looking for cues that things are indeed changing, that this initiative is not all talk. When a leader ensures immediate, positive reinforcement of employees' actions taken in support of the vision, she or he provides the clear signal that they are on the right path, and that their efforts are noticed and appreciated. This in turn will strengthen the behaviors needed to bring the organization to the vision.

Operational Considerations

In determining communication strategy, a leader must take into consideration not only her or his own personal communication style and the characteristics of the message being sent, but also the characteristics of the organization that she or he hopes will receive and embrace the message. The appropriate style and channels for the leader's communication depend on many factors, including the organization's size and structure and the geographical dispersion of its people.

Leaders often say they would prefer to communicate directly with each individual in the organization in order to feel confident that the message is understood exactly as they intended: "Direct contact is less likely to be misinterpreted than messages conveyed indirectly through management systems or staff."[15] Of course, for most organizations, this would be impossible; there simply is not enough time for a leader to speak one-to-one with everyone to secure their commitment to the vision. Instead, a leader must pay particular attention to ensuring that their direct reports have as near a perfect understanding of the vision as possible. The leader will rely on this group first to help communicate the new vision throughout the organization, and so she or he must see to it that these managers are able to echo their own message and enthusiasm throughout the organization.

A second organizational consideration is the channels the leader chooses to use when communicating. If the new vision is to become part of the culture of the organization, it is important that the leader use communication tools, processes, policies, and programs that already are in place in the organization. Although new avenues, as fitting for the message and the organization, should be considered and developed, part of making the vision "right" for employees means integrating the message into the systems that exist—the everyday bulletin boards, newsletters, memos, videos, and meetings, rather than just special mechanisms or forums.

As the organization proceeds in its journey of improvement, the leader must also ensure that the members are able to communicate with each other. This critical "work process" of communication must be both efficient and effective. To achieve these goals, many organizations have invested time and money in training all employees in common methods and a common language for pursuing quality. They have also provided mechanisms and processes for sharing information among employees. Once again, the test of the leader's commitment to the vision is in allocating resources to build the required organizational infrastructure.

SUMMARY

The tool that provides a leader with the most leverage in inspiring an organization to embrace and move toward a new vision is effective communication. Well-planned and well-executed communication will go a long way in a leader's efforts to illuminate the organization's employees with an understanding of the message of the vision, the need for it, the rightness of it, and the role that they will play in realizing it. Effective, inspirational communication by a leader can motivate employees and improve their attitudes about the changes the future will bring, thus creating the commitment needed for a successful journey to the vision beyond.

To illustrate the power of vision and the importance of commitment, we turn in the next chapter to the story of Ray Kroc and the development of McDonald's. Like many entrepreneurs, Kroc had a vision and a set of values to which he was committed; it was his genius to be able to communicate that commitment to others. As the next chapter shows, that shared commitment to McDonald's values has been responsible for the success of this business.

CHAPTER 7

RAY KROC

The Visionary at McDonald's

R ay Kroc was a believer in lifelong continuous improvement long before it was a popular topic. He repeated this
philosophy often in one of his favorite sayings: "As long as
you're green you're growing; as soon as you're ripe you start
to rot."[1] It was that belief that inspired Kroc on the day when
he first encountered the concept that would change his life
and the way America eats.

> I was a battle-scarred veteran of the business wars, but I was
> still eager to get into action. I was 52 years old. I had dia-
> betes and incipient arthritis. I had lost my gall bladder and
> most of my thyroid gland in earlier campaigns. But I was
> convinced that the best was ahead of me. I was still green
> and growing, and I was flying along at an altitude slightly
> higher than the plane.[2]

It was Kroc's vision of himself and his company as "ever-
green" that propelled him to build the largest food service organization in the world, one that would set new standards of
excellence in the restaurant business.

This chapter was written by Amir A. Iskander, an associate with Bain and
Company in Boston, Massachusetts.

THE VISION

When Kroc saw his first McDonald's restaurant in San Bernardino in 1954, he did not merely recognize that it had tremendous potential. Instead, an image actually began to form within him, an image of what McDonald's would one day become.

Long before he was known for revolutionizing the eating habits of our nation, Kroc owned a small business called Prince Castle Sales. The company sold five-spindle multimixer milk-shake machines—what Kroc believed to be the wave of the future. It was from his job as a multimixer salesman that Kroc was introduced to Dick and Mac McDonald and the first prototype of the McDonald's restaurants that are so famous today. In his book *Grinding It Out,* Kroc remembered the events that led to his discovery:

> The vibrations came in calls from voluntary prospects in different parts of the country. One day it would be a restaurant owner in Portland, Oregon; the next day a soda fountain operator in Yuma, Arizona; the following week, a dairy-bar manager in Washington, D.C. In essence, the message was always the same: "I want one of those mixers of yours like the McDonald brothers have in San Bernardino, California." I got curiouser and curiouser. Who were these McDonald brothers, and why were customers picking up on the Multimixer from them when I had similar machines in lots of places?[3]

Finally, his curiosity got the best of him and he flew out to San Bernardino to find out for himself what was so special about the McDonald brothers' operation. In a single glance, Kroc said, his imagination took over as he watched a young woman at the ten-cent hamburger stand:

> It was not her sex appeal but the obvious relish with which she devoured the hamburger that made my pulse begin to hammer with excitement. Her appetite was magnified for me by the many people in cars that filled the

parking lot, and I could feel myself getting wound up like a pitcher with a no-hitter going. . . . That night in my motel room I did a lot of heavy thinking about what I'd seen that day. Visions of McDonald's restaurants dotting crossroads all over the country paraded through my brain.[4]

Kroc recalled that he was called "Danny Dreamer," after a popular comic strip character of the day. But Kroc was more than a dreamer; he was a visionary, eager to take action to make his dream real. "The next morning," said Kroc, "I got up with a plan of action in mind. I was on the scene when McDonald's windows opened for business."[5] It was not only Kroc's dream, but his willingness to act—to take the risks associated with action—that make him, and not the McDonald brothers, the true creator of McDonald's as we know it. He recalled this telling conversation he had with the McDonald brothers immediately after discovering their business:

> "See that big white house with the wide front porch?" he [Mac McDonald] asked. "That's our home and we love it. We sit out on the porch in the evenings and watch the sunset and look down on our place here. It's peaceful. We don't need any more problems than we have in keeping this place going. More places, more problems. We are in a position to enjoy life now, and that's just what we intend to do." His approach was utterly foreign to my thinking, so it took a few minutes to reorganize my arguments.[6]

Kroc's use of the words *utterly foreign* describe with uncanny accuracy the difference between a leader with a vision and the average dreamer.

Kroc could have simply copied their production process and used a name other than "McDonald's" for his restaurant empire, but he never even considered that option. As Kroc wrote in his book, the idea alone was not enough: "There was the name. I had a strong intuitive sense that the name McDonald's was exactly right. I couldn't have taken the name."[7] Although he felt he needed to rethink his proposal, Kroc was, of course, eventually able to convince the McDonalds to sell him the rights to their name and their production process. But there was far more to Ray Kroc's vision than simply "McDonald's restaurants dotting crossroads all over the country." His vision combined fast, friendly service, with a clean eating environment, and high quality food, all at a very low price. He knew that it was this unique combination of characteristics that gave McDonald's its appeal and its strength.

Although Ray Kroc was not born with a silver spoon in his mouth, he was raised with what proved to be far more valuable than material wealth. Instilled within him while he was still a child was a solid foundation of values upon which he built not only his own future, but also the future of his company. Kroc's personal values of hard work, persistence, honesty, and self-sufficiency, combined with his strong beliefs in the free enterprise system, being the best, attention to details, quality, value, and especially cleanliness, were deeply rooted in the McDonald's culture.

Unlike many who had gone before him, Kroc's life was not dictated by the negative circumstances that surrounded him. His life and behavior were fashioned by his vision, a force that for Kroc was far more powerful than circumstance. When he was forced to use everything he owned as collateral for loans to finance the foundation for McDonald's, he revealed the power of his vision. Said Kroc, "That dream of what the company could be sustained me."[8]

Perhaps more than any other multibillion dollar organization, the McDonald's corporation is an embodiment of the strong values and beliefs of its founder. In the words of McDonald's current CEO, Mike Quinlan: "If there's one reason for our success, it's that Ray Kroc instilled within the company basic principles. Standards of excellence. Don't compromise. Use the best ingredients. The best equipment. Not galvanized metal, but stainless steel."[9]

Although Kroc died on January 14, 1984, McDonald's has gone to great lengths to preserve the legacy and memory of its inspirational founder. His spirit lives on in the McDonald's headquarters in Oak Brook, Illinois:

> Ray is not only quoted, he is, uh, sort of there in Oak Brook today. In a headquarters exhibit called "Talk to Ray," a visitor can phone up Ray, as it were, on a video screen, and with a keyboard ask him questions. Over several years, he recorded his thoughts for the company archives, and his appearances on talk shows were taped as well, so those left to carry on can find out about nearly everything they might need to know.[10]

QSC AND V

> Basic elements will insure success for a store, unless its location is unspeakably bad. . . . But the fundamentals do not spring forth, self-evident and active, from the brow of every former grocery clerk, soda jerk, military man, or specialist in one of the hundreds of other callings who join the ranks of McDonald's operators. Quite the contrary; the basics have to be stressed over and over. If I had a brick for every time I've repeated the phrase QSC and V [Quality, Service, Cleanliness and Value], I think I'd probably be able to bridge the Atlantic Ocean with them.[11]

Among the most influential of Kroc's personal beliefs were those in quality, service, cleanliness and value. Almost anyone who is familiar with the inner workings of McDonald's has heard the phrase Kroc cited above. What is it about McDonald's, however, that sets it apart from other restaurant chains that employ catchy phrases extolling the virtues of quality, value, and service? Perhaps the greatest difference is that for Ray Kroc, QSC and V was not merely a catchy phrase. It was his obsession; it was what drew him to McDonald's. From the first time he saw the two brothers' hamburger stand, he noticed that cleanliness and quality was what set McDonald's apart:

> The men in white suits were keeping everything neat and clean as they worked. That impressed the hell out of me, because I've always been impatient with poor housekeeping, especially in restaurants. I observed that even the parking lot was being kept free of litter.[12]

> Hamburgers, fries, and beverages were prepared on an assembly line basis, and to the amazement of everyone, Mac and Dick included, the thing worked! Of course, the simplicity of the procedure allowed the McDonalds to concentrate on quality in every step, and that was the trick. When I saw it working that day in 1954, I felt like some latter-day Newton who'd just had an Idaho potato caromed off his skull.[13]

Kroc was able to communicate the importance of his beliefs clearly to all McDonald's employees and franchisees. He was not merely giving lip service to these ideals. For Kroc, a breach in any one of the four fundamental beliefs was a very serious matter. He was known to pull the licenses of franchisees who consistently demonstrated an inability to meet his stringent requirements for maintaining a clean store. And Kroc was not obsessed only with quality, service, value, and cleanliness. Attention to every detail was of extreme importance to him from the very beginning.

> Sometimes Ed MacLuckie [manager of the first McDonald's store] would have forgotten to turn the sign on when dusk began to fall, and that made me furious. Or maybe the lot would have some litter on it that Ed said he hadn't had time to pick up. Those little things didn't seem to bother some people, but they were gross affronts to me. . . . Perfection is very difficult to achieve, and perfection is

what I wanted in McDonald's. Everything else was second-ary for me.[14]

Kroc spent numerous hours mopping floors and washing windows in McDonald's restaurants around the country. His willingness to roll up his sleeves to clean the floors and his rejection of a double standard for employees and manage-ment sent a strong and clear message that "QSC and V" was not merely a phrase used to keep employees busy, but an or-ganizational way of life that was to be followed by every em-ployee, manager, and owner in the McDonald's system.

GRINDING IT OUT

"You do not need to hear Ray Kroc speak for long before realizing that *Grinding It Out,* the title he has chosen for his autobiography, is not a humorous reference to the prepara-tion of McDonald's most famous product. Instead, the title brings to mind the long apprenticeship of over thirty years during which Mr. Kroc worked for others as a salesman and a sales manager and later in his own small busi-ness. . . . *Grinding It Out* also appropriately reminds the reader of the staggering investments of time, energy, and capital that were required to develop McDonald's to its cur-rent preeminence in the fast food service and franchising industries.[15]

The greatest vision in the world, combined with strong values and beliefs, will produce absolutely nothing without hard work and persistence. Throughout his book, Kroc con-tinually makes references to periods in his life when he was forced to "grind it out," or to work exceptionally hard to make it through a trying situation. Kroc recalled first starting out with McDonald's:

I did a lot of talking about the ideal way to develop McDonald's with the kind of quality and uniformity that would insure success. And when Harry [Sonneborn, the fi-nancial genius behind McDonald's long-term profitability] came up with a way to make it possible, I backed it by going into hock for everything I had—my house, my car, you name it. Talk about grinding it out! I felt like Samson with a fresh haircut.[16]

Clearly Ray Kroc was not the typical leader. His contributions place him in a class that includes few others. His dedication and persistence enabled him to keep going even during the bad times. Kroc had the following motto, entitled "Press On," framed and hung on the walls of McDonald's corporate headquarters and placed in the kitchens of McDonald's restaurants all over the world:

Nothing in the world can take the place of persistence. Talent will not: nothing is more common than unsuccessful men with talent. Genius will not: unrewarded genius is almost a proverb. Education will not: the world is full of educated derelicts. Persistence and determination alone are omnipotent.[17]

THE CULTURE OF QUALITY LEADERSHIP AT MCDONALD'S

How It All Works

On June 17, 1992, McDonald's opened a restaurant in Warsaw, making Poland the sixty-second country in which McDonald's did business.[18] There are more than 12,400 McDonald's restaurants that produce systemwide sales of more than $18 billion annually. Everyone seems to have a theory about why McDonald's is so successful, but the most frequently cited hypothesis for the hamburger maker's accomplishments is its entrepreneurial system of franchising. Much like modern-day employee stock ownership plans, which give workers a vested interest in the long-term success of the company for which they work, Kroc's plan to grow his company through a system of franchises allowed him to harness the spirit and energy of hundreds of entrepreneurs who were not only dedicated to, but are also invariably linked with the long-term success of McDonald's. "To be sure, Kroc's success with McDonald's is a story of his own entrepreneurship. But it is more. He succeeded on a grand scale because he had the wisdom and the courage to rely on hundreds of entrepreneurs."[19]

One does not need to be immensely wealthy in order to become a McDonald's franchisee. As of 1991 it only took $40,000 to lease an already existing McDonald's restaurant, and $60,000 to lease a new restaurant.[20] Far greater is the required investment of hard work and long-term commitment. As Kroc said, "A total commitment of personal time and energy is the most important thing. A person doesn't need to be super smart or have more than a high school education, but he or she must be willing to work hard and concentrate exclusively on the challenge of operating that store.[21]

A prospective franchisee must work part time for two years, without pay, before completing the requirements for becoming a McDonald's restaurant owner. After the two years, he or she must be willing to relocate to wherever the company has a store available. While McDonald's considers its franchisees' requests in making its placement decisions, it makes no guarantees. After a franchisee is assigned to a store (which may take up to three years after fulfillment of the requirements), a generous percentage of the store's gross sales is paid to the company for using the McDonald's logo as well as for national advertising, management training, and other general corporate expenses.

McDonald's is extremely selective in choosing who it will allow to be a franchisee. Each year it receives more than five thousand applications for fewer than two hundred available restaurants.[23] The interest in becoming a McDonald's franchisee is what allows the company to be very stringent about its guidelines for potential investors:

The early investors had other occupations and put money into Ray Kroc's idea looking for easy profits. Ray Kroc learned that the owner operator must be an entrepreneur willing to stake everything he owned for a chance to operate the business. Today, the franchisee is required to work full time in the daily management of the restaurant.[24]

Once a franchise is finally granted, strong incentives are provided to ensure that the owner-operator adheres to the high standards of quality that McDonald requires. "Kroc used the allocation of new restaurants as a weapon to enforce compliance. Ray Kroc understood that the overall integrity of the McDonald's system depends on the quality and uniformity of each franchise.[25] The franchising system worked so well that 1960s chairman Fred Turner limited the number of company-operated restaurants to only 33 percent of all stores. What Turner had found was that without the profit incentive inherent in the owner-operator stores, company-run stores actually had lower profit margins than the franchised units.[27]

Probably the greatest benefit of the McDonald's franchise system is what *In Search of Excellence* authors Tom Peters and Robert Waterman describe as "simultaneous loose-tight properties." The following is their definition of an organization that displays this principle:

> Organizations that live by this loose-tight principle are on the one hand rigidly controlled, yet at the same time allow (indeed, insist on) autonomy, entrepreneurship and innovation from the rank and file. They do this literally through faith—through value systems, which . . . most managers avoid like the plague. They do it also through painstaking attention to detail, to getting the "itty-bitty, teeny-tiny things" right.[28]

There is no single principle that more effectively describes the tremendous success McDonald's has enjoyed from Ray Kroc's tight, yet loose franchising system. While quality, service, cleanliness, and value are nonnegotiable and tightly-enforced standards, community involvement, employee motivation, and menu innovation are all areas in which the loose entrepreneurial spirit of the McDonald's franchisee has yielded continuous improvement.

Supplier Relationships

McDonald's created what even most of its competitors concede is the most integrated, efficient, and innovative supply system in the food service industry. Today, that system is increasingly responsible for preserving McDonald's as the industry's standard setter on uniformity of product.[29]

The chapter dealing with McDonald's suppliers in John Love's book is entitled "McDonaldizing the Suppliers." Love's creation of the word *McDonaldizing* effectively describes the transformation that McDonald's required of all its early suppliers. Ray Kroc's obsession with a quality product invariably meant that exacting demands were placed on any company wishing to supply McDonald's with the uniform, high quality ingredients upon which Kroc insisted. Not surprisingly, when Ray Kroc's company was still in its infancy, he could not find many large and established suppliers who were willing to cater to his often extreme demands. As a result, many large companies unknowingly passed up on a golden opportunity for enormous growth. Many of the smaller companies that were more accommodating of Kroc's demands, by contrast, experienced growth beyond even their wildest dreams.

One such example of this phenomenon was the Simplot company. In the early 1960s, McDonald's primarily used fresh Idaho russet potatoes to make its famous french fries. The problems was, however, that Idaho russets were only available fresh for nine months out of the year. McDonald's had to turn to California white potatoes during the summer months; unfortunately, the California white potatoes did not yield as crisp a french fry as the Idaho russets. Jack Simplot, the entrepreneurial owner of the Simplot company, approached McDonald's with an idea to use frozen potatoes for its french fries. Harry Sonneborn, then president of McDonald's, laughed at the idea. McDonald's was far more than a little picky about the way it prepared its fries. As Ray Kroc said:

> Now, to most people, a french-fried potato is a pretty uninspiring object. . . . The McDonald's french fry was in an entirely different league. They [the McDonald brothers] lavished attention on it. I didn't know it then, but one day I would, too. The french fry would become almost sacrosanct for me, its preparation a ritual to be followed religiously.[30]

Accordingly, McDonald's was not about to jump at the first chance it got to change completely the way it made french fries. Simplot, however, was not discouraged. Acting on nothing more than a handshake agreement with Ray Kroc, Jack Simplot carried the entire risk of creating a new way of producing the french fry and invested $3.5 million to put the experiment into production.[31] Kroc offered no guarantees; if Simplot's experimental production process did not produce a french fry that met McDonald's high quality standards, Simplot would have suffered a huge loss. The gamble paid off, however, and Jack Simplot went on to become a member of *Fortune* magazine's exclusive list of billionaires. Maybe it was not such a crazy risk to take after all.

In the process of reinventing the french fry, Jack Simplot and McDonald's revolutionized the potato processing industry. Not surprisingly, McDonald's had the same effect on the meat industry, also being the engine behind the move from fresh to frozen. It was the free enterprise system, which Ray Kroc so highly esteemed, that gave his suppliers the potential for business beyond what any one company could ask for.

Kroc did not offer guarantees to his suppliers, but he did offer all of McDonald's business—a tremendous payoff—if a supplier's quality met his standards. Ironically, the small suppliers not only gave Kroc the quality he demanded but, with the ongoing possibility of capturing all of McDonald's business, also gave him product innovations.

> Nowhere is the McDonald's unusual supplier dedication more evident than in the development of the new or improved products. Over the years, suppliers have become almost extensions of McDonald's product development department, willingly investing millions of dollars to develop new products or more efficient processes. The carrot has always been the knowledge that if the new product or process worked, McDonald's would give its developer all the new business it could handle.[32]

Taking advantage of nothing more than capitalism, Kroc was able to extend McDonald's culture of quality to all of his suppliers and instill within each of them the desire and willingness to continually improve the quality of McDonald's products and processes. Kroc created a model that is now the standard for relationships with suppliers in almost every industry.

McMarketing

> When it came to keeping McDonald's in touch with the market, Kroc had an innate sense—a salesman's sense—that the promotion, advertising and new product development could not be dictated by a corporate staff. To succeed in marketing, Kroc believed that McDonald's had to reach out and respond to each market. Marketing ideas had to come from the grass roots, not the blue sky. In short, Kroc realized that for McDonald's to capitalize on the market opportunity it now had, his company had to rely on the creativity of its partners—its franchisees and suppliers.[33]

Spending more than a billion dollars per year, McDonald's is easily one of the largest advertisers in the world. McDonald's advertising and marketing efforts on a national scale are funded primarily through the Operations National Advertising Fund (OPNAD), which allows the company to harness the creativity of many of its local franchises. OPNAD is funded by, and largely controlled by, individual restaurant operators who contribute a percentage of their gross sales to OPNAD as well as to 170 local advertising co-operatives.[34]

While McDonald's makes certain that during any given period all of its advertising is focused on a single idea and a consistent message, local cooperatives are free to create their own commercials and appeal to their individual clientele. Consequently, McDonald's is able to establish its image on the one hand as a large successful and respected organization, and on the other hand as a small, responsive, and innovative company that quickly adapts to the needs and desires of the individual communities in which it operates.

McDonald's chairman Fred Turner was named "adman of the decade" by *Advertising Age* in 1990. According to that magazine:

- McDonald's 1981 "Build a Big Mac" promotion popularized game-card promotions, a tactic still growing in use today.
- Its 1982 introduction of Chicken McNuggets spearheaded the growth of finger foods.
- Its creation in 1984 of Ronald McDonald Children's Charities, established in Mr. Kroc's memory after his death that year, remains a model for corporate community involvement.

It has had only four different umbrella ads since 1979, providing the classic example of the value of constancy.

McDonald's has placed among the 10 best-recalled advertisers in every monthly ad-watch survey for *Advertising Age* since the poll began in 1982.[35]

In no way is Ray Kroc's effect on the world more pronounced than it is as a result of McDonald's marketing and advertising campaigns. As the second best known brand name in the world, [36] McDonald's is able to boast that its national spokesman, Ronald McDonald, is recognized by 96% of all American children.[37] The phrases "You Deserve a Break Today," "We Do It All for You," "It's a Good Time for the Great Taste of McDonald's," and "You Know the One, McDonald's for Food, Folks, and Fun" are synonymous with McDonald's.

Community Involvement

In the wake of the verdict of the 1992 Rodney King trial, Los Angeles experienced one of the most destructive race riots in the history of the United States. Hundreds of buildings and businesses were burned to the ground, and the south-central section of the city was devastated. Amazingly, not a single McDonald's restaurant was destroyed. Nearly all of the units were open for business the day after the riots ended (except during curfews).[38] A recent article in *FW* magazine explained why McDonald's restaurants escaped the destruction:

> Why did the McDonald's units go unharmed? Lynwood, Cal., franchisee Leighton Hull says the restaurant chain's best defense was its involvement in the neighborhoods its serves. . . . He's talking about the intense involvement at the franchise level with the neighborhood schools, clubs, kids, and causes. The late Ray Kroc . . . espoused this close community involvement as savvy marketing. It has evolved, at least in the inner cities, as a plan for peaceful and prosperous coexistence between the corporation and its occasionally fractious environment.[39]

McDonald's contributions to the community and to the nation are far-reaching. The Ronald McDonald House, Ronald McDonald Children's Charities (RMCC), McDonald's All-American High School Band, the Ray A. Kroc Achievement Award, McDonald's Crew College Education Program, McDonald's Family Reading Program, and GospelFest/Gospel Connection are just a few of the many examples of McDonald's extensive contributions to our society. RMCC, perhaps the best known of McDonald's charity programs, is dedicated to helping children achieve "healthier, happier, more productive lives."[40]

MCDONALD'S TODAY . . . AND TOMORROW

Getting Ripe?

Underneath the golden gleam of the McDonald's arches, cracks are starting to appear in the foundation. As growth becomes less profitable, the logic of the company's strategy becomes questionable.[41]

—*FW* magazine

U.S. sales are still growing but they have lost their sizzle. More sophisticated consumer tastes and revved-up competition are bedeviling McDonald's.[42]

—*Business Week*

The standards at McDonald's have slipped.[43]

—Bruce Klein, former
McDonald's operations
manager

There is such a menu diversification that they've impaired
their ability to execute fast-food fundamentals.[44]

—Charles Olcott, former president of Burger King

Many sources have begun to question whether
McDonald's can sustain its long record of excellence.
McDonald's experienced phenomenal growth between 1982
and 1991. Double-digit growth in overall revenues, net profits, and earnings per share have long made McDonald's a favorite of Wall Street investors. McDonald's has had an
amazing financial record, posting 107 consecutive quarters of
record sales, income, and earnings per share.[45] But while the
company is continuing to grow, sales, profits, and earnings
per share are all increasing at a slower rate. Revenue growth
virtually came to a standstill in 1991, growing at a meager
0.8%. This slowing growth, combined with charges of dimin-
ished creativity, flexibility, and innovation at the company,
has caused many to believe that McDonald's is reaching a period of decline.

Many cite far more than lackluster performance and
lack of innovation as the fundamental disorders ailing the
company. Perhaps the most often cited concern by
McDonald's critics is the shift in the nation's eating habits
away from fast food and towards more healthy, lower-calo-
rie menus. Others point to the steady decline in sales per
store versus the initial cost of investment in the restaurant
and conclude that McDonald's has lost the ability to make
franchises as profitable and appealing to potential franchisees as they once were. "For the franchisee, opening up
a McDonald's is not what it used to be. Back in 1975, one
could reasonably hope to earn back an investment in a little over three years. Today, it would take almost six
years."[46]

Increased competition is another area of concern for

McDonald's. The upscale customer is being lured away from McDonald's by chains such as Chili's and Olive Garden, restaurants that offer full service and often more nutritious selections at only slightly higher prices.[47] At the other end of the market, Taco Bell, Wendy's, Burger King, and Kentucky Fried Chicken are often beating McDonald's on price, menu selection, and in rare instances, even fast service.

Expecting fast food customers to remain stationary in their tastes in preferences is one assumption that has recently hurt McDonald's. In 1991 Edward Rensi, the company's chief operations officer, admitted, "We got a little bit arrogant."[48] But now, said the current management team to shareholders in the 1991 annual report, "We recognize the penalty for standing still." The question then is, where do they plan to go from here?

McDonald's Tomorrow

A three-year slump in real sales growth, coupled with attacks by environmental and nutritional advocacy groups, has pierced its veil of invincibility. But Big Mac is drawing from its wellspring of innovations—particularly in menu innovations—to regain momentum.[49]

—*Restaurant Business*

At present, there's a much improved feeling. We're less rigid now. . . . I think the company is more responsive to the marketplace than ever before, in nutrition, in social issues, and in the environment. . . . If we continue what we've been doing lately, there's no stopping McDonald's.[50]

—Lyle Manchik, owner-
operator of five McDonald's
restaurants

I think there's a new attitude at McDonald's. They've
opened the floodgates to experimentation and [are] determined to be less bureaucratic, less prone to wait five years
on new products.[51]

—Ron Paul, president of
Technomic restaurant con-
sultancy

Most predictions for the future of McDonald's paint a
brighter, more hopeful picture. Having recognized the
penalty for standing still, McDonald's is now on the move. Its
strategy for future growth focuses on three key elements:
adding restaurants, maximizing sales and profits at existing
restaurants, and improving international profitability. The
vigor with which McDonald's has implemented these three
strategies has led many to conclude that flexibility and innovation are once again alive and well at McDonald's and that
the Ray Kroc legacy is still alive, too. His vision, values and
beliefs, and penchant for action can propel McDonald's into
a future that is at least as bright as its past.

PART III

VALUES:
THE FOUNDATION
FOR ACTION

CHAPTER 8

SERVING THE CUSTOMER

Beliefs and Values for a Customer Focus

"The customer comes first!" "The customer is king!" "The customer is always right!" As the familiarity of these sayings proves, an awareness of the importance of the customer is not new. In fact, the concept is so obvious as to be a matter of common sense. Without a customer, there is no business; obviously businesses must "focus on the customer."

But simply because a thing is often said does not guarantee that it is commonly achieved or even understood. How many executives have said for years that "Our people are our greatest asset," and how few have really trusted those people to act as responsible adults, welcomed their commitment, and led them to achieve organizational and personal greatness?

In the same way, where many organizations might *say* they value their customers, too few really do, at least in the sense demanded by a dedication to total quality. It is easy to pay lip service to customer satisfaction; unfortunately, it is even easier to forget, to underestimate, and to lose touch with the person without whom any business will fail—the customer.

The early months of 1993 gave us two embarrassing examples of business failures directly tied to neglect of the customer. Two days after IBM chairman John Akers announced his intention to resign as soon as his successor could be named, a story in the *Wall Street Journal* on the computer industry described how IBM had lost its way in the 1980s:

The declining cost of microprocessors, along with vicious price wars, spurred a desktop computer boom that in turn sparked another trend: the rise of small computer networks ... Big Blue, as IBM is called, virtually ignored this trend, betting instead that companies would keep using large computers the way they always had; indeed, IBM even stifled innovations that could have made it the dominant player in small computers. . . . [This] slow reaction stemmed partly from a reluctance to undermine sales of cash-cow large machines. "You have to face up to the question of destroying your product with new products," says John Morgridge, chief executive of Cisco, which makes networking hardware. "If you don't do it, someone else will."[1]

While its competitors searched the markets for the customer whose needs were not yet filled, IBM's eyes were on its products and its profits. It was in the company's interest to believe its customers would always want what IBM did best, and with its size, its power, and its record of success, it was easy to believe that what IBM wanted, its customers would want, too. By misreading the market and losing touch with its customers, IBM posted a $4.97 billion loss for 1992.

Sears, Roebuck & Company stands as another sorry example of a business who first lost its customers, then lost money, and finally lost its franchise. Twenty years ago surely very few analysts would have predicted trouble for Sears: with its history a part of American history, and its size and wealth unmatched in the retailing industry, one would expect this giant to remain the place "where America shops." But as mail-order shopping grew in the 1980s, JC Penney and other competitors moved aggressively to service "yuppies" and dual-career families who had plenty of money but too little time to spend shopping at the mall. Established and new catalog companies relied on extensive market research and new printing technology to develop specialized catalogs targeted to specific customer segments. They set up toll-free twenty-four-hour customer service centers and searched for other innovations to convince consumers that catalog shopping was safe, simple, quick, and easy.

The Sears catalog lagged behind. Some analysts blamed its demise on its failure to target specific consumer segments and change its merchandise to keep up with changing consumer tastes. In our view, however, the fundamental problem at Sears was spotlighted by its long-standing refusal to accept credit cards other than its own.[2] In that one policy the company's orientation toward its customers was clear: "we'd like to help, but you're going to have to do things our way."

In January 1993, Sears announced its intention to kill its unprofitable catalog operation, close 113 stores, and lay off fifty thousand full- and part-time employees. Two weeks later the company reported a loss of $3.93 billion for 1992, its first loss since 1933[3] and the largest yearly loss ever by a U. S. retailer.[4] Announcing quarterly results to industry analysts, merchandise group chairman Arthur C. Martinez described some of the steps Sears would take to revive its reputation with consumers. Among these moves was a decision to drop the credit card ban. An experiment conducted in six cities had showed that sales rose when stores accepted visa, Mastercard, and American Express credit cards. In Martinez's words, "I think our target consumer should have a choice of the credit vehicle she chooses."[5]

As 1993 progresses, Sears and IBM are undergoing major overhauls in their strategies, structures, and management systems. Both should stand as a warning to other companies who, despite protests of devotion to their customers, have their first priority elsewhere. Many care most about their current financial results (what is the impact on first quarter profitability?); for others, the key criterion is the strategic plan (does this fit with our objectives for the year?); and still others, like IBM and Sears, look first to serve and to protect their own products (does this undermine the success of product X)? All these things are important, but dedication to quality requires a real and literal focus on the customer. Start-up businesses fail quickly without this focus, but with success, as we have shown, this focus also can be easily lost.

Three fundamental beliefs are embedded in the concept of customer focus, and it is the responsibility of leaders to communicate them and to live by them, in order to foster their widespread adoption at all levels in the organization.

1. BUSINESS IS A CHAIN OF SUPPLIERS AND CUSTOMERS

As we described in our earlier review of the works of Deming, Juran, and Crosby, one of the basic concepts of total quality management is the definition of work as a process, a series of activities converting inputs into outputs. Businesses with a customer focus build on that concept by conceiving of a supplier on one end of the process and a customer on the other. The organization is thereby seen not only in terms of sets of related processes but also as part of a chain: with a supplier on one side and a customer on the other, the business itself is a customer and a supplier at the same time.

Leadership for quality takes as one of its objectives to strengthen the links in this chain, striving for effective communication and relationships of trust between the business and its suppliers, and between the business and its customers. Put another way, this belief implies that the most successful businesses will be those who work hard not only at being a good supplier, but at being a good customer as well.

For example, Xerox Corporation, winner of the Malcolm Baldrige National Quality Award in 1989, conceives of its business as "Team Xerox," explicitly including its suppliers in its definition of that team. Without a partnership relationship with its suppliers, Xerox knew it could never expect to achieve the significant cost savings it had estimated when implementing its just-in-time inventory systems. Accordingly, Xerox reduced the number of its suppliers from 5,000 to 480, seeking to become one of the top five customers for each supplier. Further, Xerox requires that every supplier be "process qualified." This vendor certification process involves extensive training for each supplier in quality management, and it permits Xerox to quantify and analyze each supplier's performance.

Xerox demands 100 percent quality from its suppliers. As they accept responsibility for conforming to tight Xerox standards for timely delivery and performance specifications, suppliers know that once Xerox approves a part, it will not be inspected before use on the plant floor. This partnership with suppliers has benefited all parties. Suppliers learn to improve their own performance by implementing the quality process required by Xerox. Xerox has seen defective incoming parts decline from 10,000 parts per million in 1982 to 200 parts per million in 1989. And, of course, Xerox's customers in turn have reaped benefits from more reliable products at a lower cost.[6]

The Team Xerox concept reinforces the idea of dual relationships and responsibilities. As a good customer Xerox specifies exactly what it requires, provides feedback to help the supplier achieve those specifications, and makes repeat purchases of good products. As a good supplier, Xerox must deliver the products and services to meet the expectations of their own customers.

Within organizations dedicated to quality, effective work relationships are created and sustained with the same idea: like the business itself, each employee acts every day in the interchangeable roles of customer and supplier. Take as an example a sales representative returning from a trip and completing an expense report for reimbursement. As she fills out the form in a hurry, her writing is not easy to read, and she leaves out important information required by the accounting department for tax reporting purposes. She hands in the form to the accounting clerk to carry out the required activities in the reimbursement process.

With effort the clerk is able to read the poor handwriting,

but without the required information he cannot complete the process. He returns the form with a note telling the sales representative that she will have to resubmit her expenses on a new form, properly completed. And so these coworkers, supposedly members of the same team, complete another round of a familiar duet: the clerk shakes his head in disgust and resentment of the prima-donna sales representative's arrogance and disrespect, while the sales representative reviles the stubborn, worthless bean counters and the picky little details of their stupid forms.

In far too many organizations this is a familiar story! In organizations dedicated to quality, however, it is an aberration. With an understanding of the supplier-customer relations inherent in work, both parties here take more responsibility for their actions. From the start, the accounting clerk sees the sales representative as a customer; in completing his work, he supplies a service that provides accurate and timely reimbursement for travel expenses. As a supplier, the clerk works to satisfy the customer's requirements for simple forms with clear instructions, easy and quick to complete. In turn, the sales representative sees herself as a supplier of work to the accounting clerk. If she hopes to be a customer and receive good service (a timely check), she must give the clerk what he requires: a legible, completed form that meets all specified requirements.

When people really think of their work and their coworkers in this way, they take responsibility for their own work and for effective cooperation across departmental lines, professions, and work groups. Adopting a belief in business as a chain of supplier and customer relations is a bit of a paradox; even as it identifies customers and suppliers as two distinct parties in a process, it unites them. It asks each person to think of himself or herself simultaneously as both: as we receive our work we are the customer for another supplier; and as we complete our work and it moves forward, we are the supplier to another person, who is our customer. As the example shows, even between two individuals these roles can move back and forth, changing with the context of the situation to reflect the flow of work.

At Ford Motor Company, these ideas are expressed in the following simple statement about internal customers: "Each employee is a customer for work done by other employees or suppliers, with a right to expect good work from others and an obligation to contribute work of high caliber to those who, in turn, are his or her customer."[7] This belief is a powerful one because outside the work organization, at some point almost every individual in America must think of himself or herself as a customer. We know what it is to buy a product and be dissatisfied with it, and to receive service we find too slow, too rushed, or otherwise not up to our expectations. In the same way, of course, we have known the satisfaction, the pride, and the joy of purchasing products and services that exceed our expectations. In either case, the customer-supplier relationship is one we know well from a customer's point of view.

When we conceive of work in organizations as chains of these relationships, then, we bring to the work environment a new but familiar way of thinking that leads us to see our work in a new light. It increases our sense of responsibility to our fellow workers and thereby strengthens the sense of unity across the organization. Finally, it reinforces a sense of purpose in our daily work, reminding everyone—the accounting clerk, the sales representative, and the leader—that we all work to meet the needs of our customers, inside or outside the organization.

2. THE CUSTOMER IS THE PURPOSE OF THE WORK

This concept leads to the second core belief of a customer focus. There is no higher priority, no more basic obligation, no greater end in business than to serve the needs of the customer. There are other tasks, other concerns, and many other problems, but above all of these come the demands of our customer.

As we noted earlier, these words are widely repeated, but the commitment they imply is rarely found. What does that commitment mean? First, it means that everyone in the organization recognizes that it is the customer who defines quality, no one else. In many companies the product designers, the market research analysts, or even the quality councils may lose sight of this, perhaps in the belief—often apparently justified—that they know better than the customer does what quality really is. That belief is a mistake, and any organization that makes it is not likely to retain its customers and remain in business.

We began this chapter with a look at IBM; in its devotion to its mainframe computer business, it apparently refused to recognize evident trends in consumer preferences for small computer networks. By comparison, consider the example of Gillette and its development of the "Good News" disposable razor. Gillette executives were baffled as they watched their customers turn to disposable razors in the 1970s. They knew from years of painstaking research and development that the blades and the technology of the Bic disposable were inferior to their own Trac II, resulting in a shave of such low quality that they could not understand how or why a customer would choose this product. As it tracked the sales figures, however, Gillette could see that whether it made sense to Gillette or not, the customer wanted a disposable razor. To retain those customers, Gillette would have to give them the disposable product they wanted. Knowing that the Good News razor would cannibalize sales of the Trac II and that its profitability would suffer, Gillette also knew better than to argue with its customers: no business can win that argument. The Good News razor was born, Gillette protected its consumer franchise against a serious threat from Bic, and the company then set about developing a new razor (the "Sensor") to stem the growth of the disposables.[8]

Customer focus goes beyond simply conceding to the customer the right to determine the quality of a product or service; it requires that organizations implicitly assess the value of all their actions in terms of the difference they make to the customer. If the customers really matter, if their judgment is the only one that really counts, then the organization takes pains to think about them and consider their needs not only at the point of sale, and not only at the advertisement, but in product design, testing, manufacturing, distribution—*all the time*. Beyond the daily concerns of organizational life, such as personal rivalries and political battles, people must ask first and foremost: what does this do for the customer?

GE FANUC, a joint venture between General Electric and the Japanese corporation FANUC, operates with this idea in mind. In a recent presentation at the McIntire School of Commerce at the University of Virginia, CEO Robert E. Collins described his company's customer focus with these words: "Unless we serve the need of our customer, we cannot compete. Our customers don't care about our internal concerns, only the quality of our service. If we cannot see how an activity serves our customers' needs, we either find out how it will, or we stop doing it."[9]

The ultimate goal is not just to do something for the customer, but to go beyond that. In their book *Beyond Quality*, Bowles and Hammond suggest that how far an organization goes beyond "doing something" will be the difference between companies that lead and those that just survive. These authors trace the recent movement from a goal of meeting customer expectations to one of "delighting the customer," delivering more than the customer expected. Consistently performing at that level would create a relationship of trust between the company and the customer that should ensure profitability over the long run.

It falls to the company, not the customer, to build that relationship: the company must prove itself worthy of the customer's trust. Organizations can promise to guarantee customer satisfaction, but then they must deliver on that promise. The self-confidence to make such a promise and the determination to live up to it are rare in American business, but where the 100 percent satisfaction guarantee is made and met, customer response proves its value.

The best-known example is the guarantee offered by L. L. Bean, the paragon mail-order firm. In every catalog, on every order form, the L. L. Bean guarantee promises satisfaction:

> All of our products are guaranteed to give 100 percent satisfaction in every way. Return anything purchased from us at any time that proves otherwise. We will replace it, refund your purchase price or credit your credit card, as you wish. We do not want you to have anything from L. L. Bean that is not completely satisfactory.

In our experience it seems that in almost any group of people there will be at least one L.L. Bean customer with a story of how the company lived up to that promise. Its customer service representatives are trained to implement the guarantee *according to the customer's point of view.* For example, a customer may call to complain about a pair of boots that leak after seventeen years of use; if, *in the customer's opinion,* that makes the boots unsatisfactory, the representative may send a replacement pair free of charge. Although this leaves the company vulnerable to fraud and abuse by dishonest customers, Bean reports a return rate of only 14 percent, well below the industry average.[10] Bean enjoys very solid relationships of trust with customers, in part because it has acted in ways which show that the company is willing to trust them first.

Another example is offered by Hampton Inn Hotels, which instituted the first unconditional 100 percent satisfaction guarantee in the hotel industry in 1989. Under this policy, any guest who reports a problem or complaint during a stay and is not satisfied when checking out is given a night's stay free. In an article in the *Wall Street Journal* in 1991, Ray Schultz, president and CEO of Hampton Inn

Hotels, reported excellent results from that guarantee. In addition to enthusiastic response from employees and marked improvement in performance against its own quality standards, the company's customer research revealed that 2 percent of its total room nights systemwide were purchased by customers staying with Hampton Inn *specifically because of the guarantee.*[11]

In short, leaders dedicated to moving an organization to achieve total quality must remember, through everything, that the customer relationship is the end-all and be-all of their every effort. This is a challenge for even the best-intentioned organizations. For example, Florida Power & Light, the only American company to win Japan's prestigious Deming Prize for quality, revised its entire quality process; it determined that it was spending too much time and effort meeting the requirements of the process and paying too little attention to the requirements of its customers.[12]

In a similar vein, David Luther, former vice president of quality for Corning, looked back on his work to establish Corning's quality process; his conclusion summarizes this core belief and its many challenges quite well.

> If I were going to do it again and do it differently I would make customer satisfaction a more explicit part of the basic system from the start. When we designed this sytem back in 1983, we said that one measures quality by the cost of quality. . . . But that's not the issue at all. The issue is whether or not the customer likes it. If I were able to do this over I would find some way to make happy customers the thing you're really after.[13]

3. SUCCESS COMES FROM VALUING THE VOICE OF THE CUSTOMER

The old line "The customer is always right" must be one of the most frequently repeated homilies about customers—

and, of course, it is a lie. Every waiter, every cashier, and every sales representative has at least one story to tell about customers who, for whatever reason, were just plain wrong.

One sales representative for a large chemical company told us about the irate and totally unjustified complaints he receives from some of his customers. After experiencing major problems in their manufacturing process, these customers will trace the cause to the chemicals added at a particular step. They then call the sales representative to complain bitterly about having received "bad product" and insist on immediate replacement with another shipment at no charge.

On further investigation, the sales representative discovers that the customer has changed the manufacturing process in a way that affects the chemical, perhaps by using ionized water or warmer water. The problem is obviously not a question of poor quality product, but of using the wrong product. From the point of view of the sales representative, this customer is wrong. But this does not change the fact that even when the customer is wrong, he or she is always worth listening to. Within the total quality movement, this is described as listening to "the voice of the customer."

The first step in hearing that voice is to identify the customer: who is it, exactly, whom we intend to satisfy, delight, and build a lasting relationship with? Different customers have different needs, and thinking of "the customer" as one person, group, or set of needs can result in failure to meet real needs. For example, to gain significant increases in revenue from international markets, Procter & Gamble studied the hair, skin, and hygiene habits of customers in different countries, learning to alter product formulas and marketing strategies in order to serve different customers.

Organizations that have truly "seen" their customers must then learn to hear what they have to say. This takes some effort, because customers tend not to just volunteer information on their preferences and requirements for goods and services. Even those who have experienced bad service rarely complain to the company. In repeated studies, the Technical Assistance Research Programs Institute had demonstrated that although 25 percent of a company's customers may be sufficiently dissatisfied to stop doing business with that company, only 5 percent of that group will actually register a complaint with the business; the other 95 percent will just take their business elsewhere if they can.[14]

Certainly it is possible to infer from trends and sales records the critical customer requirements and preferences, but these interpretations are obviously subject to error, as the company tends to read this information from its own, not the customer's, point of view. For example, in his book *The Service Edge*, Ron Zemke tells the story of a telephone company's efforts to improve customer service in its residential repair service. The company began by assuming that the "cycle of service" began when the customer called a repair center to report trouble with the phone. In fact, as the company later learned that *from the customer's point of view* the service cycle begins well before the call to a repair center is made. As the customer sees it, first she finds the phone is out of order; then she must determine how to contact the phone company when she cannot use her phone; and only then does she call the phone company, and not necessarily a repair center.[15] The phone company's efforts to improve residential repair service will clearly benefit from understanding that chain of events, but that is information it would not have without first soliciting, and then listening to, the voice of the customer.

In recent years many organizations have learned to develop new ways to solicit customer feedback, to enable the customer to speak more easily and more freely. For example many companies offer toll-free telephone lines for customer comments and inquiries on an ongoing basis. Other methods include the written comment cards in hotels and restaurants and follow-up telephone surveys. More elaborate customer research includes focus groups, interviews, and formal customer visits, involving visits to customers' locations and inviting them to visit one's own. The critical issue here is to make it easy for the customer to tell what he or she does or would want, like, believe or think about us and our business.

Valuing the customer's voice means going beyond mere listening to actually acting on it. Having heard what the customer has to say, the company must now do something with that information, using it to respond, to improve, and to repair or to build on the customer relationship. It is a requirement of the Baldrige award, for example, that companies monitor customer complaints and resolve them. Some companies will choose to compensate customers who complain, and to recognize and reward customers who make suggestions for improvement. The goal is to use the information inherent in customer feedback to improve the organization's ability to meet customer needs. In the spirit of continuous improvement and of employee empowerment, this information should be made widely available within the organization. The voice of the customer should be heard at all levels: "Here's what the customer thinks of us today."

Furthermore, in organizations dedicated to total quality, customers are invited to do much more than provide after-the-fact assessments of quality; they are enlisted in the product design and development process as well. Engineers work with customers in the design phase to identify critical elements of new products, seeking to ensure that these new offerings meet or exceed customer requirements.

Without question, the best example of the benefits from taking this approach is the story of the Ford Taurus. Under the leadership of Lewis Veraldi, Ford interviewed thousands of people in their middle- and upper-class conservative target market to discover what these customers looked for in a car. Specific and general open-ended questions were asked to determine precisely what the consumers wanted. Focus groups were assembled to conduct tests using Ford cars, along with Japanese and European models. In some cases Ford went back to these groups, showed them the Taurus, and allowed them to drive prototypes of the model. After the test drives, the customers made further suggestions. For example, consumers complained that the original model was too compact. To deliver a slightly larger car Ford changed the design, despite the cost. Ford listened to these customers and made the changes necessary to ensure customer acceptance of the Taurus.[16]

These efforts to involve customers so deeply in product design were then entirely new to Ford and to the entire American auto industry. In its work on the Taurus, Ford demonstrated its commitment to developing and perfecting a car to suit customer requirements. And the results of the Taurus have proved the wisdom of that approach: on its release in 1985, *Consumer Reports* states, "These new Ford products are the best-performing products we've tested."[17] *Motor Trend* awarded the Taurus its "Car of the Year" award for 1986. Even more impressive, in 1990 the same magazine stated that the Taurus "represents the established standard in the class. If you're simply shopping for the best all-around four-door, the choice remains the same as it was five years ago: the Ford Taurus LX."[18] And Ford's customers feel the same: in 1992, the Taurus was the best-selling car in America, surpassing the Honda Accord for the first time in almost a decade.

THE CORE VALUES: SERVICE, HUMILITY, INTEGRITY

A real customer focus requires leadership with these three beliefs: business is a chain of supplier and customer relations, the customer is the purpose of the work, and success comes from valuing the voice of the customer. For leaders to bring those beliefs to life, however, three personal values are essential.

The first of these is *service to others,* an interest in or an orientation to other people that places importance on their well-being. With this value it becomes natural to think about the customer and attend to customer needs, requirements, and preferences, naturally seeking to make things better for that other person. Unless the leader models a genuine interest in the well-being of the customer, people in the company will never really care about customers, seeing them only in instrumental terms: what can the customer do for me? Instead, the goal must be to think like the customer, to try to live in the customer's shoes and to see your own actions from the customer's point of view, asking, "would I want to be my customer?" Put another way, this is a value that asks us to live out in the customer relationship the Golden Rule: to do unto them as you would have them do unto you.

The second value is *humility,* or lack of pride. It takes humility to accept the fact that the customer, who is sometimes wrong, must always be listened to and attended to with respect. It takes humility to accept that it is the customer, not the engineer or the chief executive officer, who determines what quality is. It takes humility to spend a lot of money on customer research, working hard to locate and then solicit opinions from customers who often tell you only what you already know. But leadership for quality requires humility because although you probably do know what the customer wants, you could be wrong, and being wrong (failing to understand what the customer wants) is the road to disaster. Even contemplating that possibility takes humility.

Finally, there is *integrity.* To establish relationships of trust with customers requires truthfulness, honor, and responsibility in acting out these beliefs. If integrity is not important in and of itself, then long-term relationships of continuing trust will not be possible. Within such a relationship neither party seizes the opportunity to take advantage of the other; instead, each recognizes that the other's well-being is to the advantage of both.

In summary, achieving a true customer focus in a quality organization depends absolutely on leadership that holds these beliefs and values, and models and teaches them to the organization's people in both word and deed.

CHAPTER 9

FINDING A BETTER WAY

Beliefs and Values for Continuous Improvement

Continuous improvement is the only one of the three fundamental principles of total quality management to be widely known by a Japanese word, *kaizen*. As that word is loosely translated at one financial services firm we know, it means being dedicated to the concept that "every day, in every way, we're getting better and better." When expressed in those terms, continuous improvement is like the other TQM principles in this respect: it sounds wonderful, but it is an obvious (and certainly not new) concept.

Unfortunately, it is easier to claim than to carry out a commitment to continuous improvement. By analogy to sports teams, it is easy for winners to proclaim their intentions to repeat as champions next year, but how rarely do those promises come true! Too often teams and stars seem too ready to rest on yesterday's laurels, blaming injuries, the weather, or just bad luck for any decline in performance.

But this is not always the case, as we see in the example of Larry Bird, star of the Boston Celtics basketball team. Three times the league's most valuable player, member of three championship teams, and four times the league's best free-throw shooter, Larry Bird would spend hours alone in extra practice sessions, testing, practicing, and improving the accuracy of his free throws. He spoke of how his first coach with the Boston Celtics, Bill Fitch, helped direct his efforts at continuous improvement:

> He was always telling me that I'd have to learn to adjust my game. He said the opponents would never stop testing me and that I'd always have to come up with something new.... One year he told me the coaches were saying I didn't like to go to my right for a jump shot. I went home that summer and worked on going to my right. There's no problem now.[1]

Leaders seeing to imbue their organizations with a thirst for continuous improvement must look to the example of Larry Bird: it takes hard work to live up to such an ideal. In a business context, there are four core beliefs associated with a commitment to this principle. The first two focus on gaining the knowledge required for improvement; the second two focus on maintaining the spirit necessary to improve continuously.

1. YOU HAVE TO KNOW THE FACTS

There is no question about the importance of inspiration in coming up with new product ideas, technological advancements, or approaches for resolving problems, as brainstorming techniques require. In the same way, of course, we recognize that to resolve interpersonal conflicts, executives must be aware of the importance of feelings, assumptions, and other nonrational aspects of human interactions.

For most business decisions, however, there are no substitutes for the facts, and in quality organizations one typically finds a shared, deeply felt determination to get at the straight truth. There is no room for spin doctors and happy faces; what is required is only the cold, hard facts. Without the facts no leader can confidently make critical decisions, even when they are essentially judgments (such as leaving a market, closing a plant, or promoting an employee). Leaders must answer difficult questions: does this activity really add value? Can we earn the required return from this investment? Can this person deliver the results we need? In these and other important decisions, the leader must be able to ask for and get the facts to make the right call. In words and action, the leader must show the importance of knowing the facts.

Rather than disparage those who focus on the details, a leader should recognize and reward such people for attention to critical pieces of information. They know what they are talking about—not what happened ten years ago, or what one buyer said last quarter, but the information they need to support their views and proposals. In the same way, for leadership for continuous improvement, what is essential is *knowing*, rather than thinking, assuming, believing, guessing, or feeling. Continuous improvement requires knowing where we are today, knowing where we want to be tomorrow, and knowing how much progress we have already made in moving toward that goal.

Organizations dedicated to continuous improvement therefore engage in a great deal of data gathering and analysis. In the previous chapter we described the importance of soliciting and analyzing customer feedback and opinions. For example, like many hotels, Marriott Corporation leaves questionnaires in each room for guests to report their satisfaction with their stay. Data from these feedback forms are then compiled in a Guest Satisfaction Index (GSI). In 1990, Marriott's corporate Office of Consumer Affairs received more than 800,000 GSIs. The data were reviewed at the corporate level and then passed back to the individual hotels for action.[2]

In companies dedicated to quality, this kind of data collection is a critical part of everyday business decisions. American Express assesses its service quality by taking monthly measures of more than one hundred performance dimensions. These data, compiled into "Service Tracking

Reports," are used to monitor, track, and improve service quality worldwide, and a consolidated report of monthly performance results is distributed to American Express managers around the world.[3]

Xerox Corporation relies on its Customer Satisfaction Measurement System (CSMS) to gather information on customer requirements and satisfaction. The system surveys fifty-five thousand Xerox equipment owners with questions about equipment, sales and service performance. The CSMS data are then used in developing business plans and in introducing design or operating changes. In addition, Xerox uses supplementary satisfaction surveys to determine other customer perceptions: the Early Warning System measures customer acceptance of new products; the Faultless Install System evaluates installation performance; and the Post Installation Survey measures customer satisfaction with the delivery system.[4]

As we said in the previous chapter, these efforts are necessary for companies to listen to the voice of the customer. A similar phrase is used to identify a parallel requirement for continuous improvement: organizations must also listen to "the voice of the process." That is, they must make the effort to collect, monitor, analyze, and use data generated from strictly internal activities in order to achieve continuous improvements in efficiency and quality before the customer even receives the product or service.

To hear the voice of the process, quality organizations turn to the methods of statistical process control (SPC) developed and advanced by Shewart, Deming, Ishikawa, and others. For example, individual work activities are analyzed and aggregated to define a process. This process is then used to define acceptable levels of output; then a host of statistical methods are used to detect and control any deviations from the expected levels.

The effort required to study and map the many different

processes is considerable, and managers may complain that this time is not well spent because it does not benefit the customer, and because "we already know what we do." But in a presentation at the University of Virginia, Robert Collins, CEO of GE FANUC, reported excellent results from these efforts in his own organization: a 52 percent reduction in organization layers, a 25 percent reduction in approvals, and a 74 percent reduction in product development time, among others. The critical first step is in taking the time and making the effort to map the work process, because "when you study the process you usually learn there are really three distinct things: what you think it is, what it actually is, and what you would like it to be."[5]

This is why in plants, office areas, cafeterias, elevators and lobbies, total quality organizations frequently display numerous charts and graphs: having collected this information, management makes the information available to all so that everyone will know the facts. These charts are usually maintained by the employees working in the process themselves, as they are usually held responsible not only to know this information but also to use it.

At Xerox the results from this approach have been remarkable. On the assembly line in Webster, New York, a daily computerized defect report is posted at each workgroup station, specifying what the defect was, where it occurred, and how many times it happened. Employees are able to stop the line to prevent defects from occurring. As a result, defects on the assembly line dropped from 10,000 parts per million in 1980 to 360 parts per million in 1989, and defects in finished goods decreased from 36 to 8 parts per million in the same comparison years.[6]

Edward P. Stone, director of corporate quality at Varian, reported similar achievements with statistical process control at this manufacturer of gas and liquid chromatographs and mass spectrometers.

For managers and employees at Varian, SPC is very much like the speedometer giving you feedback on your driving speed. Under the old manufacturing process, it was like having the police pull you off the road to tell you about your speed and driving errors—when it was too late. Now, the charts provide feedback, and errors are prevented before they occur. Everyone takes pride in monitoring and correcting his own speed and driving, and the police are no longer required.[7]

2. REASON AND LEARN

As the Xerox example shows, from the standpoint of continuous improvement, the only real value in knowing the facts of the situation lies in using the knowledge to do better—learning from the facts how to improve. It does no good simply to collect data or to report them without framing them in a way that makes them useful. The statistical methods championed by Deming help employees understand the information they hear in "the voice of the process" and decide what to do.

The value of this methodical approach is that it demands that we reason through the problems presented by process results: why is this occurring? Is this result random, or can it be traced to a specific cause? Rather than work through a trial-and-error technique, statistical tools require a disciplined, rational analytical process. And so quality organizations invest a lot of money in training *all* employees in basic statistical tools and logical problem-solving processes. Beginning with trend charts, control charts, flow charts, scatter diagrams, cause-and-effect diagrams, pareto charts, and histograms, employees learn what questions to ask, what data to gather, how to answer their own questions, and what to do next.

The classic problem-solving process in TQM is probably Deming's "plan–do–check–act" cycle, but other examples abound. For example, Oregon State University's pilot program in total quality adopted the following ten-step problem-solving process:

1. Select critical process
2. Survey customers
3. Select the issue
4. Diagram the process
5. Establish process performance measures
6. Diagram causes and effects
7. Select data on causes
8. Analyze data
9. Develop solution: plan, do, check, act
10. Standardize improvement[8]

At Xerox Corporation, employees are trained to use a standard nine-step process for quality improvement teams, and a six-step process for problem-solving purposes. The Xerox training in these approaches is mandatory and requires thirty hours of each employee. Motorola's training in its quality problem-solving processes cost the company $70 million in 1991, but management is convinced that is an investment that pays tremendous returns.[9]

Analysis of the facts using a scientific method allows people to *learn*. With these tools, an organization can identify its problems and their causes, test new approaches, and evaluate and improve on promising innovations. The emphasis on facts and a reliance on disciplined problem-solving approaches combines in a value for learning, a thirst to know more.

Learning is the basic motivation behind benchmarking: identifying other companies who do something well, studying them, and then learning how to improve by adapting their examples. Organizations dedicated to continuous improvement admit the possibility of learning from any other organization, including competitors, suppliers, or even organizations in different industries who have struggled with similar challenges.

We can turn once again to the development of the Ford Taurus for an example of learning from one's competitors. Lewis Veraldi implemented a technique called "Best in Class" (BIC) to determine what the new Ford car would look like.[10] Ford purchased and took apart fifty of the world's best midsize cars to analyze the components of their different features.[11] The team selected the best of these features and determined to make them even better in the Taurus. For example, Ford modeled the trunk of the Taurus after that of the Audi 5000, considered to be the world's easiest trunk to operate. They used the Toyota Camry to develop a top quality hood-balancing mechanism.[12]

Xerox is the premier corporate example of benchmarking, having begun this effort in 1979, before embarking on its full "Leadership Through Quality" process. Ten years later, when it won the Baldrige Award, Xerox measured its performance in 240 key areas, with the target of achieving the level of performance of the world leader in each dimension, regardless of its industry. For example, Xerox benchmarked itself against L. L. Bean's distribution system, Federal Express's billing efficiency, and Cummins Engine Company's production schedule.[13]

In keeping with its belief in logical, rational problem-solving methods, benchmarking at Xerox follows a ten-step model. The steps are as follows:

1. Identify what is to be benchmarked.
2. Identify comparative companies.
3. Determine data collection method and collect data.
4. Determine current performance levels.
5. Determine future performance levels.
6. Communicate benchmark findings and gain acceptance.
7. Establish functional goals.
8. Develop action plans.

9. Implement specific actions and monitor progress.
10. Recalibrate benchmarks.[14]

Organizations where learning is valued are eager to identify where they have problems, to search for and study different solutions to the problem, and then apply scientific methods and disciplined problem solving approaches to achieve improvements—continually.

3. THERE IS ALWAYS A BETTER WAY

Citius, altius, fortius—the Olympic motto since 1895, meaning "faster, higher, stronger"—expresses perfectly the value of striving to attain better performance. Underlying that idea is a commitment not just to be the best, but to reach to be even better, and never to stop reaching. There is no defined end point, no upper limit to the struggle. Instead, the goal is simply to achieve ever-better performance levels. In industry, those Olympic goals for improvement are understood as *better, faster, and cheaper.*

It is easy to want to improve if one has failed, but success makes the commitment to continuous improvement much harder. We have used several examples already of very large and profitable companies who became satisfied with their successes, doubted any competitor could match their achievements, and at some basic level stopped trying: "Why should we change? Why try something new when what we have has been so successful for so many years now? If it ain't broke, don't fix it! Don't you realize we're . . ." End that last sentence with the names "General Motors," "IBM," "Sears," and others to recall the difficulties that can come with success.

We know a lawyer who tells the story of a "good" citizen who was arrested and charged with possession of controlled substances with intent to distribute. Although the charges were thrown out on a technicality, the lawyer tells us, that citizen, frightened nearly to death, learned his lesson and will never even consider repeating the behavior that almost ruined his life. Many of the leading American companies today have had parallel experiences, a brush with disaster ending in a remarkable recovery and rebirth; Ford and Xerox are two examples we have cited repeatedly.

Gillette is another such example. In 1962, when Gillette's U.S. market share was at 72 percent (its highest ever), Wilkinson Sword Ltd. introduced its Super Sword-Edge stainless steel blade, coated with a film that made the blade last two to three times longer than Gillette's comparable blade of blue carbon steel. A year later Gillette introduced its own stainless steel blade, but so did two other competitors. By 1965 Gillette's market share had fallen to 49 percent. What made this incident especially bitter for Gillette was the fact that even before the Wilkinson blade was introduced, Gillette knew that stainless steel blades would be superior. It had decided, however, that making those blades would render its own manufacturing technology obsolete. In essence, Gillette had chosen not to improve its product.

Had Wilkinson had the resources to press its advantage, Gillette might have lost its market entirely. Gillette recovered, however, and the lesson is seared on its memory; Russell B. Adams, Jr., author of a corporate biography on the company, says, "It has become part of the myth and folklore: 'This is what happens to you if you're not up there keeping ahead of the market.' " As a result, Gillette follows a policy of continuous research and development to improve shaving technology. At any point, Gillette has up to twenty experimental razors in the lab. Its most recent innovation, the Sensor razor, was introduced in 1989 after over ten years in development, and it has met with tremendous market success. Already Gillette has its successor, the Sensor II, in development.[15]

The lesson learned at Gillette was to keep pushing for improvement, not to be satisfied with what has been achieved, not to take success for granted. These same ideas were stated quite clearly in this advertisement for Motorola in 1989: "Our formula is a simple one: First, banish complacency. Second, set heroic goals that compel new thinking. Finally, raise the bar as you near each goal. Set it out of reach all over again." Motorola, the first winner of the Malcolm Baldrige National Quality Award in 1988, is an inspiring example of dedication to continuous improvement. Like the other companies, it too derived a good deal of its inspiration from a sense of impending danger, posed in this case by Japanese competitors.

In the early 1980s CEO Robert Galvin determined that Motorola had to make dramatic improvements in manufacturing efficiency to compete with low-priced, high-quality Japanese products. After two stunning successes with a cellular phone and a pager, in 1987 Galvin issued the call to quantum improvements in productivity and quality for which Motorola is now famous:

> He wanted Motorola to reduce manufacturing defects by 90% every two years, and cycle time—the time required for tasks such as filling a customer's order or developing a new product—90% every five years. by 1993, Mr. Galvin vowed, Motorola would drive its defect rate to 3.4 per million parts from 6,000, a level of near-perfection known in the parlance of engineering as "six-sigma quality."[16]

Although Motorola did not achieve its six-sigma goal by the end of 1992, it did achieve remarkable results from its total quality efforts. Between 1987 and 1992 it nearly doubled productivity, measured as sales per employee; its audit of expenses indicates that its 1992 costs were $900 million lower than they would have been without its quality efforts; and according to company estimates, its project teams produced on average four new or improved products each day.[17]

As we have said, the effort to improve requires first that we are dissatisfied with where we are and what we do now, or that we understand the fleeting nature of being number one in a field full of eager competitors. But too often, those who speak out to question the established ways of doing things are punished, threatened, or marginalized with reputations for being complainers, "negative thinkers," or just not good team players. Organizations that punish or stifle internal criticism in these ways never get the opportunity to improve.

Criticism of the status quo is therefore a requirement for organizations driving for continuous improvement. They criticize even successful results; they find fault with the best of operations, because they know what can happen in organizations that lose sight of the need to keep getting better. To paraphrase Holden Caulfield in *The Catcher in the Rye,* "first you're good, then you know you're good, then you're no good."

Leaders must create an environment in which criticism of the way things are is not only tolerated, but encouraged. They must foster the notion of dissent, of disagreement, of dissatisfaction with the "mainstream" ideas guiding the firm. Here again, Motorola provides an excellent example of valuing constructive conflict:

> Motorola makes a cult of dissent and open verbal combat. Each employee is entitled to file a "minority report" if he feels his ideas aren't being supported. . . . Engineers say they are encouraged to dispute their superiors and one another vigorously at open meetings. . . . The cult of conflict quickly identifies and fixes mistakes, unmasks and kills weak or illogical efforts, keeps top managers fully informed and sometimes unearths enormous opportunities.[18]

4. KEEP TRYING FOR PERFECTION; YOU NEVER WILL ACHIEVE IT

Parents who have taken young children on long car trips are familiar with the plaintive question from the back seat, "Are we there yet?" One father we know typically replied, "We still have a little way to go," until one afternoon, after he had given that response several times, he was surprised to hear his young son demand with obvious frustration, "Daddy, how many more ways?" The parallel to continuous improvement is clear: leaders must establish the belief that while we look forward to the end result, we must attend first to the process; the journey, and not just the destination, is important.

In placing a value on the process, leaders do not overlook the importance of the end result. At the end of the day, the product or service must be delivered to the customer. As we emphasized in Chapter 8, the most efficient and best-loved production process is worthless if its results are rejected by the customer. But leaders dedicated to quality know we bring the product or service closer to delighting the customer by improving its process, by following a quality process: gathering data, analyzing it, formulating hypotheses, testing them, and moving forward by learning how to improve.

What can be enervating in this belief is the notion that no end will ever be reached. Like the young child in the back seat, we think we will never "get there," and that can sometimes lead us to want to give up. Xerox describes the commitment to quality as "a race without a finish line"; it is reasonable to ask, what intelligent runner would choose to run that race?

Put another way, people lose heart and hope when they fear that their results will never be "good enough." Feeling a constant push to improve, and continually hearing even constructive criticism and well-intentioned suggestions for improvement, can lead employees to what we might recognize in our students as "the A-minus syndrome." Hearing only the criticism no matter what level of performance is achieved, disheartened and demoralized, they wonder, "What does it take to get an A in this course?"

It therefore becomes a critical issue to recognize achievement and effort. Although the vision is never really achieved, and as Motorola suggests, we "raise the bar" continually to push for more, each step of improvement must be recognized. Milestones must be established in the form of interim, reachable objectives so we can celebrate the progress we have made in the journey.

Without becoming too satisfied with the results of our work, we can be proud of having followed the process for improvement and for delivering evidence of it. Leaders must find ways to challenge their people to higher levels of achievement without debilitating them; to point out opportunities to do more, to do better, without demoralizing them. Even small achievements must be celebrated, and employee efforts must be recognized as examples of valuable and important steps on the neverending road to *kaizen.*

This belief recalls our earlier chapters describing the role of vision, the picture of the future described by the leader for the organization as a whole. The vision is something always *to be* achieved, always in the future. In the same way, this belief about continuous improvement is a type of "pull energy" that inspires and motivates people and sustains the organization's growth and development.[19] As the Fleetwood Mac song used as a theme for President Clinton's campaign and inaugural gala says, it is critical that people and organizations "don't stop thinking about tomorrow." Even as we celebrate where yesterday's effort has brought us today, we must return to our work to make even more progress before tomorrow.

THE CORE VALUES: HONESTY, HUMILITY, HARD WORK

In relying on a belief in facts and scientific methods, continuous improvement also relies on a value for *honesty.* There is simply no place in a quality environment for falsehood, for half-truths, deceptions, or dissimulations. Leaders must encourage people at all levels to speak the truth, even when it is unpleasant. It is too easy for people to want to conceal their errors, to withhold disappointing results, to "massage" critical customer feedback. Nonetheless, there is no progress from statistical analysis of false data, and there can be no improvement on what never really was. Leaders must emphasize and model in their own behavior the value they place on hearing the truth.

In the same way, the belief in learning relies on a value for *humility*. To even want to learn, one must first admit the possibility of one's ignorance: I don't know it all, I can learn more. And at a deeper level, it takes humility to accept the fact that one's teachers can include the most unlikely people, from new hires to retirees, subordinates and peers, white collar and blue collar, suppliers and competitors. It takes humility, in fact, to respect our competitors. Though they may move in a different way, they travel the same road, and if we can come this far, so can they.

And to complete this lesson of the tortoise and the hare, continuous improvement will always require a value for *hard work*, for an endless striving to excel. Unlike the hare, who rests to celebrate, we must keep moving forward, keep working to keep getting better. To close, here are the thoughts of Larry Bird on the importance of hard work:

> The guy who won't do his schoolwork misses the free throw at the end. In high school we used to shoot fouls at 6:30 in the morning before class, but one of my best friends never showed up. In regional finals our senior year, he missed three one-and-ones in a row and we lost in overtime. I never said nothin' to him. I just looked at him, and he knew.
>
> The thing that bothers me the most about being injured is that I can't practice. I'm not happy when I can't practice. I used to go out there thinking I'd make every shot because I'd always have the practice. I didn't, but I always thought I would. But, without practice, I really struggle out there.
>
> I believe that if you work hard, things will come out all right in the end. A lot of guys—the day of the seventh game—will come out early to shoot. Never did it all year, but now they are. That doesn't get it. I believe that you work hard all year and games like this is when it pays off.[20]

CHAPTER 10

WORKING TOGETHER

Beliefs and Values for Empowerment

As one of the premier buzzwords from the total quality movement, the word *empowerment* has been overused and sometimes misunderstood. The best definition we have found describes the concept quite simply: "the authority to plan and do the work you are capable of doing."[1] Like the concepts of customer focus and continuous improvement, this sounds familiar and sensible to many managers. For many years, most organizations and executives have publicly praised their employees in such slogans as "Our people are our most important asset." Many have adopted organizational designs that promise to put the responsibility for decision-making at the lowest possible level in the organization. And who would endorse unnecessary controls, procedures, and policies? If people are capable of doing the job, they should do it! This is just common sense.

But doubts and fears about "employee motivation" usually lurk not far behind those slogans. Giving authority to managers and supervisors is one thing, but giving it to employees is another question. Managers worry that even if employees are capable, they do not seem to care. They are there only for the paycheck, and they certainly do not care about the product or service they make or deliver, about the customer, or about the company's performance. Giving authority to employees is great in principle, but first, how do you get them to care?

In a classic *Harvard Business Review* article in the late 1960s, Frederick Herzberg drew an important distinction between satisfaction and motivation. Some factors in the work environment, such as pay or physical working conditions, could make employees dissatisfied with their situation, but could not motivate them to greater achievement. Instead, the motivating factors in a job included the work itself and opportunities for advancement, personal growth, recognition, and increased responsibility.[2] Herzberg's work therefore suggests that managers who want people to care about their work should give them responsibility for it.

Without asserting that these findings apply to everyone in all kinds of work, this idea is clearly reflected in the concept of employee empowerment. Empowerment involves giving employees more responsibility: for their own work, for the work of their groups, and ultimately for the success of the entire organization. Because this usually entails greater risk for employees, quality organizations work hard to recognize and reward those who attempt these risks in the service of organizational goals. Also, these companies attend explicitly to the development and advancement of their people.

What does it mean to have people responsible for their work? It sounds simple, but where people are really empowered—where people do the work they are capable of doing—we see things we are not used to seeing in the American workplace. Consider these two examples:

- An employee on an assembly line spots a flaw in raw materials coming through her work station. Rather than make poor quality goods with defective raw materials, she acts immediately to shut down the line and identify and correct the problem, wherever and whatever it might be.
- A customer service representative for a credit card company takes a call from an irate customer complaining about $150 in finance charges on an overdue balance.

Reviewing the account history, he decides to grant the customer a one-time concession, informs the customer, and removes the charge from the account.

In most organizations, such things are unthinkable. Where is the supervisor? How can a low-level employee know whether or not the line should be shut down, or whether that customer should get that concession? These decisions are expensive! Supervisory and management review and approval are essential! Employees making decisions like these can ruin the company!

In fact, quality organizations recognize that employees making decisions like these *make* the company successful. They empower employees to act in these situations because they know that whether it is an assembler looking for quality in materials or a service representative talking to an angry customer, that individual is the one in the best position to advance the goals of the organization: zero defects in products, and zero defections by customers. And so the assembler in the example above saves the company from wasting materials and labor on poor quality product and rework, and the service representative saves a good customer from taking her business to a competitor.

Too many companies are simply unwilling to allow their people to make such decisions. They see only the risks and the lack of controls in such practices, because they cannot see their employees as people interested in doing what is best for the company. Instead, employees are believed to have a bad attitude that they might express in this way: "So what if the customer goes somewhere else? That's management's problem, not mine." Of course, such an attitude on the part of workers anywhere is sad and ultimately self-defeating, but the same can be said of the managers who fail to see the connection between their own values and beliefs about employees and the careless, irresponsible employee behaviors they deplore.

By contrast, Timothy Firnstahl, a restauranteur, adopted a different approach with his employees:

> I believe our employees are better than most because they have the power and the obligation to solve customer problems on their own and on the spot. Giving them complete discretion about how they do it has also given them pride. Many companies have tried so many different programs and gimmicks that employees have become cynical and indifferent. The people who work for us know that we take our guarantee seriously—and expect them to do the same. We use the same ultimate strategy to satisfy both customers and employees.[3]

In organizations where empowered employees act eagerly to advance the goals of the company, leaders hold and promote the following beliefs and values, which guide the actions of every member of that organization.

1. EMPLOYEES ARE PEOPLE

As the old adage has it, sometimes we cannot see the forest for the trees, and so it is helpful to begin by stating the obvious: employees are people. It is too easy for leaders to forget this. If you are high enough in the organization, after a while everyone beneath you becomes mere "headcount." And headcount from that perspective is a cost, almost always rising too fast, and therefore typically the prime target for cuts in tough times. Leadership for empowerment requires that we see people behind those numbers. Leaders who had adopted the style of "managing by walking around" actually see their employees in their workplaces and may even come to know the tasks and responsibilities of each. They may even know their names.

Even leaders who can discern the worker behind the variable cost must learn to see the person in the worker; it is too easy to see employees only as their jobs. On meeting strangers, how many of us pose the first question, "So, what do you do?" Especially of lower-level workers, many people tend to say, "She's *only* a secretary," or "He's *just* an operator." These definitions limit and diminish the very people whose efforts are critical to an organization's success—those who make the products and provide the services to customers. In a quality organization these people are as valued as the vice president of marketing. Each person is capable of understanding and contributing to the mission of the organization. As Ricardo Semler, president of Semco S/A, Brazil's largest marine and food-processing machinery manufacturer puts it, leaders must remember that employees are adults. With that in mind, Semler

> replaced all the nitpicking regulations with the rule of common sense and put our employees in the demanding position of using their own judgment. . . . We also scrapped the complex company rules about travel expenses—what sorts of accommodations people were entitled to, whether we'd pay for a theater ticket, whether a free call home meant five minutes or ten. We used to spend a lot of time discussing stuff like that. Now we base everything on common sense. . . . If we can't trust people with our money and their judgment, we sure as hell shouldn't be sending them overseas to do business in our name.[4]

2. PEOPLE ARE BASICALLY GOOD

At the heart of empowerment is the conviction that people are good. Although we sometimes fail, and we sometimes make mistakes, we mean to do good. As sensible, thinking beings, it is our natural inclination to want to succeed in our work.

Leaders who would empower others must take this almost as an article of faith. As Jeffrey Gandz has said, faith goes deeper than trust, which is built on good experiences and can be shattered with bad ones. To empower others, leaders must simply believe that "over time, most people will, most of the time, exercise power in the pursuit of a vision and be guided by good values."[5]

This conviction about the nature of human beings should remind us of Douglas McGregor's description of "Theory Y" managers, who believe that people actually want to work and, under the right circumstances, will strive to achieve good results.[6] Under this set of assumptions about people, it is easy to see why empowerment is described as "liberation." Rather than attending to means of controlling, checking, verifying, and overseeing the actions of the people who work in the organization, leadership for empowerment trains and equips employees with all they need to accomplish the task, points them in the right direction, and lets them do all they can.

Because the concept of empowerment begins with this idea that people want to do good work, it implies that managers no longer need to devise methods to induce workers to exert effort. Instead, they must make sure that people have the knowledge and the tools required for the job, and then they must support employee efforts by removing any obstacles that prevent excellent performance. Managers who once asked "What can I do to motivate these people?" should now ask "What am I doing, and what is this organization doing, that kills their desire to excel, or interferes with their effort?"

3. BUREAUCRACY KILLS INITIATIVE

Ralph Waldo Emerson wrote that "society everywhere is in conspiracy against the manhood of every one of its members," and correcting for sexism, the same might be said of work organizations today. When they ask "Why don't people care?" leaders should look at their organization's policies, practices, systems, and procedures to see how the latter discourage or prevent people from doing all they can to help the company achieve its goals. In too many little ways, employees hear the subtle messages that destroy initiative, innovation, and creativity: just do what you're told; you're not paid to think. Mind your own business, do your own work, and we'll take care of the rest.

Consider the last line of many job descriptions: "performs other tasks as directed." Even if this phrase is included for legal reasons only, many employees may hear this message: do these other things we tell you to do, but do nothing unless you are told. The same message can be conveyed by the ubiquitous "suggestion box." Highlighting extraordinary contributions in a destructive way, suggestion boxes can give the message, "In the unlikely event that you should have an idea, write it on this form, put the form in this box, and get back to work."

Features of the organizational structure itself can drive this message home in the same way. For example, an extensive hierarchy of job grades and levels in organizations may reinforce the message that greater contributions are expected only from those higher in the hierarchy. For example, we have worked with organizations where users calling the MIS department would refuse to speak with analysts or programmers whose job grade was lower than their own, no matter how skilled or knowledgeable the individual might be.

The single most damaging aspect of organizations where there is no empowerment is in the multiple layering of managerial levels. Each level is required to review, monitor, and approve the work of the level below it. These middle levels of management are the ones attracting attention today as contributing less value than employees on the front line while costing far more in salaries, all because the organization is built on the assumption that employees at lower levels (and, in particular, their work) must be watched and verified closely to ensure quality and avoid mistakes.

By contrast, empowerment returns all that responsibility to employees themselves. Employees are taught how to monitor their own work, and the work of their team. They learn to gather and interpret performance data themselves, making any necessary adjustments to their work process that are indicated. Employees thereby gain greater motivation in their work because they are responsible for it, and the organization captures significant savings by eliminating layers of managerial fat. Schlesinger and Heskett point out that elimination of managerial layers, accompanied by expanded employee responsibilities, will result in substantial labor cost savings and higher profits, even after investing in training and in wage increases for the empowered workers.[8]

To achieve these benefits for their organizations, leaders must begin by identifying those aspects of the organization that, however ostensibly efficient, teach employees *not* to do, *not* to try, and *not* to care about their work.

4. THE MANAGER'S JOB IS TO PROVIDE TRAINING, TOOLS, AND SUPPORT

Having accepted the ideal of empowerment, and having realized how the current ways of operating act against it, leaders will naturally arrive at the conclusion that major changes are required both of the organization and of its people. They must also accept, however, that these changes, because they are so fundamental, will take time and effort to succeed. Policies, procedures, and practices that frustrate employee initiative must all be changed.

Resistance to these types of changes is natural and will occur for reasons that are entirely predictable. As Kotter and Schlesinger point out, people resist change because they do not understand it, because they fear the unknown, and because they fear they will lose something in the new order.[9] Supervisors and employees alike will most likely resist empowerment for the same reasons.

Supervisors and managers have to learn entirely new roles. Used to monitoring, reviewing, approving, and making decisions, they need to help employees learn to do all those things for themselves. For many supervisors, this brings a feeling of obsolescence and fears of impending job loss: if they are doing my job, what am I supposed to do? Indeed, leaders who are honest will admit that the size of the supervisory and management work force is likely to shrink as empowerment results in bigger work groups, wider spans of control, and flatter organizations.

As for employees, they must learn to accept responsibility for the problems they had always been able to pass up to the supervisor for resolution. It is far easier to sit on one's hands, wait for decisions from above, complain about how long it takes for a decision to be made, and in the end, point out its flaws. With empowerment, employees have to face the fact that there are no perfect solutions to many problems, and to live with the best workable solutions they themselves can devise. The supervisor is no longer the scapegoat; the fault lies in themselves.

Among both groups there is a shared fear of the new role, and an anxiety about needing to learn new ways of working; a shared sense of loss for what was comfortable, however flawed it might have been; and a shared fear of failure as empowered employees and coach-supervisors.

Accordingly, every organization with a successful quality effort has invested millions of dollars and thousands of hours in training for everyone, managers and employees alike. When Xerox began its Leadership Through Quality program it began with training for the highest levels of management and moved through each level until every Xerox employee was trained in the company's new quality philosophy and problem-solving processes.

Once leaders perceive the innate talents and potential in their people, they must then invest resources to develop and utilize those capabilities in the service of the organization's goals. As H. Thomas Johnson puts it, leaders must see their people as "a bundle of opportunities to be developed and enhanced for the purpose of serving customers."[10]

In all respects, Motorola provides an excellent example of an organization that provides the tools and the training to empower its people to do what they are capable of doing. Robert Galvin, Motorola's former chairman, believed that his employees were willing to take responsibility for their actions, and that they were capable and willing to work. To create an environment where employees and managers could work together, he instituted Motorola's Participative Management Program (PMP). The program forms employee teams to achieve objectives set by management; if the teams exceed the goals, all individuals in the team share a bonus based on the savings or profits generated from their efforts. Within these teams, the "I Recommend" system encourages employees to put forward their ideas on improving quality, achieving cost reductions, or other improvements. Unlike the traditional suggestion box, this system promises a response from management within seventy-two hours of the suggestion, and if the employee does not agree with the response the question is discussed immediately.[11]

In addition to PMP, Galvin also instituted what is known as "Tool Management Culture" (TMC) at Motorola. Essentially, this culture focuses on management's commitment to provide employees with the latest and most advanced equipment, and its demand that employees devise and suggest new tools, learn more advanced techniques, and communicate their views to management.[12] Finally, as we noted in Chapter 9, Motorola invests heavily in human resources development and training. It sets aside about 1.5 percent of its payroll to maintain employee competency levels,[13] with a training program that provides education for everyone, from the newest maintenance employee on the shop floor to the CEO.[14]

In addition to tools and training, leaders must also provide support throughout the change process as people actually try to operate in new ways. Inevitably, in taking these risks and in making decisions on their own, some people will fail. And when new things fail, most people naturally tend to rush back to what is familiar, what "always worked before," and give up on the new way of doing things.

Therefore, paradoxically, in the early stages of the change to empowerment, leaders must support failures as they wait for successes they can recognize and reward. In fact, failures must be allowed to occur; supervisors must not rush in to override employee decisions except to avoid the most disastrous consequences. And even then, the employee who sticks her or his neck out and makes a decision—even if it ends in a financial loss for the company—must not be made to feel stupid or ashamed for what she or he tried to do. Instead, leaders should set the example for supervisors in this regard, discussing with the employee what went wrong so that next time the employee's decision might be more successful. For individuals, early mistakes must be learning experiences; for the organization as a whole, they must be symbolic evidence that the risk of making decisions without prior approval does not extend to risking one's job. Ray Schulz, president and CEO of Hampton Inn Hotels, found it necessary to encourage his employees to implement the company's satisfaction guarantee:

> We had to assure our employees that we would stand behind their decisions 100%. An employee who judiciously breaks the established "rules" in the interest of service— even if it means returning a guest's money—merits a commendation from our owners and managers.[15]

THE CORE VALUES: HUMILITY AND HONESTY

It is impossible to empower people unless one has faith in them, removes the constraints that organizations place on them, and invests heavily in their continuing development and capabilities. Leaders who act on those beliefs implicitly hold two core values: humility and honesty.

McGregor's "Theory X" managers believe that because human beings are on the whole lazy and irresponsible, they require and even prefer close supervision.[16] Of course, most managers who subscribe to this theory believe it applies to everyone but *themselves,* and the conviction that they are special cases guides their interactions with others in the workplace. Leadership for empowerment demands the opposite view. If we accept that people generally seek to do good work, then we should also accept that they will try to find good ways to do it. Once we recognize that employees as well as managers have the ability to think, to analyze, and to make their own decisions, we must admit the possibility that their ideas and decisions may sometimes be better than our own. Otherwise, why would we give them the responsibility to act based on their best judgments?

This value of humility can be difficult to accept. Many managers have made their reputations by stepping in to save the day, and the fantasy of the superhero coming to the rescue exerts a strong appeal to many egos. It can be hard to check the impulse to simply take control, to make all the decisions for everyone. And this myth of the mighty leader can just as easily debilitate employees, who may buy into a picture of themselves as weak and dependent to avoid the greater risk associated with decision making.

This is exactly what happened at Johnsonville Foods, a very successful company in the Midwest. In 1980 Ralph Stayer, the CEO, seized on the idea of empowerment as a way to increase his employees' involvement in decision making and their commitment to the company. He told his top management team to take responsibility for making their own decisions, but two years later, he had to replace all three members. Stayer blamed both the managers and himself for that failure:

> I went from authoritarian control to authoritarian abdication. . . . I had trained them to expect me to solve their problems. I had nurtured their inability by expecting them to be incapable; now they met my expectations with an inability to make decisions unless they knew which decisions I wanted them to make. . . . In a way they were right. I

didn't really *want* them to make independent decisions. I wanted them to make the decisions I would have made. Deep down, I was still in love with my own control; I was just making people guess what I wanted instead of telling them.[17]

Empowerment requires leaders to refuse to accept the notion that they alone can make decisions, judge, think, and act. Instead, where appropriate they will return problems and questions and decisions to the people who asked them, saying, "What do you think? You decide, and let me know." The purpose here is to build confidence at lower levels of the organization. Because she or he values people, she or he knows perhaps better than the employees do that they really are in a position to make the best decision, and she or he is willing to risk learning after the fact that they actually did so.

This same leader, having removed herself or himself from the decision, will not reappear to reap any reward or recognition for having made that judgment. If the division thereby achieves its highest levels of customer satisfaction and the president comes to present a corporate award, the leader will be sure that that recognition goes not to herself or himself as representative of the group, but to the people who deserve it.

As another example, if an employee team in his or her department develops a strong quality improvement proposal requiring significant capital investment, rather than take the materials to the executive committee to make the presentation—and gain the glory—himself or herself, an empowering leader asks the team to repeat the presentation to the committee. While the leader loses an opportunity to shine (and risks a second-rate presentation made by nervous and inexperienced employees), the employees gain valuable experience in developing their presentation skills, an awareness of how major investment decisions are made in the corporation, and valuable exposure to leaders outside their own areas.

Humility requires that leaders give credit where credit is due. To empower employees is to have them take risks, and where those risks pay great rewards, leaders must be sure that employees share in them. As one leader has told us, "My job is to make my people famous."

The second basic value, honesty, requires that leaders tell the truth to their people—and, equally important, that they allow their employees to tell the truth to them. Without this value, empowerment will fail. Leaders who express a faith in people and a willingness to let others make decisions can still undermine empowerment by withholding from employees information critical to effective decision-making.

In describing this decade as "the empowerment era," Jeffrey Gandz has described empowerment as "the integration of thinking and doing."[18] Byham and Cox note that this differs from the typical business operation, where managers do the thinking, supervisors do the talking, and employees do the doing.[19] According to such a scheme, employees might collect data and then hand it up to supervisors. This level might perform preliminary analysis and then hand it up to managers, who would weigh that against other data, incorporate additional analyses, and announce decisions and directives for the employees to follow. Clearly, if employees are to be given responsibility for making these same decisions, they need access to the same data, the same analytical tools, and the same analyses.

This can be quite a hurdle in some organizations. For years management has largely denied the possibility that employees could think at all, except for the highly unusual "flash-in-the-pan" idea to be duly deposited in the suggestion box. Further, management has actively distrusted employees. Even if information might be understood by lower-level employees, they might choose to divulge it to competitors. Worse, they might "misunderstand" it, question some of our assumptions, and judge our effectiveness—they could use it against us.

Leadership for empowerment disallows such thinking. First, because we have faith in people, we do not fear self-destructive behavior on the part of employees: they will want to advance the company's market position, not weaken it. Further, because we seek to have them make the decisions best made at their levels, we see the sense of giving them all the training, the resources, and the information required to do so.

There remains the unfamiliar prospect, however, that informed employees will be able to make judgments about management effectiveness. Leadership for empowerment accepts that as a cost—and a benefit—of this new way of operating. Managers have accepted the judgments of superiors without question; what could be so damaging in the judgments of subordinates? Again, with humility, we accept that others (even those beneath us in the management hierarchy) might just have better ideas than we do. Perhaps their analysis of operating information might result in a new and better way of doing business.

Leadership for empowerment requires leaders to welcome this possibility. Empowered employees are likely to say and do things because they are right, because they should be done. They will be less likely to concern themselves with political consequences or issues, as those subordinates closest to the leader may be. They may question you; they may challenge you. But for empowerment to mean anything, it must mean that employees have the chance to tell the truth and know the truth. And as the biblical admonition states, the truth will set them free.

The beliefs and values outlined above must inform and direct the human resources initiatives required for successful implementation of empowerment. It is useful to distinguish here between the companywide efforts the leader should initiate and fund, and the individual efforts of the leader as a person that can help make the difference in empowering employees.

Companywide Initiatives

We have already suggested some of these in the preceding section; a brief overview follows.

1. *Process analysis/organizational analysis.* The leader must initiate a study of current operating procedures to identify where required approvals, quality checks, and supervisory or management intervention would be unnecessary with empowered employees.
2. *Job redesign.* Human resources specialists must redefine the responsibilities, authority, and performance expectations for all jobs in the new work process. This may also involve establishing new specifications and qualifications for recruiting new hires.
3. *Training.* Current employees and their supervisors must be trained in the new jobs. Beyond this, as we have already stated, all members of the organization must receive training in the need for empowerment, the goals and the benefits it will bring, and the impact it will have on their work.
4. *Recognition and support.* After the training, employees must be offered continuing help and support in trying to adjust to their new roles. Those who take responsibility, and who act in pursuit of the organization's goals, must be recognized and supported, no matter what the outcome; those who thereby deliver outstanding results must be rewarded. The same applies to managers and supervisors, who must also learn to adopt new roles and functions in an empowered organization.
5. *Assessment and redeployment.* At the same time, leaders must recognize that some people will never be effective managing or working as a member of an empowered work force. Employees may reject the additional responsibility offered to them. Many managers will struggle with this, learning at last the lesson one shared with us:

"You can't empower anybody; they have to empower themselves." On the other side of the coin, managers and supervisors may refuse to relinquish authority to empowered employees who, as they should, just take it. After training, and after counseling, support, and other assistance have failed to help these people adjust to the change, those who cannot function should be reassigned or removed.

Individual Initiatives

On a personal level, as individuals, leaders must act to advance empowerment in the organization. In all their actions, they must strive to show visible personal support for the concept. They can do so in many ways.

First, the leader should attend training sessions and speak about the value of the change effort. A leader's presence lends credence to the importance of what is taking place, and in the initial training, credibility is essential. In resisting the change, many people (employees and supervisors alike) will doubt the sincerity and the persistence of such an effort. Where the leader attends and participates in the sessions, such doubts are much harder to adopt.

Along the same lines, the leader should attend any recognition ceremonies, personally giving any awards or congratulations to employees, and speaking again to the group of the value of these efforts. Again, simply by being there, the leader demonstrates to everyone the importance of the proceedings and the value of the individual effort or achievement being recognized by the organization.

Finally, the leader should try to spend time in the workplace among the employees doing the work. Executives who can find time to sit with customer service representatives working on the telephones, or who can walk through and visit the pickers and packers in the warehouse, visibly demonstrate that they do in fact value the efforts and contri-

butions of the people who make the difference in their organizations. In short, most employees know that where the
leader is, there is power. The leader should demonstrate in his
or her person that this is true by spending time where the
power is: with the frontline employee empowered to make
decisions on the company's behalf.

In closing, let us admit that the concept of empowerment
is a paradoxical one: it implies that leaders give something to
employees (power, authority, or responsibility) when actually
it is more a question of taking something away: the constraints and limitations imposed by unnecessary controls and
bureaucracy. We compare leadership for empowerment with
the story of the Wizard of Oz. At his direction, Dorothy, the
Scarecrow, the Tin Man and the Lion worked as a team, accomplishing a task they first thought was impossible. In
achieving their goal they needed brains, and heart, and
courage, the very things they had come to the Wizard to obtain. In the end, he gave them nothing that they did not already have; he only gave them work that allowed them to
find what they sought inside themselves. Of course, we also
learn at the end of the story that the wizard is no wizard at
all, only a man. Even as we point to great leaders like Sam
Walton, Ray Kroc, Walt Disney, David Kearns, and others, we
should remember that they too are not wizards, only men
who have learned how to lead.

PART IV

COURAGE:

REALIZING YOUR VISION

CHAPTER 11

THE CREDIT BELONGS TO THE COMPETITOR IN THE ARENA

Successful leadership that results in quality performance be-gins with a vision of what the leader and his or her fol-lowers intend to accomplish, but having a vision is no guarantee of success. As we have said before, there is no shortage of ideas and visions in the world. If a vision is all an individual has, then he or she is a dreamer, not a leader. A leader must communicate the vision, and his or her commit-ment to it, in such a way that those who must follow under-stand what it is, know why it is important to the company and to them personally, and become committed to the process of making it a reality.

Beyond the essential element of vision, successful leader-ship requires the development and communication of strongly held values and belief. All these define what the or-ganization represents, what it stands for, and what makes it different from and better than other organizations. Thus, they are absolutely essential for effective leadership. In this book, we have focused on three fundamental beliefs that are indispensable if the leader's goal is to produce quality results. They are a belief in serving the customer, a belief in continu-ous improvement, and a belief in the empowerment of em-ployees.

Values and beliefs may be thought of as the glue that unites people as they undertake the process of realizing a vision. Unless values and beliefs are specified and communicated and become part of the organization's character, guiding day-to-day decision making, people in the organization will not and cannot truly commit to the vision. They will lack direction and focus, and ultimately much of their effort and energy will be wasted. Eventually they will become frustrated and disillusioned, and many of them will lose interest in the vision and give up.

But even a compelling vision and strongly held values and beliefs cannot ensure effective leadership. The leader must also be able to harness and direct his or her own effort and energy, and the effort and energy of others, to realizing the vision. Harnessing effort and energy and focusing them on a predetermined target is the action phase of leadership, and it separates mere thinkers from leaders. It also separates the people who are more interested in possessing a title (or *being* something) from those whose primary interest is in *doing* something. An old Irish proverb says, "You'll never plow a field by turning it over in your mind." Ultimately, leaders must do things, and that is why they are so important.

THE ACTION ORIENTATION

As we mentioned in Chapter 1, Theodore Roosevelt described leadership in action as well as anyone could have when he said:

> It's not the critic who counts, not the man who points out how the strong man stumbled, or where the doer of deeds could have done better. The credit belongs to the man who is actually in the arena; whose face is marred by dust and sweat and blood. Who strives valiantly; who errs and comes short again and again . . . who knows the great enthusiasms, the great devotions, and spends himself in a worthy cause. Who at the least knows in the end the triumph of high

achievement; and who, at the worst, if he fails at least fails while doing greatly, so that his place shall never be with those cold and timid souls who know neither victory nor defeat.[1]

There will always be critics. Anyone attempting to do anything significant will experience his or her share of abuse. Many of your colleagues and associates would rather spend their time and energy criticizing and ridiculing what you are trying to accomplish than to attempt to do anything significant themselves, mostly because of their own fears of failure. Leaders must face their own fears, as well as deal with the ridicule and the resistance that stems from others. Leaders in organizations are on a playing field of sorts, and the outcome of the game is dependent to a large extent on what they do or fail to do. It is the leader's thoughts and actions that will guide an organization's achievements.

Roosevelt uses the arena, or field of play, as a metaphor. Most of us have attended football games and heard a few spectators condemning the coach, the players, and the officials. No matter what play the coach called, it was the wrong play. No matter what ruling the official made, it was incorrect. No matter how well the quarterback played, he should have played much better. But have you ever wondered how many of those spectators have actually played football? How many of them, for example, know how it feels to run wind sprints in August in 95 degrees Fahrenheit and 95 percent humidity? How many of them can remember how it feels to be standing on the field virtually unconscious for a few minutes because someone has hit you so hard that it almost knocked you out?

We doubt many of the spectators we are talking about could relate to these experiences. And it would be unconscionable if the rewards went to the people in the stands who are just watching the game, instead of the players on the field who have invested all they have in the sport and are risking their health. In business, the players may not be risking their health, but they are betting their careers and their professional reputations every time they say, "I have an idea, and I would like to give it a try."

We think that is what Roosevelt is saying. Those people who are striving to accomplish something worthwhile in an organization, who give all they have to offer and are determined to stay the course until victory is secure—they are the ones who deserve the credit and the rewards. They are not perfect; they will make mistakes, and they will get a little bloody from battle. But there can be no victory without them. Such people, no matter what their titles, are true leaders.

Roosevelt's description of the people who are not players in the game, the spectators, is quite interesting. He refers to them as "cold and timid souls who know neither victory nor defeat." These are the people who spend their time and energy criticizing what others are doing rather than doing things themselves. They rarely lack intelligence and ability, but they have a serious deficiency nonetheless. They do not possess the desire, determination, persistence and courage that successful leadership demands. In Chapter 7, we included the following quote from Ray Kroc:

> Nothing in the world can take the place of persistence. Talent will not: nothing is more common than unsuccessful men with talent. Genius will not: unrewarded genius is almost a proverb. Education will not: the world is full of educated derelicts. Persistence and determination alone are omnipotent.[2]

This is not to say that it is wrong to criticize. In fact, as we have stated many times, a belief in continuous improvement is fundamental to producing quality results, and an essential tenet of this belief is that everything we do must be reviewed (that is, criticized) constantly. But leaders do much more than just criticize. They focus and direct criticism toward achieving improved results. Ultimately, they will be the force behind the changes that must occur in our society if we are to have any hope of competing in the rapidly changing global economy.

THE ACTIVITY TRAP

Achieving quality results is not easy; if it were, everyone would do it. Quality is the product of dedication and commitment over a long period of time, and it requires leadership. Absent the influence of leaders, most people in businesses would be perfectly happy doing things the way they have always done them. Business as usual, employing tried-and-true approaches, would be the norm.

There are tremendous differences between activities that produce lots of movement but few worthwhile results and focused activities that culminate in accomplishment, yet many people are unable to distinguish between the two. The inability to tell the difference between activity and accomplishment is endemic in the United States, and it has affected the performance of our businesses in profound ways.

The growth of bureaucracies in U.S. businesses since the end of World War II has produced lots of activity, and bureaucracies have been responsible to a large extent for our performance problems and for our apparent shortage of leaders as well. People who work in overly bureaucratic organizations find that there is always plenty to do. There are reports to write, meetings to attend, directives to prepare and disseminate, and so on. It is no wonder little of importance is accomplished in most organizations by many of their people. They are too busy performing fruitless activities to spend time doing the things that are essential for success. Today, major corporations across the country are realizing that their bloated bureaucracies have effectively stifled creativity and innovation and caused them to be less competitive in the global market than they need to be. For our own sake, this must change. A Dennis the Menace cartoon we once saw made this point very well. Dennis was walking in the woods with his pal Joey. Dennis's remark, "We may be lost but we're makin' good time!" is a sad but fitting depiction of life in many U.S. businesses: people scurrying around doing things very quickly and perhaps even efficiently, but accomplishing little or nothing.

Under the leadership of Jack Welch, General Electric identified the problem of non-value-added activities and started to deal with bureaucracy more than a decade ago. Welch realized that multiple layers of managers between the people at the bottom of the organization who were actually doing the work and the people at the top of the organization were making GE less efficient, less innovative, and less agile in responding to rapid changes in the global economy. To combat the problem, GE started to downsize by reducing the number of middle-level managers. It also sold off pieces of its business that did not fit with its strategy and bought other businesses that did fit. *Reorganizing* is the word used to describe this overall activity; the word *downsize* was replaced later with the more accurate term *rightsize* to show that bigger did not necessarily mean better. In effect, GE was righting itself instead of reducing its size. This effort has resulted in a leaner and more efficient GE, more decentralized decision-making throughout the company, and more rewarding and challenging jobs for GE employees. Today, GE is well-regarded for producing products and services that are of very high quality at competitive prices.

ECONOMIC EFFECTS OF CORPORATE INACTION

The success of this approach at GE has led other firms to consider using a similar strategy in dealing with their bloated bureaucracies. From the perspective of both short-term profitability and long-term competitiveness, this approach has worked well. In December 1992, IBM announced that it would lay off twenty-five thousand workers to streamline operations, reduce costs, and increase competitiveness. Although IBM had used early retirements, reassignments, and restructuring for several years in a vain attempt to solve its problems without reneging on its long-standing policy of avoiding layoffs, it had to confront the unpleasant reality of the need for streamlining operations more drastically. IBM was simply too big and had become too bureaucratic for incremental solutions to work.

The effect of this delayed realization, according to Michael Schrage has reduced IBM "to a stumbling corporate Cyclops: an object of pity and concern desperately struggling to regain its lost vision."[3] He attributes the computer giant's current difficulties to an unwillingness to bite the bullet much earlier, and the lack of courage on the part of its leaders to "redefine itself as a company that offers the best computing value per dollar."[4] This is probably an accurate assessment given the changes that have taken place in the computer industry, where small firms emerge almost overnight and within a few months consume market niches that had traditionally belonged to the larger firms in the industry.

John Burgess and Dan Southerland also suggest that IBM's problems are rooted at the top of the organization. They say that IBM's leaders . . . drifted along for years believing they still owned the industry—as they had, for many years."[5] Instead of focusing and redirecting its resources to a small number of market segments in which it could play the leading role, IBM continued to try to be all things to all people. As a result, "Nobody knows what IBM stands for."[6] As Schrage says, "In this era, 'wanting it all' is less a sign of strength than a signal of immaturity."[7]

Ironically, pressure from the investment community played a large part in IBM's decision to face reality. The executives at IBM could have made this decision on their own several years earlier, but they did not act. As a result, others acted for them.

Cutbacks, layoffs and plant closings at firms like GE, IBM and AT & T have put a real strain on the U.S. economy. They have caused unemployment to rise to an unacceptable level, and as president of the United States, in November 1992 George Bush paid the political price for these business problems. As unfortunate as these consequences certainly are and as unpleasant as these decisions are to make, they are necessary if we are to regain our competitive position in the global economy.

As we said earlier, GE has made great progress since the early 1980s in solving its problems and is now focused and competitive. GM and IBM are now beginning to move in the right direction, but they both have a long way to go. Many U.S. firms have not yet realized the extent to which their bloated bureaucracies and their lack of vision are hampering their competitiveness. Yet some are beginning to move in the right direction.

SUCCESSFUL CHANGE DEMANDS
DETERMINATION, PERSISTENCE, AND COURAGE

To infuse an existing organization with that can-do spirit and courage to take action is very difficult. People develop routines and rules of thumb quickly in organizations to help them get their jobs done effectively and efficiently. Over time, the appropriateness of these tools declines rapidly, but the people's commitment to them does not.

As organizations grow, their bureaucracies become more powerful and begin to dictate what will and will not be done. When this happens, these rules and routines become governing criteria. They define the organization's character and its purpose, and they stifle the creative activity that is essential in achieving quality results. Unfortunately, because of the time it takes to develop such a structure, the structure itself is almost always out of date for the environment that the organization is currently facing. It is probably more difficult to change these rules and routines than it is to change anything else in corporate life.

The poem that follows (by an unknown author) illustrates this point. It shows in an entertaining way how organizations evolve over time, and it depicts how much easier it is to follow a proven path then it is to blaze a new trail. Following the existing path is much safer in the short term than taking chances by venturing into uncharted waters. Yet if people in your organization are unwilling to even consider new and possibly better ways of doing things, your organization will eventually become less competitive in the global market and will suffer greatly as a result. If left unchecked, this behavior will result in obsolescence and eventually failure. Leaders must be on the alert and be determined to counter these natural tendencies if they hope to produce quality results.

The Primeval Calf

One day through the primeval wood
A calf walked home as good calves should;
But left a trail all bent askew,
A crooked trail as calves all do.

A dog took up the trail next day
A bear, too, went along that way.
And then a wise bellwether sheep
Pursued the trail o'er vale and steep.

And drew his flock behind him too
As good bellwethers always do.
And from that day, o'er hill and glade
Through those old woods a path was made.

And many men wound in and out
And dodged and turned and bent about.
And uttered words of righteous wrath
Because 'twas such a crooked path.

The forest path became a lane
That bent and turned and bent again.
And this, before men were aware,
Became a city's thoroughfare.

And soon the central street was this
Of a renowned metropolis.
A hundred thousand men were led
By one calf, near three centuries dead.

For men are prone to go it blind
Along the calf paths of the mind
And work away from sun to sun
To do what other men have done.

They keep the path a sacred groove
Along which all their lives they move;
But how the wise old wood gods laugh
Who saw that first primeval calf!

LEADERSHIP IN ACTION

Our goal in this book has been to explain what is required from leaders whose vision it is to develop performance excellence and to produce quality results. We have described two examples in detail: those of Sam Walton and Ray Kroc, both men of vision whose businesses have changed their industries, and America, for the better.

Throughout the book we have also cited examples from many companies including Xerox, Motorola, and Ford Motor Company. Each of these companies fell on very hard times, and then leaders emerged to guide them through difficulties to the path that leads to quality results. All three compete in very rapidly changing industries, and they will continue to face stiff competition and business cycle fluctuations. Thus, the importance of leadership in these companies will intensify over time. Their leaders must maintain their vigilance, or they could find themselves in the position of being unprepared to adjust to the ever-changing terrain on which competitive battles are fought.

Without a doubt, Sam Walton (the subject of Chapter 3) was a good example of leadership in action. He may have been one of the best communicators of all time. Walton was able to extract a level of commitment from his associates that borders on fanatical. His company is a symbol of what he stood for and believed in; his vision, his belief in the importance of customers, his belief in empowering his people, and his penchant for continuous improvement are all evident at Wal-Mart.

Leaders who would move their organizations to achieve quality would do well to emulate Sam Walton. But now the man is gone, and his company must move on without him. The great question for Wal-Mart is, can the organization continue to excel in the absence of the leader? David Glass, CEO at Wal-Mart, has done a remarkable job in the early 1990s of continuing Walton's legacy. He is definitely off to a good start, and there is every indication he will continue, but only time will tell.

To deal with this question, we conclude this book with the story of one company with a history of prosperity, decline, and renewed prosperity. Under Walt Disney's leadership, his company did amazing things. After his death, the managers who took over the company tried to do the things they thought Walt would have done, not realizing that Walt was constantly innovating. Thus, without its founder, the Walt Disney Company became stagnant and did not change significantly until Michael Eisner joined the company almost twenty years later.

CHAPTER 12

WALT DISNEY AND MICHAEL EISNER

Leadership at the Walt Disney Company

If we try to coast, we'll go backward.[1]
—Walt Disney

Of all the things I've done, the most vital is co-ordinating the talents of those who work for us and pointing them at a certain goal.[2]
—Walt Disney

I'm afraid if I'd been running this place we would have stopped several times en route because of the problems. Walt has the stick-to-itiveness.[3]
—Roy Disney

Walt had set the standard, and that way of doing things persists to this day: it must be the very best you can do; and, if properly prodded, you can always do far better than you think you can.[4]
—Disney animator

The chronicle of the Walt Disney Company's rise to the top of the entertainment industry begins with the story of a creative genius who relentlessly pursued his dreams and, more broadly, the triumph of the American entrepreneurial spirit.

This chapter was prepared by Joanna Blattberg, who is an associate at Carter, Ledyard & Milburn in New York.

Simply stated, Walt Disney's vision was to bring warmth, laughter, and amusement to audiences around the world; his medium of communication would be an enterprise known for its quality, attention to detail, and constant striving for improvement, even during times of financial difficulty.

Walt belonged to a breed of leaders possessed by a distinctively American idea. The modest concept is that it takes one good idea, accompanied by unswerving determination, to succeed. Indeed, Walt became a hero of American popular culture, legendary for his visionary approach to entertainment. But his ability to lead, to encourage and direct the talents of his employees, was the key factor in the success of his business and the key to the fulfillment of his dreams.

In the early days, as Walt fought with skeptical bankers and experienced competitors, he developed the theory that the key to success in the entertainment industry was the establishment of a reputation for quality, even if a constant drive to improve products meant sacrificing sizeable immediate profits. He was convinced that superior performance would elicit the maximum consumer response and thereby render his company irresistible to investors and consumers.

According to Walt, quality resulted from "the four C's": curiosity, courage, confidence, and constancy. Building on those concepts, he developed a set of company standards that would motivate his employees to care about the quality of their work. He encouraged constant innovation, improvement and attention to detail, efficiency without compromising quality, creative freedom, teamwork, and a willingness to take chances and diversify. Walt lived by these principles, embedded them in his company culture, and in the process built an international entertainment conglomerate.

THE BIRTH OF WALT DISNEY PRODUCTIONS

Walt learned the value of hard work and perseverance at a young age. He was born in 1901 into a struggling midwestern farming family. As a child, Walt labored along with the rest of his family, and he watched his father fail in a struggle to secure financial stability for his family.

Fueled by clever concepts and an innovative spark, young Walt worked as a cartoonist for a Kansas City newspaper and created animated shorts for local movie theatres. When his early business ventures failed, however, the twenty-one-year-old dreamer left for Hollywood to pursue what had eluded his father for a lifetime: the American dream.

Once in Los Angeles, Walt went into business with his older brother Roy. Together they formed the "Disney Brothers" and immediately began work on their first series of shorts. Though Walt was rich with enthusiasm and ideas, he was practically penniless and hardly experienced in a film industry characterized by tight budgets and limited contracts. His progress was gradual and at times frustrating. As the company grew, Walt struggled with competitors, unions, critics, skeptics, and uncooperative financiers, but he endured because he believed in his vision. As Walt said, "I have been up against tough competition all my life. I wouldn't know how to get along without it."[5] His tenacity and extraordinary fighting spirit carried the company through trying times.

Inspired by the moderate success of their first series, entitled "Alice in Cartoonland," the brothers next created "Oswald the Rabbit." Disaster struck, however, when a New York distributor stole the series along with all of its animators. Disappointed but not defeated, Walt renewed his search for fresh concepts. He developed the idea for Disney's earliest character, Mickey Mouse, on the train trip back to Hollywood.

> But was I downhearted? Not a bit! I was happy at heart. For out of trouble and confusion stood a mocking, merry little figure. Vague and indefinite at first. But it grew and grew and grew. . . . The idea completely engulfed me. The wheels turned to the tune of it.[6]

Ironically, New York distributors were uninterested in "Plane Crazy," the first silent short to spotlight the mouse that would become one of Disney's most endearing and timeless characters. Nonetheless, the brothers persevered and featured Mickey in a new film, "Steamboat Willie," which was an immediate success when it was released the following year. As Walt alone had provided the inspiration for the studio's first major hit, he renamed the company Walt Disney Productions.

Instead of worrying about whether audiences would grow tired of Mickey, Walt set out to develop new characters. His quest for aesthetic and stylistic diversification took courage and confidence. When Walt entered the film industry, most studio leaders showed neither the desire nor the aptitude for improvement. Walt, on the other hand, was restless by nature. He once admitted, "I can never stand still. I must explore and experiment. I am never satisfied with my work. I resent the limitations of my own imagination."[7] He continually searched for improved methods, fresh concepts, and ways to diversity and to distinguish the work of his studio from that of his competitors.

From the beginning, it was Walt who handled the production of cartoons, while Roy was relegated to the secondary but necessary role of arranging the financing for Disney animation. Walt was interested in more than mere commercial prosperity. Money, he believed, was merely a means of funding the development of new ideas and enterprises. He once said, "Money—or rather the lack of it to carry out my ideas—may worry me, but it does not excite me. Ideas excite me."[8]

Walt was a gambler. When he had faith in an idea, he was determined to expose it to the public. Although he appreciated the importance of running a profitable company, he refused to compromise his vision by producing low quality products in return for high profit margins. With these standards, Walt provided the direction and inspiration in Disney's quest for long-term improvement and innovation, not simply instant profits and commercial success.

Walt had a taste and gift for technical innovation. He once described his incessant search for novelty: "We're searching here, trying to get away from the cut and dried handling of things all the way through . . . and the only way to do it is to leave things open until we have completely explored every bit of it."[9] His obsession with new technology was driven in part by a desire to elevate the work of his studio, and partly by the challenge and potential for transformation of the art of animation itself.

Walt insisted that his employees have the most sophisticated equipment and elaborate machinery available. He provided his staff with the best working conditions in the industry, and in return he expected each of his employees to work as hard and care as much about quality as he did. Walt also understood, unlike his competitors, that to produce better quality he would have to use unorthodox training methods to improve the skills of his employees. He discovered that teachers of animation shared his quest for enriched craftsmanship, and he hoped that night classes would generate the enthusiasm, inspiration, and ability necessary to obtain higher quality.[10] Following the elaborate art classes, Disney employees were encouraged to experiment with lavish cartoons and new techniques at any expense.

Walt's drive for technological novelty not only made Disney into the leading studio in innovative animation, but also transformed the film industry. The studio pioneered the use of full color, synchronized sound, and serious music in animation. But Walt did not stop once he had found success with shorts, for he had a broader vision. He moved on to a novel and colorful enterprise: the production of full-length feature. In 1937 Disney released *Snow White*, the first full-length animated film in the industry. The movie was also the first to feature the revolutionary multiplane camera, which produced the illusion of depth in figures on screen.

The studio had a similar commitment to innovation in its true-life adventure movies. In preparation for films, Walt required cameramen and artists to study the anatomy and locomotion of animals in their natural habitat. He made sure that his naturalist photographers had the best available equipment and more than enough time and space to do their work. His insistence on increasingly realistic reproductions of nature generated a revolutionary product that was wildly appealing to audiences around the world.

Continuous Improvement and Attention to Detail

What distinguished the Disney studio from its competitors was its commitment to constant improvement and attention to detail. Disney employees maintained that under Walt, nothing was permanent; there was always room for improvement and time to make the requisite changes. As one commentator suggested, "It was typical of him that anything he went into had to be the best, and not just the best of what was currently being done, but the best it was possible to do."[11]

Walt's films developed a reputation for superior staging, extravagant detailing, and highly effective conveyance of the feelings of his characters. An animator who worked on *Pinocchio* told a story that illustrated Walt's remarkable regard for details: when presented with a series of experiments on the use of line and color, Walt surprised the animators by praising the airiness of certain bubbles and criticizing the heaviness of others.[12] Indeed, the overwhelming success of Walt's typical film rested on the extraordinary details, the "small touches that one scarcely notices on its first viewing but that must finally be seen as the movie's true subject matter."[13]

Flexible and Creative Approach to Increase Efficiency

Walt's single-minded pursuit of quality and innovation in the studio meant that during the early years Disney operated on borrowed money. On the brink of bankruptcy, the company responded to crisis with flexibility, as Walt found clever ways to cut costs without sacrificing the quality of his product. For example, he reduced production costs by streamlining the ideas in his films. Such a simplification allowed the studio to avoid time-consuming efforts, including the development of extra scenes and characters, that would not have improved the quality of the result. Instead, Walt encouraged a heightened use of repeat action and cycles. One animator explained the development: "The new ideas, the better pictures, the things that paid off with an audience, and even the training of his staff—this is where he spent every nickel he could get. We were asked many times to find more economical ways of working, but never to compromise the quality of the product."[14] To cut costs, Walt would also purchase cheap literary properties, which he would then present to his writing staff and artists for their stylistic trademarks—a process of "Disneyfication."

Walt's obsession with order played an important role in cutting costs through increased organizational efficiency and productivity in the studio. Initially the Disney staff invented stories as it went along, hoping that the ideas would fall into place on their own. Frustrated by the inefficiency and randomness resulting from this traditional yet chaotic system, Walt imposed order when he decided early on that stories would be outlined in preliminary meetings. He separated the creative stages of production while insisting at the same time that there be ample interaction among the artists.

Also, as Disney continued to grow in success and size, Walt made sure that most of the growth came from the bottom. The number of animators, creators, and craftsmen increased at a much greater rate than that of executives, managers, and administrators. The studio thereby had a source for novel ideas without excessive bureaucracy and burdensome salaries. In a way, Walt turned the studio into a rationally composed factory, vital yet efficient.

Another illustration of Walt's flexibility was his response to the war years, when all entertainment enterprises lost business. Walt turned the near disaster into a chance to diversify and experiment. To maintain his cash flow, continue building a name for his company, and experiment further with innovative techniques, he accepted government contracts for propaganda and training films. While fulfilling these contracts, Walt tinkered with novel modes of film production, including live action.

It was during these early financial difficulties that Disney first implemented its cross-promotional efforts by licensing Mickey Mouse and other cartoon characters. Finally, in order to alleviate the burden of bank loans, Disney went public in 1940. Creative business planning coupled with quality products helped to pull Disney out of debt.

SHARING THE VISION

But the company may very well have failed had the Disney staff not shared Walt's excitement for and dedication to the creative process of experiment, exploration, and discovery. The Disney studio was full of exuberance, and the staff worked long hours and studied new techniques in animation, particularly during times of stiff competition and financial instability.

As Walt's employees began to grasp his vision, they grew increasingly excited and captivated by the potential of their work. According to one animator, "When it came right down to it, most of us were more interested in keeping animation alive than we were in making money. We were beginning to sense the magnitude of the art form that we were discovering, and its potential held us like a magnet."[15] His staff was convinced that Walt ran the best studio in the world, and that their work would develop into a form of expression that would transform mass media worldwide.

The Leader as a Stimulator and Coordinator

Walt was a strong and effective leader, but not through complete control of the creative process. Once he provided a concept, Walt expected his employees to build on it, polishing and adding their own touches. He selected a staff that he expected would grow, develop, and improve along with him. He did not elevate himself above the other participants in the creative process. As a result, Walt's mind remained open to what was new, and he continued to learn from his staff. He sat in on everything and constantly dropped by to visit his employees to observe their progress firsthand.

The studio had a youthful, fast-paced, and informal atmosphere. His colleagues described Walt as frequently resorting to mimicry and pantomime with his restless, fidgety hands to convey certain ideas. Disney associates reported that Walt was relaxed, down-to-earth, and accessible; he would sit on the lawn outside of his office after lunch and chat with his employees, whom he insisted call him by his first name. Walt once explained his role in a company by telling the following story:

> You know, I was stumped one day when a little boy asked, "Do you draw Mickey Mouse?" I had to admit I did not draw anymore. "Then you think up all the jokes and ideas?" "No," I said, "I don't do that." Finally he looked at me and said, "Mr. Disney, just what do you do?" "Well," I said, "sometimes I think of myself as a little bee. I go from one area of the studio to another and gather pollen and sort of stimulate everybody. I guess that's the job I do."[16]

Walt believed that his most important contribution to the success of his company was his ability to coordinate the talents of his employees and inspire them to produce the best. Although highly creative, he did not fancy himself an elite artist. His goal was to amuse and bring pleasure to his audience rather than to express himself with obscure artistic impressions.[17] Walt left the formal development of animation to his staff, while reserving for himself the role of coordinator and stimulator. One Disney producer accurately insisted that without Walt's supervision and insistence, the crucial developments would have never occurred.[18]

Faith in the Talent of Employees

Walt searched for ways to maximize his employees' talents and to foster greater group commitment and involvement. He hated firing staff members; instead, he reassigned unsuccessful employees to new projects, generally to reveal undiscovered talents. A production supervisor said of this uncanny gift for steering the movement of employees and finding the most productive spot for creative talent:

> if the "lost soul" didn't make it in [one] department, Walt wouldn't give up on him; we would have to try yet another spot. To my amazement, some of these "lost souls" became valuable contributors towards our production progress. And most others would find a niche that satisfied the studio and them.[19]

Walt's flexibility and commitment to his people often paid off. The consensus among Disney artists was that one "of Walt's greatest gifts was his ability to get you to come up with things you didn't know were in you and that you'd have sworn you couldn't possibly do!"[20] He demanded and extracted more and more from his staff, pushing them to think for themselves, to create and innovate to the best of their abilities.

Walt supplied the framework, and he encouraged his employees to use their expertise to polish his concepts and supply the details. One animator wrote, "Walt always could show you exactly how the business should be done, but the animator was expected to go further with the idea, to come up with something of his own, some touch or bit of timing or an expression that would make it not only personal but special."[21] He did not want his employees to try to discern what he wanted or to anticipate the results he desired. Instead, he wanted them to use their own skills to solve problems and originate and execute ideas. Walt encouraged his craftsmen to throw away a day's worth of work if they were dissatisfied. He refused to install time clocks or to impose minimum output requirements on his employees.

Walt himself was an inventor and tinkerer, and he applied those same standards to his employees. By giving his employees the freedom to play and create, he not only gained their loyalty but also extracted a better product.

Teamwork

In his exuberant and growing organization, Walt made sure to keep the lines of communication open. He was in regular contact with his staff, who tended to discuss studio problems constantly and informally over lunch or in the halls. Walt sent an unending trail of memos from his office to all levels of the company. Fortunately, however, Walt understood that a set of rigid controls would stifle the production of quality craftsmanship and undermine loyalty and camaraderie among employees. He avoided excessive bureaucracy in favor of group work and freedom. Instead of rigid procedural requirements, Walt allowed the freedom for ongoing discussion, evaluation, and argument. This way, he hoped, his employees could learn from each other and work together more productively.

Walt's idea was to create a stimulating environment in

which an exchange of ideas and collaboration among artists would flourish. Team effort was the basis of the Disney system. Walt wanted each employee involved in the creative process to express himself or herself freely. Building on the give-and-take basis of his democratic story conferences, Walt had an "infectious enthusiasm for ideas, even bad ones, that kept the ideas bouncing until, somehow, the plot or situation or character was sharpened to a satisfactory but not necessarily preordained point."[22]

Walt believed that an employee who was not keenly interested in the entire process and who did not proudly contribute, even at the risk of failure, was a mere laborer.[23] He wanted each person to believe that his or her contribution was indispensable, and he wanted no one person to take credit for the success of the resulting product.

As a result of Walt's persistence and the dedication of his team, when most major studios were suffering financial setbacks, Disney was gaining stability and loyalty among consumers. One reason was that when it came to values, tastes, and prejudices, Walt was an unstudied mainstream American. Mass appeal was essential to the success of any studio, and Walt had the intuitive ability to identify broad audience tastes.

Walt confidently believed that if he and those working with him liked an idea or an image, the public would like it as well. He avoided the intellectualism of the arts and instead focused on what he, and by implication the public, would enjoy. He once said, "We seem to know when to 'tap the heart.' Others have hit the intellect. We can hit them in an emotional way. Those who appeal to the intellect only appeal to a very limited group."[24] While Disney's competitors began to focus on more sophisticated themes, Walt sensed that the public yearned for fairy-tale pictures built on warmth, tenderness, and sympathy. Yet again his intuition proved correct, as audiences flocked to take part in his timeless brand of family entertainment.

Walt continued to produce films that had widespread appeal, while his competitors were forced to speculate about audience opinions and morality. He did not have to waste time monitoring customer expectations, because he embodied those expectations. Instead, he focused on delivering quality products and services.

Strategy of Diversification

To distribute its increasingly popular films and secure financial independence, Disney formed its own distribution subsidiary, Buena Vista. Walt had not forgotten his father's dependence on bankers as a farmer in debt, nor had he forgotten the disaster that occurred when he lost the rights to his first Disney series. One animator said of a 1929 conversation with Walt, "He was determined that he would no longer be dependent on a distributor or a victim of his chicanery."[25] Walt insisted that control of distribution would allow the company to maintain its autonomy, protect itself from interference by outsiders, and oversee carefully the pricing of Disney products.

Once Walt secured financial independence, stability, and a solid reputation, he was prepared to convert his narrowly based organization into a broader operation by expanding into other facets of the entertainment industry. He decided upon a courageous plan that called for both a return to the traditions underlying his business and for diversification.

Disneyland: A Revolutionary Amusement Park Experience

Shortly after the formation of the family business, Walt began to develop his dream of building a new kind of amusement park, of unprecedented dimension and quality, for the enjoyment of American families. For more than twenty years Walt worked on the concept as a hobby until he had produced a sketch for the theme park in 1952.

People thought Walt was crazy when he announced he would build a different kind of park, with revolutionary machines and rides—in essence, a new instrument of entertainment. The Disneyland concept was unimaginable to all but a few of Walt's most creatively adventurous associates. Roy, who considered the concept to be another of "Walt's screwy ideas," would invest only $10,000 of Disney studio money in the risky project. Similarly, members of the financial community thought Walt's ideas were farfetched. But Walt knew all too well that his imagination was far more venturesome than that of Wall Street analysts. Determined to realize his vision, Walt came up with the rest of the capital he needed by borrowing on his life insurance policy.

The goal at Disneyland was to ensure that guests enjoyed an educational and friendly escape. To that end, permanent park employees, or "people specialists," were required to undergo days of training and indoctrination at the "University of Disneyland" before appearing in public to entertain guests. Once again, Walt realized that he would have to train his people by his own methods to ensure consistently high quality customer service. The staff was polite, friendly, courteous, well groomed, and eager to share facts and anecdotes glorifying the folklore of the park.

The attention to detail and quality was as apparent at the theme park as it was in the studio. One novelist described Walt's obsession with the constant improvement, indeed perfection, of Disneyland: "Walt feels about Disneyland the way a young mother feels about her first baby. He coddles it, pampers it, fusses at it, bathes it, dresses it, undresses it, peers at it from all directions . . . "[26] To be sure, Walt worried over the tiny details of the construction of each of the park's attractions. He spared no expense in demanding that the rides be authentic as possible.

Similarly, he aggressively sought the development of life-like audio-animatronic figures as the centerpieces of Disney shows. While in Europe in 1948, Walt had stumbled upon an automatic whistling bird and, as an inveterate fan of mechanical gadgets, purchased it immediately. He presented the bird to the head of the machine shop, a man for whom Walt's extraordinary requests had become routine. Before long the shop discovered the secret of the automated bird and applied the principles to full-life figures that became the source of constant amazement for Disneyland guests.

Walt created a magical fantasy world that showcased his values and vision, and he presented it to the public for its approval and enjoyment. At the opening in 1955, Walt promised that "Disneyland will never be completed, as long as there is imagination left in the world."[27] Within one year of its opening, the gross annual revenues from the park totaled $10 million and accounted for roughly one-third of overall sales at Disney.[28] Disneyland stands to this day as a monument to Walt's gift for maximizing technological innovation and consistently investing in training, precision, and attention to detail.

Development of a Promotional Television Strategy

As Walt was building Disneyland, the newly developed television industry supplied increasing competition to his and other entertainment companies. Instead of ignoring it, Walt realized that he could—in fact, had to—use the medium to his benefit.

Walt's development of an effective television strategy took more than five years, during which time he was driven by the conviction that the success of his long-held vision, Disneyland, relied on television. He developed a series of syndicated shows that were a source of free and liberal publicity for Disney films, theme parks, consumer products, and publishing. Once again, Walt's insight and perseverance paid off as television programming became the cornerstone of the company's promotional efforts.

DISNEY IN TRANSITION

During his last years, Walt began to concentrate on real estate ventures. He also focused on his private dream of an unprecedented kind of community, a utopian environment in which artists could come together to share their work and leisure time. He developed his idea into the concept for Walt Disney World, a futuristic theme park that would feature not employees and customers but rather "cast members" and "guests."

When Walt died in 1966 after more than forty years of hard work and struggle, his business was flourishing. The standards he formulated and articulated had been applied to almost every medium of mass communication. He had been resourceful and determined, yet flexible and openminded in his quest to create, and maintain an entertainment machine whose parts worked together in harmony and strength.

The Disney point of view had become so influential and pervasive that his death left an emptiness in the hearts of consumers everywhere. As a *McCall's* reader responding to a poll wrote:

> Sometimes I feel there is a conspiracy to seduce and ruin our youth. I'm sick of sick pictures, offensive sex, and bad taste. . . . The movies these days seem more interested in turning your stomach than in warming your heart. And over and over again: What's going to happen now that Walt Disney is dead?[29]

Indeed it was unclear whether the company could produce leaders capable of leading it into the future with the innovation and imagination that had characterized Disney from the start.

BACK TO THE BASICS: REVIVAL UNDER MICHAEL EISNER

During the next two decades, Walt's successors insisted on a rigid adherence to traditional formulas. In the film division, the studio's brand of wholesome and predictable entertainment generated increasing revenues, but as the tastes of moviegoers began to change, the studio's market share fell. Moreover, although the opening of Walt Disney World was an important source of revenues, the company took on a huge amount of debt to finance construction work at the Environmental Prototype Community of Tomorrow (EPCOT). By the early 1980s, as the need for significant change at Disney became apparent, the blockbuster movie *E.T.* removed any doubts; within the industry, that film became known as the "best movie Disney never made." It was time to recapture that lost ingredient, that special something that made Disney the great company it was under Walt.

Disney managers struggled to regain the balance and creativity that had seemed to flow so easily under Walt's direction. The battle over whom to entrust with the revival of the company was fought between two factions: the financial "Roy men" and the creative "Walt men." The latter group, which argued that the most suitable leaders for an institution like Disney were "creative crazies," triumphed.

Michael Eisner emerged as the new chairman. Like Walt Disney, Eisner was a man driven by ideas. As president of Paramount Pictures Corporation, he had proven that he had the common touch, a natural aptitude for pop programming through simple storytelling techniques.[30] When interviewing for the position at Disney, Eisner reasoned with one of the company's largest shareholders: "It's going to take a creative person to run this company.... Look at the history of America's companies. They have always gotten into trouble when the creative people are replaced by the managers."[31] Like Walt, Eisner had a creative flair and an uncanny connection with the attitudes and tastes of the public. Eisner was widely perceived as one of the most creative executives in Hollywood.

He was joined by Frank Wells, a consultant to Warner Brothers, who would handle Disney's financing as president and chief operating officer. Wells was the perfect complement for Eisner: detail-oriented, pragmatic, and with the business sense to translate Eisner's concepts into profitable realities. Eisner and Wells were an attractive and suitable combination for the task of resurrecting Disney, particularly because of their resemblance to the founding brothers.

Unlike Walt and his immediate successors, however, Eisner had the wherewithal and desire to cultivate Wall Street, and he brought in a new chief financial officer who could structure the necessary creative financial deals. Although Eisner was a "Walt man" at heart, he was well aware that a public company in the 1980s was by necessity operating in a more threatening investment environment. Moreover, he had inherited a company plagued by falling stock. Eisner believed that it would no longer be enough for Disney's leaders to simply provide wholesome family entertainment; to remain competitive, Disney's leaders needed to promote the company image confidently to investors.[32]

The Disney board had finally found a high-powered team of executives to update the business while maintaining its traditional commitment to quality and innovation. In a strategic maneuver that symbolized Disney's new approach to the investment community, at the 1986 annual meeting the name Walt Disney Productions was dropped in favor of the Walt Disney Company.

In addition to bringing in top-flight executives, Eisner began to change the management style at the company. Significantly, he began to refer to Disney managers collectively as "Team Disney." Eisner placed a greater emphasis on group encounter meetings to generate ideas more efficiently for movie scripts and creative business strategies. Typically, a group of the company's most creative talents would meet on Sunday mornings to brainstorm. During these meetings, which came to be known as "gong shows," a head executive would require each attendant to offer a new idea; those that fell below group standards would be rejected with a gong. This system illustrated a return to the traditional Disney willingness to experiment with fresh ideas, even at the risk of failure. By infusing Disney with new executives, a fresh approach to the investment community, and a highly creative format for generating new ideas, Eisner had positioned the company to expand its studio, theme park complexes, and consumer product divisions into the 1990s.

UPDATING THE FILM DIVISION

Eisner quickly began a search for a "Walt man" to fill the leadership vacuum in the studio. In order to lure the best, he secured a promise from the board to approve a larger salary and bonus package than ever before. The commitment to pay what had become customary in the industry proved worthwhile when Disney signed Paramount executive Jeffrey Katzenberg as president of the studio. In Hollywood, Katzenberg was known as the "golden retriever" because of his uncanny aptitude for sniffing out directors and agents with hot scripts. Renowned for his tough negotiating and relentless work ethic, Katzenberg routinely arrived at work before seven o'clock, even on holidays and weekends. Disney subsequently developed an unwritten rule that studio executives must arrive early, stay late, and work weekends.

Under its new leadership, Disney promoted a second label that had been created by Disney before the Eisner-Wells team arrived, Touchstone Pictures, through which the company could produce the racier movies that were in vogue with American audiences. Katzenberg began his reign at Disney by exploiting the new label and signing a deal for the studio's first R-rated film, *Down and Out in Beverly Hills*. Disney's more daring approach remained consistent with the company's fundamental commitment to creativity and innovation, and Touchstone Pictures increased profits without compromising the unique Disney flavor.

The company had rebounded, but Eisner was not satisfied. Like Walt, Eisner was dedicated to constant improvement. In a drive to create new assets, he encouraged the film division to begin work on new Disney characters. Before long, animators had come up with an idea that developed into the central character of its next live-action animated film. Innovative and racy, *Who Framed Roger Rabbit* was an immense success for the studio. Similarly, Disney's next character, featured in *The Little Mermaid,* was reminiscent of the Disney classics and was heavily promoted in the consumer product as well as the theme park division. Under new leadership, Disney was once again turning out fresh and marketable assets.

Innovative financing was essential to the studio's turnaround. In producing its films, Disney not only showed restraint and efficiency but also proved that its retreat from creative corporate structures had merely been temporary. Significantly, the studio began to rely heavily on investors to fund its film projects; the company was thereby able to increase output while relinquishing neither control nor high returns.

The studio's insistence on long hours, good scripts, and fresh ideas paid off: by late 1988 Disney was making and marketing traditional family-oriented films, as well as twelve films per year under the Touchstone label. Eisner and Katzenberg wanted to increase the number of movies produced, but they knew that studios that grew too large inevitably sacrificed quality. As a result, they launched Hollywood Pictures, a third Disney film unit that, like Touchstone, would produce light adult entertainment with simple story lines and tight budgets.[33] This strategy allowed the film division to increase output and target a different audience while maintaining a commitment to quality.

Disney's overall film division produced a steady stream of successful films featuring top talent, strong writing, and original formats. When Team Disney faced its first major film slump, however, management responded with resourcefulness and flexibility. The studio began by cutting back on costs involved in making and marketing Disney films. In a 1991 memorandum to his staff, Katzenberg wrote, "We have slowly drifted away from our original vision of how to run a movie business." He went on to articulate the studio's revised mission: to return to "the kind of modest, story-driven movies we tended to make in our salad days."[34]

The studio continues to implement the policy of producing films with tight budgets and correspondingly reasonable returns rather than hit-or-miss blockbusters, like *Dick Tracy*, that cost more than $100 million to make and market; at Hollywood Pictures, the average film budget has been cut from $20 million to $15 million.[35] The studio's overall strategy is to avoid expensive flops by sticking to budgets that fall below Disney's average budget in previous years, as well as below the industry averages.

DIVERSIFICATION STRATEGY: EMPHASIS ON MEASURED EXPANSION

Eisner has pursued a strategy of diversification, with a steady expansion into the recording, consumer products, radio, home video, and network, cable, and syndicated television industries. This drive, reminiscent of Walt's tactics, has resulted in a steady growth of profits and expansion into new industries and markets. Under Eisner, the drive to diversify wisely emphasizes international (and particularly the Japanese) markets, where Disney products are extremely well received.

For example, with the formation of Hollywood Records in 1991, Disney entered the mainstream music business, a $25-billion-a-year industry characterized by low overhead and comparatively high rewards.[36] In furtherance of its goal to become a major competitor in the worldwide pop music business and in anticipation of a dramatic expansion of the international music industry, Hollywood Records has opened an office in Great Britain.

Eisner has also focused on the sale of consumer products in both domestic and foreign markets, which serves not only to generate significant revenues for the company but also to promote Disney resorts, theme parks, and characters. Disney has 123 stores, including four successful international divisions. Eisner intends to set up and operate 100 stores in Japan, the world's second-largest toy market.[37]

Furthermore, Disney has expanded its licensing operations. The company licenses not only the name "Walt Disney" but also its characters, literary and visual properties, and music to consumer manufacturers, publishers, and retailers around the world. As a means of quality control, Disney participates in the development, approval, and generation of new characters that will be licensed under Disney's name.[38] Eisner, like Walt Disney, is unwilling to produce, market, or sell a cheap, low quality product simply because of a high profit margin.

Finally, Disney is eager to accelerate the company's distribution of television shows and movies. Deal making is expected to continue, but the studio has made it clear that efficiency and restraint will continue to be important values. Furthermore, studio management has suggested that an evolving hands-off policy will lead to more autonomy for Disney executives and a more dynamic creative process.

Although it has been rumored that Eisner is considering the addition of a second cable channel, he has said that an expensive acquisition is not Disney's mission: "It's not to be the biggest, to have the most toys, to own things writers think are important and sexy like networks, cable companies, satellites and countries. Our mission is to grow our own. We can have a nice respectable 20% without having to impress anybody."[39] True to the Disney tradition, Eisner favors long-term progress over quick profits.

Expansion of theme parks and resorts under Team Disney has underscored the increasing importance and attractiveness of foreign markets. Disney capitalized on the prospects for growth abroad by opening its first international theme park, Tokyo Disneyland. From the start, attendance in Tokyo threatened to surpass that at the original Disneyland, and it has continued to climb, setting records along the way.[40]

Next Disney capitalized on the inviting European market by opening a park just outside of Paris. In the company's 1991 annual report, Eisner called Euro Disneyland "the most wonderful project we have ever done. . . . [a] theme park jewel, a creative extension of Walt's first park utilizing new technology."[41] Once again, Team Disney insisted on a flexible, creative approach to financing the $3.6 billion operation. They were determined to retain control as well as a healthy share of the profits generated by a new European park, but they also wanted to minimize the company's risk by sharing costs with the maximum number of participants; to do so, they would have to rely on a new corporate structure.[42] In yet another innovative financing maneuver, Disney set up a French version of a limited partnership to be managed by Euro Disneyland, a publicly held French company in which Disney now owns a 49 percent equity interest.[43]

The success of Disney's international operations confirmed Eisner's intuition that Disney's brand of family entertainment was marketable worldwide. Before increasing activity in overseas markets, however, Eisner streamlined operations by selling Arvida, a real estate development company it had purchased several years earlier.

By 1986, Disney's real estate division began to reassess the value of owning Arvida. Eisner thought that Disney should develop only its own hotels; he also worried that Arvida's Florida land was a liability considering the volatile and increasingly soft real estate market. In 1987 Disney sold Arvida to JMB Realty Corporation in a move that reflected the company's financial flexibility and willingness to shed assets that no longer suited its long-term plans.[44]

In 1991, Disney's theme park and resort division showed decreases in overall revenues and profits. Disney management addressed the problem of falling attendance at its theme parks in a cautious but effective and often resourceful manner. First, the company departed from former policy and raised ticket prices in small increments to avoid negative publicity. Instead of tarnishing Disney's friendly image and thus exacerbating the decline in attendance, the price increase strategy led to soaring revenues.

Next management directed the Imagineering design team to create new theme park attractions that would appeal to teenagers. Disney has also sought to augment attendance by aggressively investing in advertising campaigns. Eisner, wearing Mickey Mouse ears, appeared in advertisements to encourage the use of Walt Disney World for business conventions.[45]

Also, Disney initiated a discounting program. Guests at the Disney-MGM Studios in Orlando received free videos of *Fantasia,* while visitors holding $25 receipts from Vons grocery stores in southern California gained free admission to Disneyland.[46]

FUTURE EXPANSION AND INNOVATION

The theme park division will remain the central focus at Disney. At a 1990 press conference, Eisner announced Team Disney's intent to "do nothing less than reinvent the Disney theme park experience."[47] Management has identified its theme parks as the linchpin for Disney's other divisions and has pledged to add not only new attractions but also increase accommodations. Team Disney will also continue to explore the enormous potential for growth in unexploited international markets.[48]

To ensure continued creativity, Eisner has encouraged Disney executives to develop the "Disney Institute," a think tank in Orlando, and "The Workplace," an entertainment and educational facility focusing on manufacturing plants.[49] Eisner's focus is once again reminiscent of Walt Disney's vision of a utopian studio in which artists and technicians would flourish.

Under its founder's leadership, Disney developed a reputation for aesthetic and technological quality and innovation. As Walt Disney's true successor, Michael Eisner has managed to replicate that essence while developing tactics to address the changing world. He has pledged to continue a strategy of diversification, expansion of foreign projects, commitment to excellence and innovation, and concentration on theme parks as a wellspring for Disney's other services and products in an increasingly globalized economy. He has continued the traditions that keep the Walt Disney Company at the heart of the entertainment industry. Eisner, referring to the 1990s as the "Disney decade," has said that only "a lack of continued creativity and nerve can impede us as we move into the 90s."[50]

Eisner's success at Disney is heralded as a monumental achievement. He brought back the vitality and the spark that we associate with great leaders. According to Christopher Knowlton, "Disney's uniqueness stems from having a creative executive—not a finance man or a lawyer—in charge. [Eisner's] chief duty at Disney is to lead creatively, to be a thinker, inventor, and cheerleader for new ideas—in Walt's own words, to be an imagineer."[51] The Walt Disney Company today stands as an example for all American businesses, including other great companies like Wal-Mart and McDonald's, for it has achieved something even they have not: rejuvenation through new leadership.

As we have described, when Walt Disney died, his company did not die with him: Disneyland, Disney films, and other products continued to earn money. The corporation kept moving forward, but after a time the momentum began to slow. It became clear that simply doing what had always been done was no guarantee of continued success—in addition, it was a betrayal of what Walt Disney had stood for. New leadership was required, and it was provided by Michael Eisner. Eisner created a new company within the old, one that was true to the vision, the values, and the beliefs of Walt Disney himself.

While Wal-Mart and McDonald's are great companies, it is yet to be seen whether or not they can make this transition. In the absence of effective leadership, all their assets, market power, and history of success could not keep Sears, IBM, or General Motors from losing their markets to competitors. As the Walt Disney Company has done with Michael Eisner, these companies must find and follow a leader with a vision, values, and courage to act to retain their place among the world's greatest corporations.

DEMING'S GUIDELINES FOR TRANSFORMATION

The Fourteen Points:

1. *Create consistency of purpose for improvement of product and service* with the aim to become competitive, to stay in business, and to provide jobs. This is a radical departure from the historic purpose of American business, which is generating profit. If a company is to remain competitive and survive over the long term, it must allocate resources for innovation, research, and education, and constantly improve the design of products and services. (Two of Deming's "deadly diseases" also address this topic.)

2. *Adopt the new philosophy.* The new philosophy of quality improvement must be adopted in full. It is a philosophy that does not tolerate previously acceptable levels of mistakes, defects, poor workmanship, improper tools for the job, or flawed work processes.

3. *Cease dependence on mass inspection.* Rather than inspecting quality into a product at the end of the production line, a company must build quality into the product from the start. With end-of-line inspections, a company is "paying workers to make defects and then to correct them. Quality comes not from inspection but from improvement of the [work] process,"[1] reducing the costs of scrap and rework.

4. *End the practice of awarding business on the basis of price tag alone.* Purchasing procedures that award orders on the mere basis of low price will result in poor quality supplies, which will in turn result in poor quality products. Companies should move toward using single suppliers who supply high quality materials and who will work with the company con-

tinually to improve that quality. This means building long-term, mutually beneficial relationships with these suppliers.

5. *Improve constantly and forever the system of production and service* to improve quality and productivity, and thus constantly decrease costs. Continuous improvement must become the unceasing goal of every work process within a company, whether it is part of manufacturing or administration.

6. *Institute training.* Workers must be properly trained to do their jobs. Too frequently job training comes from other workers who themselves were poorly trained. This creates a continuing problem of poor work performance, which in turn results in poor quality output. Job training at every level must provide employees with the knowledge they need to do the job right and meet management expectations.

7. *Institute leadership.* The old management role of supervision—telling, auditing, and controlling—is ineffective. Management must take on a leadership role: guiding their employees, and removing the barriers to and providing the resources for doing a good job.

8. *Drive out fear.* Fear prevents effective work. In an environment that contains fear, employees are aware of problems, yet are afraid to step forward and "rock the boat." Or employees may feel inadequately trained for the job, but are afraid to bring attention to their performance. "The economic loss of fear is appalling," writes Mary Walton. "It is necessary for better quality and productivity that people feel secure."[2]

9. *Break down barriers between staff areas.* Relations between different organizational groups are often strained, and competing goals make it difficult for different groups to work together as a team. These barriers must come down so that cross-functional teams can use their collective knowledge to identify and solve quality problems.

10. *Eliminate slogans, exhortations, and targets for the work force.* Posters and slogans are targeted at the wrong people. Even

if they want to, workers cannot fulfill the slogan's message (and thus management's expectations) because the constraints to trouble-free performance are embedded in the work system, which they are powerless to change. This renders slogans and targets useless.

11. *Eliminate numerical quotas.* Management reaps the performance it rewards. If it requires and rewards quotas, employees will meet quotas, regardless of the waste and inefficiency that comes from doing so. Quotas are, says Deming, "totally incompatible with never-ending improvement." This point also applies to numerical goals, such as percentage of sales increases, for managerial/professional employees. Leadership must be substituted for the traditional management-by-numbers.

12. *Remove barriers to pride of workmanship.* As with the preceding point, this applies to both hourly and managerial/professional employees. For managerial/professional employees, the barrier is the annual rating of performance. For hourly employees, barriers are anything that prevents the employee from doing a good job: poor work systems, bad equipment, or defective materials.

13. *Institute a vigorous program of education and improvement.* Everyone in the organization must be trained in the subjects and skills necessary to implement quality improvement. These include statistical techniques, teamwork, and problem solving.

14. *Take action to accomplish the transformation.* Management must develop a plan and then implement that plan to accomplish the transformation into a quality organization.

THE DEADLY DISEASES

The following self-inflicted problems are often more threatening to a company than competition:

1. A lack of consistency of purpose to improve products and services by providing resources for long-term planning, research, and training.

2. An emphasis on short-term profits.

3. Using individual performance evaluations through merit ratings and annual reviews.

4. Instability resulting from the mobility of managers.
5. The misuse of data.
6. Excessive medical costs.
7. Excessive legal liability costs.

THE OBSTACLES

The following can impede productivity and the adoption of the philosophy:

1. Impatience for quick results

2. A dependence on technology to solve problems

3. The tendency to rely on examples of other companies' improvement methods rather than developing one to fit the organization.

NOTES

Preface

1. McKenna, Joseph F., "Bob Galvin Predicts Life After Perfection: Motorola's Executive-Committee Chairman Sees Quality of Leadership," *Industry Week*, January 21, 1991, p. 12.

Chapter 1

1. *Time*, "Sam Walton Recounts the Life of a Salesman," June 15, 1992, p. 52.
2. WEFA Group, *U.S. Long-Term Historical Data*, second quarter 1991.
3. Gorman, Joseph T., "Facing Facts and Foreign Agendas," *Vital Speeches of the Day*, December 1, 1991, 58: 124–26.
4. Parts of the material in this section are derived from an article by Neil H. Snyder, Bernard A. Morin, and Marilyn A. Morgan that was published in the April–June 1988 issue of *Business*, pp. 14–19. The title of the article is "Motivating People to Build Excellent Enterprises."
5. Dill, W. R., "Environment as an Influence on Managerial Autonomy," *Administrative Science Quarterly* (1958):404–43; Kast, F. E. and James E. Rosenzweig, *Contingency Views of Organization and Management* (Chicago: SRA, 1973); and Paul Lawrence and Jay Lorsch, *Organization and Environment* (Homewood, Ill.: Irwin, 1969).
6. Kanter, R. M., *The Change Masters* (New York: Simon and Schuster, 1983), 17–18.
7. Daniel, D. R., "Managing the Creative Organization Implications for Business Schools," *University of Virginia Darden Report* (Winter 1985): 12–13.
8. Ibid.
9. Bennis, Warren, "The Pivotal Force," *Enterprise* (September 1985): 9–11. Much of the material in this section was published in an article by Neil H. Snyder titled "Leadership: The Essential Quality for Transforming United States

Businesses" that appeared in the April 1988 issue of *SAM Advanced Management Journal,* pp. 15–18.

10. Glen, Pascall, *The Trillion Dollar Budget* (Seattle: University of Washington Press, 1985), p. 152.

11. Zaleznik, Abraham, "Managers and Leaders: Are They Different?" *Harvard Business Review,* March–April 1992 pp. 129, 131.

12. Stewart, Thomas A., "Why Nobody Can Lead America," *Fortune,* January 14, 1991, pp. 44–45.

13. Hyatt, James C., and Amal Kumar Naj, "GE Is No Place for Autocrats, Welch Decrees," *Wall Street Journal,* March 3, 1992, p. A1.

14. Nanus, Burt, "Futures-Creative Leadership," *Futurist* (May–June 1990): 13–17.

15. Bennis, Warren, "Managing the Dream—Leadership in the 21st Century," *Training* (May 1990): 46.

16. Peters T. J. and Waterman, R. H., *In Search of Excellence* (New York: Harper and Row, 1982), p. 282.

17. Selznick, Philip, *Leadership in Administration* (New York: Harper and Row, 1957), 28.

18. Mason, George, *The Virginia Bill of Rights,* Williamsburg, VA., June 12, 1776, p. 5.

19. Watson, Thomas, Jr. *A Business and Its Beliefs* (New York: McGraw-Hill, 1963), 4–6.

20. Peters and Waterman, p. 285.

21. Fisher, George, from a videotape of a speech delivered at the University of Texas, Arlington, on September 18, 1990.

22. Nanus, *Futurist,* p. 14.

23. Roosevelt, Theodore, from a speech before the Hamilton Club, Chicago, Ill., April 10, 1899.

Chapter 2

1. *International Quality Study: The Definitive Study of the Best International Quality Management Practices, Top-Line Findings,* a joint project of Ernst & Young and the American Quality Foundation, 1991.

2. Ibid.

3. Fuchsberg, Gilbert, "Quality Programs Show Shoddy Results," *Wall Street Journal,* May 14, 1992, p. B1.

4. Byrne, John A., "High Priests and Hucksters," *Business Week Special Issue: The Quality Imperative,* October 25, 1991, p. 52.

5. Fuchsberg, p. B1.

6. "The Curmudgeon Who Talks Tough on Quality," *Fortune,* June 25, 1984, p. 119.

7. Deming, W. Edwards, *Out of the Crisis* (Cambridge: Massachusetts Institute of Technology, 1986), ix.

8. Most of this information is common to numerous sources. The most comprehensive and interesting write-up on Dr. Deming's background is found in chapter 1 of Mary Walton's book, *The Deming Management Method* (New York: Putnam Publishing Group, 1986).

9. These summaries are a compilation from Deming's description in *Out of the Crisis,* Mary Walton's book *The Deming Management Method,* and our own interpretation.

10. Deming, as quoted by Walton, p. 26.

11. Interview with Joseph M. Juran, "From the Great J. M. Juran: How to Manage for World-Class Quality," *Boardroom Reports,* May 1, 1990.

12. J. M. Juran, *Quality Control Handbook,* 3rd Edition (New York: McGraw-Hill, 1974) Chapter 11, p. 5.

13. Juran, J. M., "Universal Approach to Managing for Quality," *Executive Excellence,* May 1989.

14. Juran, J. M., "Managing for Quality," *Journal for Quality and Participation,* March 1988.

15. Jespersen, Fred F., "Once More with Feeling: Quality Starts at the Top," *Business Week,* August 1989, p. 65.

16. Most of this information is distilled from Philip Crosby's books *Quality is Free,* (New York: McGraw-Hill, 1979) and *Quality Without Tears,* (New York: McGraw-Hill, 1984). More recent comments and clarifications from Crosby are noted where appropriate.

17. Crosby, Philip, "By George, I Think I've Got It!" *HR Focus,* December 1991, p. 23.

18. Crosby, as quoted by Jespersen, p. 65–66.

19. Philip Crosby, "Quality Comes from Policy and People," *Executive Excellence,* March 1990, p. 7.

20. Deming, *Out of the Crisis,* p. 23.

Chapter 3

1. Reed, Susan, "Talk About a Local Boy Making Good," *People,* December 19, 1983, p. 133.

2. Ibid., p. 54.

3. Ibid., p. 56.

4. Ibid., p. 59.
5. Reier, Sharon, "CEO of the Decade: Sam Walton," *Financial World,* April 4, 1989, p. 56.
6. Huey, John, "Will Wal-Mart Take Over the World?" *Fortune,* January 30, 1989, p. 52.
7. Gilbert, Les, "Wal-Mart Scores and Soars," *Weekly Home Furnishings Newspaper,* June 18, 1990, p. 10.
8. Zellner, Wendy, "OK, So He's Not Sam Walton," *Business Week,* March 16, 1992, p. 56.
9. Trimble, Vance, *Sam Walton: The Inside Story of America's Richest Man,* (New York: Signet Books, 1991), p. 132.
10. Zellner, p. 56.
11. Lawrence, Jennifer, "Sam Walton Reshapes Retailing Environment," *Advertising Age,* December 23, 1991, p. 5.
12. Huey, p. 56.
13. Trimble, p. 328.
14. Teutsch, p. 87.
15. Huey, p. 52.
16. Reier, p. 56.
17. Ibid.
18. Trimble, p. 327.
19. Mason, Todd, "Sam Walton of Wal-Mart: Just Your Basic Homespun Billionaire," *Business Week,* October 14, 1985, p. 142.
20. Huey, p. 52.
21. Teutsch, p. 151.
22. Huey, p. 52.
23. Mason, p. 142.
24. Zellner, p. 56.
25. Mason, p. 142.
26. Reier, p. 56.
27. Saporito, Bill, "Is Wal-Mart Unstoppable?" *Fortune,* May 6, 1991, p. 51.
28. Salk, George, "Competing on Capabilities," *Harvard Business Review,* March–April 1992, p. 58.
29. Trimble, p. 235.
30. Barrier, Michael, "Walton's Mountain: Wal-Mart Founder Sam Walton," *Nation's Business,* April 1988, p. 18.
31. Hayes, Thomas, "Behind Wal-Mart's Surge—A Web of Suppliers," *New York Times,* July 1, 1991, D, 1:3.
32. Barrier, p. 18.
33. Huey, p. 52.
34. Trimble, p. 181.

35. Barrier, p. 18.
36. Huey, p. 52.
37. Barrier, p. 18.
38. Wal-Mart public relations information, p. 4.
39. Barrier, p. 18.
40. Helliker, Kevin, "Closing the Books: Sam Walton, Founder of Wal-Mart, Dies," *Wall Street Journal,* April 6, 1992, p. A1.
41. Huey, p. 52.
42. Reier, p. 56.
43. Lawrence, p. 5.
44. Trimble, p. 183.
45. Helliker, p. A1.
46. Saporito, p. 58.
47. Huey, p. 52.
48. Teutsch, p. 85.
49. Trimble, p. 331.
50. Stalk, p. 59.
51. Huey, p. 52.
52. Trimble, p. 177.
53. Teutsch, p. xiii.
54. Gilbert, p. 10.
55. Helliker, p. A1.
56. Rudnitsky, Howard, "How Sam Walton Does It," *Forbes,* August 16, 1982, p. 142.
57. Huey, p. 52.

Chapter 4

1. Senge, Peter, *The Fifth Discipline* (New York: Doubleday Currency, 1990), 205–226.
2. Bennis, Warren, "Managing the Dream—Leadership in the 21st Century," *Training,* (May 1990), p. 44.
3. Stewart, Thomas A., *Fortune,* "Why Nobody Can Lead America," January 14, 1991, p. 44.
4. Tichy, Noel, and David Ulrich, "The Challenge of Revitalization," *New Management,* no. 3 (Winter 1985): 53–59.
5. Bennis, Warren "The Pivotal Force," *Enterprise,* September 1985, p. 10.
6. Kiechel, Walter, III, "A Hard Look at Executive Vision," *Fortune,* October 23, 1989, p. 208.
7. Gardner, John P., *On Leadership* (New York: Free Press, 1990), 21.

8. Kotter, John P., *A Force For Change: How Leadership Differs From Management* (New York: Free Press, 1990), 36.
9. Senge, *The Fifth Discipline,* p. 210.
10. Senge, *The Fifth Discipline,* p. 210.
11. Smith, Bryan, "Vision: A Time to Take Stock (Organizational Visioning)," *Business Quarterly,* Autumn 1989, p. 81.
12. Rockefeller, John D., III, *The Second American Revolution* (New York: Harper and Row, 1973), p. 11.
13. Main, Jeremy. *Fortune,* "Wanted: Leaders Who Can Make A Difference," September 28, 1987, p. 94.
14. Ibid.
15. Zaleznik, Abraham, "Why Managers Lack Vision," *Business Month,* August 1989, p. 63. (excerpts from his book *The Managerial Mystique).*
16. Kiechel, p. 209.
17. Alexander, John W., "Sharing the Vision," *Business Horizons,* May-June 1989, pp. 56–57.
18. Kotter, p. 56.
19. Senge, *The Fifth Discipline,* p. 105.
20. Kotter, p. 75.
21. Senge, *The Fifth Discipline,*
22. Senge, Peter M., "The Leader's New Work: Building Learning Organizations," *Sloan Management Review,* Fall 1990, p. 13.
23. Ibid.
24. Alexander, pp. 57–58.
25. Senge, "The Leader's New Work," p. 13.
26. Ibid., p. 9.

Chapter 5

1. *The Living Webster Encyclopedic Dictionary of the English Language* (Chicago: English Language Institute of America, 1977).
2. J.F.T. Bugental, as quoted by Hitt, D., *Thoughts on Leadership,* (Cleveland: 1992), Battelle Press, 26.
3. Ibid.
4. Huibregtsen, Mickey, "Memo to a CEO: Putting Your Organization on the Move," *McKinsey Quarterly,* 1991, no. 3, p. 55.
5. Ibid.
6. Stayer, Ralph, "How I Learned to Let My Workers Lead",

Harvard Business Review, November–December 1990. p. 80.
7. Kouzes, James M., and Barry Z. Posner, *The Leadership Challenge* San Francisco: Jossey-Bass Publishers, p. 198.
8. Stayer, p. 72.
9. Reier, Sharon, "CEO of the Decade: Sam Walton," *Financial World,* April 4, 1989, p. 56.
10. Senge, Peter, *The Fifth Discipline: The Art and Practice of the Learning Organization,* (New York: Doubleday Currency, 1990), p. 6.
11. Senge, Peter M., "The Leader's New Work: Building Learning Organizations," *Sloan Management Review,* Fall 1990. p. 9.
12. Kouzes and Posner, p. 10.
13. Johnson, Ollie, and Frank Thomas, *Disney Animation: The Illusion of Life* (New York: Abbeville Press, 1981), p. 25.

Chapter 6

1. Limerick, David C., "Managers of Meaning: From Bob Geldof's Band Aid to Australian CEOs," *Organizational Dynamics,* Spring 1990.
2. Ibid.
3. Presentation by Xerox Corporation, Western Region Customer Quality Day, October 16, 1990, Seattle, Washington.
4. Joiner, Charles W., *Leadership for Change,* (Cambridge, Mass.: Ballinger Publishing, 1987), 57.
5. Xerox, op. cit.
6. Kouzes, James M., and Barry Z. Posner, *The Leadership Challenge,* (San Francisco: Jossey-Bass, 1987), 126.
7. Robbins, Stephen P., *Essentials of Organization Behavior,* Second Edition, Prentice Hall, New Jersey, 1988, p. 98.
8. Umsot, D. D., *Understanding Organizational Behavior,* (St. Paul, Minn.: West Publishing, 1984).
9. Ibid.
10. This material has been summarized from that developed by Robbins, op. cit.
11. Hopen, Deborah L., "The Process of Communicating," *Quality Progress,* 24 (6): 49.
12. Conger, *The Charismatic Leader,* (San Francisco: Jossey-Bass Publishers, 1989) pp. 73, 74.
13. Hopen, p. 49.
14. Connellan, Thomas K., "Interpersonal Feedback," *Quality Progress,* (6): 20.

15. Badaracco, Joseph L., Jr., and Richard R. Ellsworth, *Leadership and the Quest for Integrity,* Harvard Business School Press, Boston, 1989.

Chapter 7

1. Kroc, Ray, *Grinding It Out: The Making of McDonald's,* (Chicago: Contemporary Books, 1977), 6.
2. Ibid., p. 13.
3. Ibid., p. 6.
4. Ibid., p. 6.
5. Ibid., p. 8.
6. Ibid., p. 11.
7. Ibid., p. 68.
8. Ibid., p. 82.
9. Moser, Penny, "The McDonald's Mystique," *Fortune,* July 4, 1988, p. 112–16.
10. Moser, p. 114.
11. Kroc, p. 85–86.
12. Ibid., p. 7.
13. Ibid., p. 66.
14. Ibid., p. 75.
15. Ibid., p. 2–3 (foreword).
16. Ibid., p. 82.
17. Boas, Max, and Steve Chain, *Big Mac: The Unauthorized Story of McDonald's,* (New York: E.P. Dutton, 1976), 7–8.
18. McDonald's 1992 second quarter report.
19. Love, John F., *McDonald's: Behind the Arches,* (New York: Bantam Books, 1986), 5–6.
20. McDonald's customer relations information, 1991.
21. Kroc, page 168.
22. Noren, D. L., p. 60–62.
23. Ibid., p. 60.
24. Ibid., p. 61.
25. Ibid., p. 62.
26. Ibid., p. 62.
27. Love, p. 292.
28. Peters, Thomas and Waterman, Robert, *In Search of Excellence* (New York: Harper and Row, 1982), p. 318.
29. Ibid., p. 326.
30. Kroc, p. 9–10.
31. Love, p. 334.

32. Ibid. p. 329.

33. Ibid., p. 276.

34. Hume, Scott, "Adman of the Decade, McDonald's Fred Turner: Making All the Right Moves," *Advertising Age,* January 1, 1990. p. 6.

35. Hume, Scott, pp. 6 and 17.

36. McDonald's 1990 annual report, Oak Brook, IL.

37. McDonald's customer relations information, Oak Brook, IL.

38. Ibid.

39. Linsenmayer-Hardman, Adrienne, "Out of the Ashes: What the Los Angeles Riots Are Teaching Corporate America," *FW,* June 9, 1992, p. 18–19.

40. McDonald's customer relations information, Oak Brook, IL.

41. Ozanian, Michael K., "Why McDonald's Has Hit A Mid-Life Crisis", *FW,* August 21, 1990, p. 31–33.

42. Therrien, Lois, "McDonald's Isn't Looking Quite So Juicy Anymore," *Business Week,* August 6, 1990, p. 30.

43. Therrien, Lois, "McRisky," *Business Week,* October 21, 1991, p. 114.

44. Ibid., p. 115.

45. McDonald's 1991 annual report, Oak Brook, IL.

46. Ozanian, p. 32.

47. Therrien, "McRisky," pp. 114–115.

48. Ibid., p. 116.

49. Scarpa, James, "McDonald's Menu Mission," *Restaurant Business,* July 1, 1991.

50. Ibid.

51. Hume, Scott, "McD's Sizzles with New Ideas," *Advertising Age,* September 3, 1990, p. 1.

Chapter 8

1. Zachary, G. Pascal, and Stephen Kreider Yoder, "Order from Chaos: Computer Industry Divides into Camps of Winners and Losers," *Wall Street Journal,* January 27, 1993, p. A1.

2. Schellhardt, Timothy D., "Sears Trims Operations, Ending an Era," *Wall Street Journal,* January 26, 1993, p. B1.

3. Patterson, Gregory A., "Sears Registers Quarterly Loss of $1.8 Billion," *Wall Street Journal,* February 10, 1993, p. A3.

4. Mathews, Jay, "Sears Rallying, Will Expand Clothing Sales, Analysts Told," *Washington Post,* February 11, 1993, pp. B1, B10.

5. Ibid., p. B1.

6. Carbone, James, "Purchasing Helped Xerox Win the Baldrige," *Electronics Purchasing,* March 1990; DeYoung, H. Garrett, "Back from the Brink: Xerox Redefines Its Notion of Quality," *Electronic Business,* October 16, 1989. (Reprints provided by Xerox Corporation.)
7. From a presentation by Ford Motor Company executives at the Third Quality Forum, 1991.
8. Ingrassia, Lawrence, "Keeping Sharp: Gillette Holds Its Edge by Endlessly Searching for a Better Shave," *Wall Street Journal,* December 10, 1992, p. A1.
9. Presentation at the McIntire International Case Competition Forum, McIntire School of Commerce, University of Virginia, Charlottesville, February 5, 1993.
10. Bowles, Jerry, and Joshua Hammond, *Beyond Quality* (New York: G. P. Putnam's Sons, 1991), p. 75.
11. Schultz, Roy, "Satisfaction Guaranteed for Customers and Crew," *Wall Street Journal,* January 28, 1991.
12. "The Cracks in Quality," *Economist,* April 18, 1992, p. 67.
13. Ciampa, Dan, *Total Quality: A User's Guide for Implementation* (Reading, Mass.: Addison-Wesley, 1992), 162.
14. Zemke, Ron, with Dick Schaaf, *The Service Edge* (New York: Penguin Books, 1990), 4.
15. Ibid., p. 21.
16. Doody, Alton F., and Ron Bingaman, *Reinventing the Wheels* (Cambridge, Mass.: Ballinger, 1988), 16–17.
17. "This Time, Ford Has a Better Idea," *U.S. News and World Report,* December 15, 1986, p. 54.
18. Taub, Eric, *Taurus: The Making of the Car That Saved Ford* (New York: Penguin Books, 1991), 69.

Chapter 9

1. Ryan, Bob, "Apple of Teacher's Eye," *Boston Globe,* February 4, 1993, p. A17.
2. Bowles, Jerry, and Joshua Hammond, *Beyond Quality,* (New York: G. P. Putnam's Sons, 1991), p. 70.
3. Ibid., p. 73.
4. DeYoung, H. Garrett, "Back from the Brink: Xerox Redefines Its Notion of Quality," *Electronic Business,* October 16, 1989. (Reprint provided by Xerox Corporation.)
5. Collins, Robert, "Continuous Improvement," presentation at McIntire School of Commerce, University of Virginia, Charlottesville.

6. Sheridan, John H., "America's Best Plants," *Industry Week,* October 5, 1990. (Reprint provided by Xerox Corporation.)
7. Stone, Edward P., "Employee Support and Interaction Are the Keys to an SPC Program," *Quality Progress,* vol. 24, no. 12, p. 56, 1991.
8. Coate, L. Edwin, *An Analysis of Oregon State University's Total Quality Management Pilot Program* (Corvallis: Oregon State University Press, 1990), 5.
9. Hill, G. Christian, and Ken Yamada, "Staying Power: Motorola Illustrates How an Aged Giant Can Remain Vibrant," *Wall Street Journal,* December 9, 1992, p. A18.
10. Taub, Eric, *Taurus: The Making of the Car That Saved Ford* (New York: Penguin Books, 1991), 56.
11. Petersen, Donald E., and John Hillkirk, *A Better Idea: Redefining the Way Americans Work* (Boston: Houghton Mifflin Company, 1991), 72.
12. Easterbrook, Greg, "Have You Driven A Ford Lately?" *Washington Monthly,* October 1986, p. 27.
13. Cauldron, Shari, "How Xerox Won the Baldrige," *Personnel Journal,* April 1991, p. 98.
14. Bowles and Hammond, pp. 133–34.
15. Ingrassia, Lawrence, "Keeping Sharp: Gillette Holds Its Edge by Endlessly Searching for a Better Shave," *Wall Street Journal,* December 10, 1992, pp. A1, A8.
16. Hill and Yamada, pp. A1, A18.
17. *Ibid., p. A18.*
18. *Ibid., p. A18.*
19. Ciampa, Dan, *Total Quality: A User's Guide for Implementation,* (Reading, Mass.: 1992), Addison-Wesley, 117.
20. Ryan, Bob, "Bird On . . . ," *Boston Globe,* February 4, 1993, p. A20.

Chapter 10

1. "A Report on the Total Quality Leadership Steering Committee and Working Councils," Procter & Gamble, November 1992, p. 2–10.
2. Herzberg, Frederick, "One More Time: How Do You Motivate Employees?" *Harvard Business Review,* January–February 1968.
3. Firnstahl, Timothy W., "My Employees Are My Service Guarantee," *Harvard Business Review,* July–August 1990, pp. 28–32.

4. Semler, Ricardo, "Managing Without Managers," *Harvard Business Review*, September–October 1989, p. 79.
5. Gandz, Jeffrey, "The Employee Empowerment Era," *Business Quarterly*, Autumn 1990. pp. 74–79.
6. McGregor, Douglas, *The Human Side of Enterprise* (New York: McGraw-Hill, 1960).
7. Emerson, Ralph Waldo, "Self-Reliance," in *Essays 1st and 2nd Series*, (New York: E.P. Dutton, 1914), p. 32.
8. Schlesinger, Leonard A., and James L. Heskett, "The Service-Driven Service Company," *Harvard Business Review*, September–October 1991, p. 79.
9. Kotter, John P., and Leonard A. Schlesinger, "Choosing Strategies for Change," *Harvard Business Review*, March–April 1979.
10. Johnson, H. Thomas, *Relevance Regained: From Top-Down Control to Bottom-Up Empowerment* (Boston: Harvard Business School Press, 1992).
11. Weisz, William J., "Employee Involvement: How It Works at Motorola," *Personnel*, February 1985, p. 29.
12. Gomersall, Earl S., "How Motorola Manages to Introduce Change," *Management Review*, September 1983, p. 32.
13. Brody, Michael, "Helping Workers to Work Smarter," *Fortune*, June 8, 1987, p. 87.
14. Therrien, Lois, "Motorola Sends Its Work Force Back to School," *Business Week*, June 6, 1988, p. 80.
15. Schultz, Ray, "Satisfaction Guaranteed for Customers and Crew," *Wall Street Journal*, January 28, 1991.
16. McGregor, Douglas, *The Human Side of Enterprise* (New York: McGraw-Hill, 1960).
17. Stayer, Ralph, "How I Learned to Let My Employees Lead," *Harvard Business Review*, November–December 1990, p. 68.
18. Gandz, pp. 74–79.
19. Byham, William C., and Jeff Cox, *Zapp! The Lightning of Empowerment* (New York: Harmony Books, 1988).

Chapter 11

1. Roosevelt, Theodore, from a speech before the Hamilton Club, Chicago, April 10, 1899.
2. Boas, Max, and Steve Chain, *Big Mac: The Unauthorized Story of McDonald's*, (New York: E.P. Dutton, 1976), p. 7–8.
3. Schrage, Michael, "IBM Must Face the Fact That It Can No

Longer Play in Every Market," *Washington Post,* December 18, 1992, p. B11.

4. Ibid., p. B11.
5. Burgess, John, and Dan Southerland, "Intel: The 'I' That Has It," *Washington Post,* December 20, 1992, p. H1.
6. Ibid., p. H1.
7. Schrage, p. B11.

Chapter 12

1. Schickel, Richard, *The Disney Version: The Life, Time, Art and Commerce of Walt Disney* (New York: Simon and Schuster, 1968), 284.
2. Ibid., p. 171.
3. Ibid., p. 284.
4. Johnson, Ollie, and Frank Thomas, *Disney Animation: The Illusion of Life* (New York: Abbeville Press, 1981), 258.
5. Ibid., p. 23.
6. Schickel, p. 116.
7. Johnson, p. 25.
8. Ibid., p. 186.
9. Ibid., p. 509.
10. Ibid., p. 71.
11. Ibid., p. 29.
12. Ibid., p. 258.
13. Schickel, p. 219.
14. Johnson, pp. 86–87.
15. Ibid., p. 23.
16. Schickel, p. 33.
17. Johnson, p. 23.
18. Ibid., p. 39.
19. Ibid., p. 186.
20. Ibid., p. 25.
21. Ibid., p. 41.
22. Schickel, p. 174.
23. Johnson, p. 188.
24. Ibid., p. 119.
25. Ibid., p. 87.
26. Schickel, pp. 316–317.
27. Ibid., p. 315.
28. Ron Grover, *The Disney Touch: How a Daring Management Team Revived an Entertainment Empire* (Homewood, IL: Richard D. Irwin, 1991), 8.

29. Schickel, p. 339.
30. Grover, p. 30.
31. Ibid., p. 23.
32. John Taylor, *Storming the Magic Kingdom* (New York: Alfred A. Knopf, 1987), 247.
33. Grover, p. 222.
34. Grover, p. 281, from Jeffrey Katzenberg memo to staff, "The World Is Changing: Some Thoughts on Our Business," January 11, 1991.
35. Turner, Richard *Wall Street Journal,* "Lost Sparkle: Disney Hits Bad Patch After Eisner's Six Years of Giddy Expansion," November 12, 1991, A1, A10.
36. 1991 Walt Disney Company annual report, p. 3.
37. *Wall Street Journal,* November 12, 1991, pp. B1, B6.
38. 1991 Walt Disney Company form 10-K, p. 5.
39. *Wall Street Journal,* November 12, 1991, p. A1, p. A10.
40. Walt Disney Company 1984 Annual Report, p. 9.
41. 1991 Disney annual report, p. 4.
42. Grover, p. 190.
43. 1991 Disney form 10-K, pp. 2–3.
44. Grover, pp. 211–212.
45. Taylor, p. 242.
46. pp. A1, A10.
47. Grover, p. 270, from Michael Eisner press conference, Swan Hotel, Orlando, Florida, January 14, 1990.
48. "Disney Net Fell 25 Percent in Fiscal 4th Quarter as Economy Sags," pp. B1, B6.
49. Grover, p. 276, from Benedick, Robin, "Disney Serious about Making Osceola Dream City a Reality," *Orlando Sentinel,* July 25, 1990, p. 1.
50. Grover, p. 270, from Michael Eisner press conference, Swan Hotel, Orlando, Florida, January 14, 1990.
51. Knowlton, Christopher, "How Disney Keeps the Magic Going," *Fortune,* December 4, 1989, p. 111.

Appendix

1. Walton, Mary, *The Deming Management Method* (New York: Perigee Books, 1986), 35.
2. Ibid., p. 72.

INDEX